Palgrave Studies in Audio-Visual Culture

Series Editor
K.J. Donnelly
School of Humanities
University of Southampton
Southampton, United Kingdom

The aesthetic union of sound and image has become a cultural dominant. A junction for aesthetics, technology and theorisation, film's relationship with music remains the crucial nexus point of two of the most popular arts and richest cultural industries. Arguably, the most interesting area of culture is the interface of audio and video aspects, and that film is the flagship cultural industry remains the fount and crucible of both industrial developments and critical ideas.

Palgrave Studies in Audio-Visual Culture has an agenda-setting aspiration. By acknowledging that radical technological changes allow for rethinking existing relationships, as well as existing histories and the efficacy of conventional theories, it provides a platform for innovative scholarship pertaining to the audio-visual. While film is the keystone of the audio visual continuum, the series aims to address blind spots such as video game sound, soundscapes and sound ecology, sound psychology, art installations, sound art, mobile telephony and stealth remote viewing cultures.

More information about this series at
http://www.springer.com/series/14647

Beth Carroll

Feeling Film

A Spatial Approach

Beth Carroll
Southampton, United Kingdom

Palgrave Studies in Audio-Visual Culture
ISBN 978-1-349-71177-2   ISBN 978-1-137-53936-6   (eBook)
DOI 10.1057/978-1-137-53936-6

Library of Congress Control Number: 2016959960

© The Editor(s) (if applicable) and The Author(s) 2016
The author(s) has/have asserted their right(s) to be identified as the author(s) of this work in accordance with the Copyright, Designs and Patents Act 1988.
This work is subject to copyright. All rights are solely and exclusively licensed by the Publisher, whether the whole or part of the material is concerned, specifically the rights of translation, reprinting, reuse of illustrations, recitation, broadcasting, reproduction on microfilms or in any other physical way, and transmission or information storage and retrieval, electronic adaptation, computer software, or by similar or dissimilar methodology now known or hereafter developed.
The use of general descriptive names, registered names, trademarks, service marks, etc. in this publication does not imply, even in the absence of a specific statement, that such names are exempt from the relevant protective laws and regulations and therefore free for general use.
The publisher, the authors and the editors are safe to assume that the advice and information in this book are believed to be true and accurate at the date of publication. Neither the publisher nor the authors or the editors give a warranty, express or implied, with respect to the material contained herein or for any errors or omissions that may have been made.

Cover illustration: © World History Archive / Alamy Stock Photo

Printed on acid-free paper

This Palgrave Macmillan imprint is published by Springer Nature
The registered company is Macmillan Publishers Ltd.
The registered company address is: The Campus, 4 Crinan Street, London, N1 9XW, United Kingdom

WEBSITE DETAILS

Supportive material for this book, such as the appendices and virtual reconstructions (VR 1, VR 2, VR 3) referred to throughout, can be found at: www.feelingfilm.weebly.com.

It is recommended that this be explored alongside the book.

Acknowledgements

Thanks need to go to Palgrave for their help and support. Thanks too should go to Michael Williams, Lucy Mazdon and Shelley Cobb, as well as the Film and English departments at the University of Southampton. Kevin Donnelly should be especially thanked for the constant belief and encouragement he has provided in both getting my research turning and this book published.

Thanks go to Emilio Audissino, Elena Caoduro, Zubair Jatoi, Alican Pamir and Daniel O'Brien who have been fantastic throughout, proving helpful words when needed. The students I have taught at Southampton should be thanked for the insightful comments.

My family and friends deserve a debt of gratitude for their timely distractions. Special thanks go to Brendan and Brigitte Carroll who have only ever once fallen asleep reading my material; this book is dedicated to you. Particular thanks go to Peter Girdwood for his constant reassurance and assistance.

Contents

1 A New Methodological Approach — 1

2 Theoretical Approaches — 29

3 Sound Space — 49

4 Visual Space — 89

5 Audio-Visual Space — 141

6 What Next? — 181

Bibliography — 195

Index — 205

List of Figures

Fig. 3.1	Graph showing the number of shots within 'Cvalda', the time they occur, and the length of the shot in seconds	72
Fig. 3.2	Graph showing the different parts of the song overlaid onto Fig. 3.1	73
Fig. 3.3	A virtual recreation of the 'Cvalda' number from *Dancer in the Dark*	75
Fig. 3.4	Spectrograph showing changes in sound volume throughout the 'Cvalda' number	77
Fig. 3.5	Percentage of total shots in 'Cvalda' sequence as split between the different types of shot	78
Fig. 5.1	Spectrograph demonstrating sound levels in 'Supersonic Sam's Cosmic Café' number	172
Fig. 5.2	Spectrograph demonstrating quieter section of 'Supersonic Sam's Cosmic Café' number	172

CHAPTER 1

A New Methodological Approach

An aesthetic appreciation of film is often of secondary concern to the dominant theoretical strains running through the discipline. How the filmic elements of sound and image combine to engender a narrative that is comprehensible to the audience is frequently a guiding question that runs through academic works. What happens, however, when we make aesthetics the very object of study, when we explore the elements of film language not in the service of another goal but in their own right? The short answer is that a form of impasse is reached with the traditional and dominant theoretical methodologies no longer providing the tools necessary. Cognitivism, semiotics and narratology no longer suitably serve our purposes, for they all encourage a contextual reading of aesthetics that lead back to story and the role aesthetics play in constructing it. My desire to explore aesthetics in isolation comes down to an essential belief in the Gestalt rules of perception; that a form of perception happens before cognition and that this perception can involve an (un)conscious appreciation of aesthetics. When we watch a film we understand it on more than a narrative level, we simultaneously experience it on an aesthetic level. How we understand this aesthetic engagement is my primary concern.

The purpose of this book, whilst multifaceted, essentially comes down to a desire to explore a new methodological approach to the study of film aesthetics, or, as I shall also call them, 'abstract aesthetics', as they are removed from their narrative context. Discerning what such a methodology should look like took a considerable amount of time and many false starts. Eventually it became clear that in order to explore the relationship between the different elements of film language a spatial approach was needed, for it enabled an understanding of the negotiated interactions between sound and image on a complex level. Space, and the different ways of reading its representation and changes, is the essential focus of this book and I argue that a spatial reading is best understood through the senses.

My desire to explore this new spatial methodology on a holistic level, paying attention to sound, image and their interactions, encouraged me to take the musical as the book's case study in order to demonstrate how such an approach might be applied at the level of genre. It quickly became apparent that attempting to formulate a spatial reading of films through the senses without restricting my corpus of films, would quickly become unwieldly. A generic case study, as a lens through which to explore this new methodology, would enable me the ability to highlight variations and important considerations in its construction. The choice of the musical is severalfold, but essentially comes down to my desire to demonstrate two things. Firstly, that the musical genre's aural focus provides us with exaggerated examples of the audio-visual relationship to explore (such as the long-standing debates regarding diegetic sound), and secondly, that the musical, often excluded from generic theorising, is not as dissimilar to other genres as at first it might appear; what I discuss in terms of the musical can, to either a greater or lesser extent, be applied to other genres.

As result of this I did not want to follow a traditional book structure of each chapter exploring specific filmic case studies, but rather each chapter studies the theoretical approaches and implications of spatial readings before providing brief analysis in order to demonstrate how such theories can be applied to different song sequences from the musical. As such, they are not meant to be complete examples of analysis, but rather suggestions of how it might be performed given different foci. At this point it is essential to restate that, whilst the musical as a genre has been taken as a case study, a spatial methodology should not be seen as unique to the genre. Though any genre's idiosyncrasies will have an effect on the methodology's nuances, it can be applied to film more generally. It is my hope that other theorists will be encouraged to explore how these peculiarities and features of other genres impact on spatial readings.

In order to realise this new spatial methodology, I utilise a range of new or underused theoretical approaches; one innovative approach includes the use of virtual reconstructions to explore and analyse spatial representation. Textual analysis, whilst important for illustrating how spatial analysis can be achieved, will play a supportive role to the exploration of spatial theories more widely. Although the spatial methodology discussed can be applied widely to Film Studies, genres often contain an amalgamation of characteristics that enable them to differentiate themselves. When utilising this methodology in a thorough manner, it is therefore necessary that it should be adapted and pay attention to the peculiarities of the different genres, in our case: the musical. Consequently, it is important to consider the musical's generic and theoretical context.

Context

Though the innovation of this book is its ability to synthesise theories of space into a methodological approach, it does not exist in isolation. Indeed, important to any holistic approach is the pooling of a range of ideas both directly and tangentially related to the topic at hand. The musical's theoretical and structural concerns need to be considered in the adoption of a spatial methodology and its subsequent emphasis. On what terms we consider genre and how it is applied to the musical is therefore of importance.

Rick Altman writes that for too long the history of the musical has been discussed and written about almost without issue, when in actuality such terms as 'musical' and 'history' are inherently problematic.[1] For Altman, the musical genre is 'a fascinating multi-media celebration constituting the world's most complex art form'.[2] The musical thus offers a fantastic opportunity to explore a spatial methodology that will permit the subsequent adaptation into other generic conventions. This is in large part possible due to the ambiguity of the genre. Indeed, Altman argues that there are several means of defining and creating a corpus of films that might be defined as members of the musical genre, and these vary depending upon their source: producer, consumer, and/or critic.[3] In both form and content the musical can differ widely and yet to the producer and consumer categorisation can appear straightforward. 'The musical, according to the industry, is a film with music, that is, with music that emanates from what I will call the diegesis.'[4] Such a definition illustrates the difficulties presented to the critic—one might also widen this term to our status as theorist—that may be omitted by the industry and/or consumer, for it provides neither, as Altman states, 'a method for dealing with its functioning or even justifying this particular delimitation of the genre'.[5]

Altman's issue with such definitions, whilst shared by other theorists of the genre, are often overlooked in theoretical discussions. Steven Cohan, despite deliberating over the genre's peculiarities in *The Sound of the Musicals*, makes no attempt at definition.[6] The same is true of Bill Marshall and Robynn Stilwell's *Musicals: Hollywood and Beyond* in which they concede that whilst Altman has added much to the understanding of the 'large-scale workings of the genre, [they] are lacking markedly in the specifics which give such distinction and pleasure'.[7] This omission of genre debates should not be seen so much as a dismissal of the inherent problems, but as an unwillingness to contend with them. My assessment of the two such approaches is that they both provide fruitful avenues of discussion as they permit a variety of foci. It is important to synthesise the two; simultaneously assessing the difficulties characteristic of the genre but not making it the primary emphasis. As such, I want to provide a methodology for reading the musical genre that considers the peculiarities through a reading of its representation of space but does not make the peculiarities the main priority; after all this is not a book on the musical, but rather on spatial methodologies that uses the musical as a test case.

There has been limited discourse on the spatial idiosyncrasies of the musical genre beyond its relationship to diverse temporal structures. In this study I want to make a case for how space is represented through the symbiotic relationship between sound and image within the specific context of the musical number, thus discussing and acknowledging the characteristics of the genre that permits such structural delineation. My main approach for achieving this is through close analysis, referred to throughout the book as 'forensic analysis', of abstract aesthetics of the musical numbers. Academic discussion of space seen through the lens of abstract aesthetics has been unexplored in the study of the musical genre before this point.

The popularity of the film musical has been in a state of flux for more than half a century. After the success of the Hollywood musical under the studio system however, with such stars as Judy Garland, Fred Astaire and Doris Day each producing several popular musicals a year, it is, in many ways, a surprise that this should be the case.[8] It is important to concede that the musical's status as an all but sure box-office success in many respects declined alongside classical Hollywood.[9] Despite this, the oft-held adage of the 1980s and 1990s that the 'musical is dead' seems to have been laid to rest. The musical genre has been experiencing a renaissance and a renewed popularity. Films such as *Les Misérables* (2012) and

Mamma Mia! (2008) have been exemplars of a genre that is growing in box-office success, and theorists have been keen to ride this trend into academic discourse.[10] In recent years, discussions on the genre have become more wide ranging than ever before. Whereas previous theorising on the classical Hollywood musicals of old were largely restricted to topics of auteurism (c.f. work on Busby Berkeley by such theorists as Martin Rubin) and genre studies, epitomised by Rick Altman's *Film/Genre*, recent discourse on the musical has been eager to challenge established readings.[11] Such analyses promote re-readings of canonical texts through alternative theories such as camp or queer theory, an example of which would be Steven Cohan's work on the musical as holding a sub-cultural status in the gay community.[12] It is in this re-evaluating of canonical texts that analyses of the peculiarities of the genre are frequently omitted.

Running concurrently to this resurgence has been an increase in academic interest in Film Music and Sound Studies more generally. After Claudia Gorbman's seminal book on music in cinema, *Unheard Melodies*, which provided a catalyst for the sub-area within Film Studies, more and more theorists turned towards sound and music.[13] Gorbman's book, however useful, took as its basis Literature Studies. Though effective, there were numerous shortcomings that needed to be addressed in subsequent theorising. One such example would be the issue of technology and its development over the decades. Work on stereo sound, surround sound and different sound systems could provide insight into how films could be read differently by audiences.[14]

The use of music and sound in films largely followed the same model of representation; that is, the study of how sound and music's function aids in the understanding of narrative development and its forms of representation. I want to move away from the dominance of narrative and, rather than analyse how the different elements of film language aid in representation, make them the subject of analysis themselves: elements of film language are analysed on an abstract aesthetic level. My disavowal of narrative primacy, in terms of methodological approaches to the study of the musical, permits a wider discourse that is not constrained by the overarching framework of representation that narrative has offered. Without narrative as the defining methodological approach it is important to outline how I will delimit the musical genre. In short, through necessity I contradict myself and take as my cue Marshall and Stilwell's definition: 'any film in which music is an integral part of the narrative'.[15] Altman argues that it is the theorist not the consumer who struggles with a definition of the genre; this is undoubtedly true in my case. I worry over what is and is not a musical and, at my most anarchic, whether we should consider the musical a genre at all. Though this is not the argument I want to make here, I do want to promote a broadening of the musical genre. A broadening that may well make even audiences question the clarity of the term and the genre. Despite this, in this book I take examples of musicals that make little challenge to audience's perceptions of the genre with a view to encouraging a gradual re-assessment of modes of reading musicals. This notwithstanding, the use of films, which would not traditionally be defined as musicals, as supportive material show how the methodology and findings could be applied more widely. The filmic examples will be used to demonstrate how the different methodological approaches used in the study of the space of musical numbers can be applied.

In the rest of this introduction I want to contextualise my approach to the study of musical numbers in relation to wider academic Film Studies discourse and argue that a forensic analysis of abstract aesthetics can offer an alternative reading of the genre. Furthermore, it is important to engage with the structural issues of the genre by justifying the specific study of musical numbers rather than whole musical films.

My aims with this book are to explore the representation of space in musical numbers through a forensic analysis of abstract aesthetics. It therefore differs from other studies of the musical that focus on narrative and analyse a film's aesthetics in order to aid readings of camp, gender, Marxism and heterosexuality, amongst other approaches. I do not look at aesthetics in the service of narrative, but rather as an end in themselves and within the context of space. I therefore, call them 'abstract'.

This study does not exist in a vacuum. It is worth noting, however, that this study does not fit neatly into a single collection of work on a particular topic. As I will subsequently show, an array of diverse theories and theorists have been utilised, expanded upon and synthesised. As a consequence of the large range of theories used, I want to deal specifically with both the bigger, more influential theories utilised, and the less well known. My intention being that the reader will be given an understanding of how this work fits within theories that they may be well versed in, and a brief introduction into why the lesser-known theories will be important. Though I am in danger of fatiguing my reader with a cataloguing of the various theoretical strands of interest to this study, there is an element of necessity. This book is outlining a methodology; what that might look like and the tools that are needed in its development and implementation are essential to our discussion; so too are the type of discourses that a spatial methodology springs fourth from and engages with. We can be like the proverbial plaster, however, and make it as swift as possible.

Genre/The Musical

The musical is undoubtedly one of the archetypal genres of Hollywood cinema. Although I was determined not to restrict my analysis to Hollywood musicals in order to demonstrate the value of a spatial methodology to film more broadly, the main body of theoretical work on musicals in the western world has. Genre theory itself is problematic due to its polyvalent nature; its very definition is not without issue.

As previously mentioned, Rick Altman has a prolific body of work, on both genre theory more widely and the musical more specifically, and his work provides a useful overview. There are a variety of approaches to genre that Altman outlines. In his book *Film/Genre* he synthesises a large body of work on the subject and simplifies the general findings into four different definitions of genre; namely, 'genre as blueprint', 'genre as structure', 'genre as label' and 'genre as contract'.[16] Part of the longevity of genre studies is due to its amorphous nature, or perhaps more accurately, its ability to be manipulated to meet the ends of the theorists utilising it. Altman describes it as 'only slightly short of magical in its versatility [...] because of its ability to perform multiple operations simultaneously'.[17] This is arguably, however, where film genre differs from its literary counterpart. The breadth of the 'production-distribution-consumption process', as Altman dubs it, is not seen in Literary Studies to the same degree.[18] This breadth, however, is not without difficulty. Each time theorists choose to use genre theory, in terms of the musical Jane Feuer or Steven Cohan provide a useful example, restrictions must be made upon it. This may take the guise of restricting the work to a particular director's oeuvre, the canon, a particular filmic period, or creating further sub-units within a genre, such as those found in the musical (i.e. the 'back-stage' or the 'integrated' musical). Problems thus ensue as each time an approach is selected an alternative may counteract the findings. Of importance, however, is understanding genre theory as a contention between production and consumption categories, whether the latter be by audiences or theorists.

Whilst I am not aiming to promote one approach of genre studies over another—this debate may safely be left to other more inclined theorists— I will, however, primarily make use of the 'genre as structure' approach that details a framework that forms individual films. This is not through any desire to endorse structure over other approaches, indeed I will adapt and utilise some aspects of a structural approach to genre over others included in the rubric, but rather it better suits a more abstract aesthetic-based focus. Furthermore, I strongly believe that the versatility of a spatial methodology is illustrated by these taxonomies however useful or not you might think them. In short, a spatial reading can be conducted at either the macro- or micro-level; for instance, it may be applied to a director's oeuvre, a national cinema, an historical period or a generic sub-category of film. Choice and adaptability is what it offers. The emphasis on genre that I take in this book is just one possibility.

One argument frequently levelled at 'genre films'—a term often used disparagingly—is that there is little variation amongst the films. Genres often have common themes, plots and structures—aspects that make them identifiable to the viewer and aid in the creation of expectations. A consequence of this is their repetitive nature. Altman describes how 'both intratextually and intertextually, the genre film uses the same material over and over again'.[19] The result is, unavoidably, that plots lose their importance. The ending becomes not something that is anticipated, but rather known from the beginning. 'Genre films', as Altman states, therefore 'depend on the *cumulative* effect of the film's often repeated situations, themes and icons'.[20] An important aspect of this study is the disavowal of the importance of narrative readings and the promotion of abstract aesthetics. Genre theory thus becomes key to the promotion of this way of reading films. By removing the narrative emphasis I am neatly sidestepping the historical concerns and changes that genre theory tries to contend with; however valid such an approach is. As such, I am going to differ from much of the literature on the musical by not utilising a genre theory approach in my readings of musical numbers. Whilst this may at first appear problematic to a study of the musical, I hope it has the opposite effect. As this study seeks to convey an original methodology and discourse, analysing the musical without the overarching genre theory framework provides a more open means of viewing such films. The musical number can then be compared to other instances in films outside of the genre's framework; such as scenes within horror or action films, and indeed widened to films that have music as an essential part of the narrative. After all, if the example of Bollywood cinema is taken, the concept of genre and the musical is complicated. Genre theory is, however, not discarded; it informs the understanding of the musical without restricting analysis and it is important that subsequent work on space in film complicate this further.

Altman is an unusual theorist in that he very early took the musical as a case study in the exploration of genre.[21] Though the musical is archetypal, it is not unproblematic. If one looks at introductory film theory texts that shed light on genre for students new to Film Studies, it is clear that dealing with the musical as an example of genre does not have a high level of importance.[22] As has been previously demonstrated, the musical does not fit easily into conventional generic categorisation.[23] Thus, the argument to remove genre theory's framework is further supported.

Steven Cohan has stated that (in reference to classical Hollywood): 'In promoting an upcoming musical, a studio's theatrical trailers often focused more on the film's musical spectacle [...] than its story.'[24] The emphasis on spectacle rather than narrative adds further claim to an abstract aesthetic. Altman too claims that narrative is not the primary concern of the musical: 'Whereas the traditional approach to narrative assumes that the structure grows out of *plot*, the dual-focus structure of the American film musical derives from *character*.'[25] Altman is a key theorist for developing and rethinking the musical as a theoretical trope; his own understanding on the subject having changed over time.[26]

Cohan describes how the 'tradition of spectacle'—an idea that may be traced alongside Tom Gunning's 'cinema of attractions'—affects the musical: 'any attempt to account for its form as a mode of potent cultural representation needs to consider the significance that numbers bear whether analysed along, in sequence, or as elements in a larger formal structure that includes but is not dominated by narrative'.[27] This study can, therefore, be seen as my exploration into the creation of space within the 'spectacle'. This 'tradition of spectacle' is perhaps more important for the formation of an understanding of the musical than narrative. Bill Marshall and Robynn Stilwell state that the musical has arguably remained popular for 'the spectacle, the music, the enjoyable predictability of the outcome weighted against the pleasure of the varied details'.[28] This emphasis on the variation of details rather than the overarching structure is a key aspect of genre, and the musical largely holds true to this.

Understanding the musical as 'different' is a trope found within the literature on the genre. The musical, despite being an often overlooked genre within genre theory, does have both a core and ever-growing number of theorists dedicated to unlocking its secrets. The more established theorists include Rick Altman with his seminal book *The American Film*

Musical, Jane Feuer with *The Hollywood Musical*, and K. J. Donnelly with *British Film Music and Film Musicals*, amongst others.[29] Much of the work of Rick Altman and Jane Feuer in particular, though varying in their emphasis, may be generally defined as attempts to understand the musical on a structural level. Altman argues that the musical follows a different temporal structure from other genres, one based upon a dual focus narrative that works upon simultaneity rather than a linear time frame.[30] A key aspect of Altman's work is the theory of the 'audio-dissolve', which may be defined as the moment when there is a change in emphasis behind what is driving the scene, specifically in terms of sound.[31] He gives the example of Fred Astaire in *Top Hat* (1935) and the moment when Astaire's walking, rather than being driven by the character's motivations, becomes driven by the non-diegetic music; he begins to walk and eventually sing and dance in time to the music. What occurs is, therefore, a moment when the narrative (here seen as the character's motivations as described by the diegesis) fades into the background and what was once (apparently) non-diegetic—a better term may be Claudia Gorbman's 'meta-diegetic'— music is heard by the character who begins to dance in line with its time signature.[32] The notion of the audio-dissolve is important, whilst it is not unproblematic—I take issue with the notion on various levels—it does provide a good springboard for not only delineating the musical number from that which surrounds it, but also understanding its interplay between image and sound. The audio-dissolve is a liminal space where the interplay between sound and image is ambiguous.

Jane Feuer's *The Hollywood Musical* argues for a musical that is complex: that tries to deny its artificiality by making the song numbers appear spontaneous (often casting the characters as amateurs), however, they are often performed under a form of proscenium arch, making them appear more like consummate performers.[33] Feuer's exploration into the amateur/professional dichotomy is important for understanding the use of space between spectator and performer and this will be effectively combined with Adrienne McLean's work on Rita Hayworth to create a new reading that is found in the Chapter 4.[34] Though not the emphasis of her book—it being more an exploration into Rita Hayworth's career and star persona more widely—McLean does suggest that Hayworth was able to control her own representation within musical numbers. This control often saw her star image subverted due to the emphasis on being a consummate performer. It is this use of the multiple versions of a star—star, character, performer, amateur, etc.—within the musical numbers that relate it so well with Feuer's work and allows a synthesis of the two that has as yet not been approached by scholars. I will use it to understand how the space between the audience and performer is constructed, negotiated and, potentially, even controlled.

The musical does have a constantly growing body of work developing with many theorists attempting to provide new readings on a range of different films (both long theorised and new). Whilst this growing trend is to be encouraged and delivers much valuable theorising on the musical, it at times proves to be of limited use to our current discussion. One such example is Steven Cohan's edited collection, *Hollywood Musicals: The Film Reader*, which sees a range of topics debated including: gender politics by Patricia Mellencamp, feminism by Lucie Arbuthnot and Gail Seneca, sexual difference by Steven Cohan, and camp by Jack Babuscio.[35] These ideas are important and a book such as Cohan's is significant for developing these ideas, however, their use in the understanding of abstract aesthetics of space (audio, visual and audio-visual) is minimal as they privilege narrative.

Consequently, this study clearly demonstrates my desire to move away from what may be dubbed the 'traditional' discourse on the musical genre—one based upon narrative and semiotics—and towards a reading that focuses on space: its creation and representation. Understanding space, and its different 'realms' is, however, not without issue.

SPACE

Space benefits from being a subject that has been theorised in a variety of different ways, using a range of different approaches. There are, what one might call, the 'grand theories of space', such as those written by the French theorist Henri Lefebvre in *The Production of Space*.[36] Lefebvre's argument may be simplified as follows: every culture produces a unique space in its own way. Space, therefore, is a social product that affects practices and perception. It is thus intrinsically linked to politics as the space may be used to aid capitalism and the ruling classes. Lefebvre's theories are far ranging, seminal, influential, and ultimately of little use to me at this point. Though they affect the wider understanding of space, their ability to translate to abstract aesthetic representations of space is minimal. Lefebvre is not the only theorist who deals with political and cultural space. Others include, but are not limited to: Pierre Bourdieu, Judith Butler, Michel Foucault and Edward W. Said.[37] As with Lefebvre, these theorists provide background but are of little actual use here due to their focus on social understanding rather than the aesthetic construction and representation of space. These approaches will become increasingly useful as the spatial methodology develops with time and theoretical discussions. Space should be understood as a palimpsest and the work of Lefebvre et al. will add to the understanding of these different layers.

Different approaches to space may be found in different disciplines. In Anthropology there is the theory of proxemics that, even within its original discipline, remains little known. Unlike the 'grand theories of space', proxemics is, however, exceedingly useful for an understanding of abstract space. Proxemics was a term coined by the social anthropologist Edward T. Hall to describe the spatial, and indeed temporal, relations between people. He believed they can be read as a form of communication and he devised a form of notation that this study utilises. Edward T. Hall's work is not without the caveat of it being culturally specific; however with sensible application it proves to be very revealing. Hall's work, examples of which include: *The Silent Language* and 'A System for the Notation of Proxemic Behaviour', provides actual methods of recording and analysing space.[38] The usefulness of these methods is demonstrated in subsequent chapters.

Hall's work complements the work by theorists such as Mark Baldassare who argues that humans have a spatial behaviour that has important communicative values, both for observers and participants.[39] Although these theories are not without ambivalence, especially within the social sciences where it is claimed they lack sociological relevance, they provide interesting models of spatial understanding.[40] Through the use of proxemics, I am able to explore the spatial interactions between characters and their surroundings, and indeed, between characters and spectators (both internal and external) and, furthermore, record the data in new ways enabling further analysis. What proxemics offers, therefore, is an understanding of space on multiple levels.

Though it is true that many of the theories of space I employ are synthesised and adapted from other disciplines, Film Studies does have a small body of work on the subject that is of use. C. S. Tashiro's *Pretty Pictures: Production Design and the History Film* works to isolate set design from its narrative function in order to 'understand the image's impact beyond the story'.[41] Set design's function has long been associated with the narrative (c.f. Léon Barsacq). Tashiro's ability to separate the narrative, whilst remaining sympathetic to it, therefore provides a good model for me to work with.[42] He looks at space on a more abstract aesthetic level, creating a taxonomy of different types of space, such as 'Delimited space' that is either 'framed' or 'window'. Framed, he describes, is the 'movement of images *towards* (centripetal) centre of frame'; Window, on the other hand, is movement '*away* (centrifugal) from centre'.[43] Tashiro's taxonomy and analysis of space has not had the impact it deserves. Its flaws notwithstanding, its emphasis away from the traditional Film Studies' focus of narrative, has meant that it has gone largely unnoticed despite being used by such theorists as David Bordwell.[44] Tashiro's ideas and the way in which they disavow narrative will be of use.

David Bordwell explores space in terms of set design and mise-en-scène in his book *Figures Traced in Light: On Cinematic Staging*. He argues that 'deep or shallow, cinematic staging relies on a perspectival projection of space'.[45] The book takes as case studies a series of unrelated films; they vary in genre, period, director, style and studio. This broad range of case studies has inherently influenced my belief that a breadth of films can be explored through a single methodology. Like Bordwell, I am taking unrelated films (other than their ability to be placed along the musical genre's spectrum), and seeking to understand their musical numbers' representation of space in order to provide examples of how theories of space may be applied; with further work it is hoped that the methods can be extrapolated. In *Figures Traced in Light*, Bordwell breaks down average shot lengths and shows how they have changed over time. This, he argues, is an intrinsic part of a film's style and thus is important to a reading of film. Style, he argues, 'is the tangible texture of the film, the perceptual surface as we watch and listen, and that surface is our point of departure in moving to plot, theme, feeling—everything else that matters to us'.[46] Bordwell's use of terms such as 'tangible texture' and 'perceptual surface' are important features when discussing film's space, and are related to the theory of the haptic. I hope to further Bordwell's close analysis by looking beyond average shot lengths (though useful) to camera position and movement as well as sound levels.

HAPTICS

The theory of haptics is a marginal concept in Film Studies, though one that has the potential to uncover innovative and valuable readings and approaches to film. It is better known in the neurosciences and sciences more generally where there are studies into the senses.[47] Although peripheral there are a small, but devoted, group of theorists continuing to act as advocates. These include, but are not limited to: Laura Marks, Jennifer M. Barker, Giuliana Bruno, Yvette Hatwell, Arlette Streri and Édouard Gentaz.[48] The haptic has been described by the latter three as: 'tactilo-kinesthetic or active touch perception'.[49] Haptic images can, therefore, be seen as images that invite a sense of touch. Though the different aspects and approaches to haptic cinema will be looked at in more detail in Chapter 4, it is important here to note that one of the key aspects of the haptic is movement. Touch, unlike vision, requires contact and this contact can be felt throughout the body. Jennifer M. Barker describes how 'vision and touch are married in the experience of cinema, as are mind and body'.[50] Cinema spectatorship involves embodied acts of expression and perception, and as Barker describes, 'cinematic tactility occurs not only at the skin or the screen, but traverses all the organs of the spectator's body and the film's body'.[51] The body thus has the ability to 'feel' the film. Movement is important to this as vision is kinaesthetic through its registering of movements of the body. Consequently, as the eye perceives the movement of the images, it is picked up tangibly and tactilely by the body of the spectator; hence the embodied act of spectatorship. Audiences experiencing a film are doubly situated, existing in two places at once without leaving their seats.[52] They are experiencing the world of the film at the same time as experiencing the world of the cinema.

If one were to generalise, there are two key strains to haptic cinema; firstly, haptic images, and secondly, haptic experience. They are undoubtedly linked to one another. The latter is demonstrated by the embodied experience of films that is felt by the body. A key theorist that will be used in conjunction with this is Vivian Sobchack whose book *The Address of the Eye* argues for a form of spectatorship anchored in the senses; one that links the external audience with the onscreen images, characters and causes; in one sense, a single mode of viewing. The viewer is thus able to enter the cinematic space, and 'negotiate it'.[53] Sobchack's work is instrumental to my understanding of haptic experience. Haptic images, conversely, whilst still enabling haptic experience, can be looked at less abstractly. Theorists such as Antonia Lant have argued that the term 'haptic' has been misused in cinema.[54] She suggests that at the beginning of cinema, film was at its most haptic. With the discovery of depth of field, space and lighting techniques such as chiaroscuro, cinema moved more towards an optical form of cinema.[55] Haptic images, using Lant's evocation of the term, are images that suggest texture and detail. Both types of haptic cinema, however, are important for understanding the space represented in musical numbers as they give a means of understanding how the space between film and spectator is bridged, negotiated, or even subverted. A synthesis of the various strains of haptic cinema will provide new ways of interpreting musical numbers. Furthermore, it is important to extend the study of the haptic into the realm of sound and argue that haptic cinema can be created through sound space.

Sound

Whilst many theorists on sound begin their discussion lamenting the lack of theorising on such an important aspect of film, it is perhaps time to leave such frustration behind.[56] Although it is true that the study of sound in Film Studies, and indeed by theorists in Music and other disciplines who study films, has historically taken a back seat to the image, and still does (the rhetoric and language alone that dominates is proof of this), it would be misleading to suggest that sound theory is where it was twenty or so years ago.

One of the most seminal works regarding sound and music in film is Claudia Gorbman's previously mentioned *Unheard Melodies*. This book was a catalyst for theorising on sound and music in Film Studies, particularly in Anglophone academia. Gorbman deals with music as an important device within film; she both traces its history and its use. Gorbman argues that the 'traditional' understanding of music as 'background' sound is perhaps not accurate when one takes a historical approach and looks at its use across various periods.[57] Though Gorbman's *Unheard Melodies* and later work are important for numerous reasons, there is one in particular that makes it especially valuable here: the 'meta-diegetic'. Gorbman creates a taxonomy of uses of music—or perhaps more specifically their place—in film that includes diegetic, non-diegetic and meta-diegetic. Though diegetic and non-diegetic are basic terms used throughout Film Studies, Gorbman development of the term meta-diegetic to explain that, arguably, intermediary space is important. The meta-diegetic can be applied to images as well as sounds; in terms of sound, however, it is the sounds heard by characters within their own internal world. These sounds may be music, sound effects or dialogue. Indeed K. J. Donnelly has stated that 'Whereas it might easily be argued that all sonic aspects in cinema are sound effects, [...] I approach sound effects and dialogue more as music, or at least as retaining an aesthetic sensibility that might in some way be related to music'.⁵⁸ The process of characterising the previously mentioned sounds as meta-diegetic is not without difficulty, especially when used in the context of the musical genre. The musical often sees character's seemingly spontaneously break out into song. These outbursts may take place, as in *Oklahoma!* (1955) for instance, in outside rural areas; where does the sound come from? Where is the orchestra? Gorbman's term the meta-diegetic may be useful here, for the music is arguably imagined, but what happens when the musical number becomes a chorus of voices or dancers? Are they performing to a collective meta-diegetic?

The same claim that can be laid at much of genre theory can also be laid at Gorbman's door: the initial approach is one based in literary theory. Gorbman's taxonomy of the diegetic takes as its basis the narrative as told by the image. The image is still, even in a book dedicated to sound, given dominance. The taxonomy is relative to the images seen. If it is meta-diegetic it is because other characters cannot see it, or the audience cannot see it. As K. J. Donnelly argues:

> There are a handful of crucial, defining characteristics that mark out sound film [...] as a unique aesthetic and perceptual entity. They are all thought via sound although defined via image: non-or extra-diegetic status (where sound appears not to emanate from the world on-screen), off-screen sound (where the audience does not see the origins of the sound but assumes it to be near to what we see on screen), and synchronisation and asynchrony (where sound can match events on-screen or appear to a lesser or greater degree to be unconnected).⁵⁹

Gorbman's meta-diegetic can, however, be productively explored in conjunction with Altman's 'audio-dissolve'. Both these ideas will be used and placed within the context of an abstract audio-visual space that exists between audience and performer thus furthering our reading of these liminal spaces.

Furthering the discussion on the relationship between image and sound is Michel Chion's acousmêtre; the most important aspect of his work for a spatial methodology. The acousmêtre has been defined by Chion as:

> The acousmatic character whose relationship to the screen involves a specific kind of ambiguity and oscillation [...]. We may define it as neither inside nor outside the image. It is not inside, because the image of the voice's source—the body, the mouth—is not included. Nor is it outside, since it is not clearly positioned offscreen in an imaginary "wing," like a master of

ceremonies or a witness, and it is implicated in the action, constantly about to be part of it.[60]

The 'acousmatic character' is the sound 'one hears [...] without seeing its cause'.[61] Chion highlights how when we listen to the radio or a sound recording we are listening acousmatically.[62] Musicals often present the audience with sounds whose sources are hidden. The acousmètre is, therefore, an important theory for attempting to understand the sonic spaces of musical numbers. As outlined previously, space is more than the tangible space of set design; it is also the location of sounds, how they travel, how they are perceived and how the audience interacts with them. An exploration into the acousmètre will allow for an understanding into sources of sounds, especially those that are not visualised. Herein lies a problem with the acousmètre, however. Like many studies on the subject, the categorisations of sounds are often relative to their position with the image. Although film is undeniably an audio-visual medium, allowing image to be the primary base to compare sounds against does nothing for altering its supremacy in terms of theory that sound theorists have so long lamented.[63]

Expanding discussions on audio-visual space to include opera is valuable. Its long-standing theorising on the interaction between music, dialogue and set design can offer a productive approach to understanding the spatial negotiations that audiences participate in. Geraldine P. Dilla describes how

> In a typical drama there are three elements: words, acting and scenery. This might be called a kind of three-dimensional art, logical and consistent. Colour and lighting are accessories to the scenery; a dance may make part of the acting; the words may become poetry. But music comes into the drama as a sort of fourth or extra dimension.[64]

Opera and musicals are not the same entity, but they exist along the same spectrum. Utilising the understanding of the interaction between these elements is a useful exercise, and so too is the promotion of the musical as a spectrum.

Opera also offers long-standing theorising on the division of aria and recitative. An aria may be defined as an expressive piece, generally for a solo voice accompanied by an orchestra, while recitative resembles sung speech. The composer Richard Wagner explored the interaction between the two in his work *Opera and Drama*.[65] Wagner formed the idea of the *Gesamtkunstwerk* ('total work of art') that would be used to describe a work that was a synthesis of many art forms. Put simply, all the aspects would work together to meet the same ends. As such, the typical distinction between recitative and aria becomes (it perhaps always was) highly problematic.

Though the interaction between sound and image contributes to the development of filmic space, so too do aspects specific to sound that theorists, utilising a range of different approaches, have tackled. One such method is to analyse the technology used within films to create the soundtracks: Mark Kerins and Gianluca Sergi are two such examples.[66] Their work looks into the Dolby Surround Sound (DSS) technologies in particular and argues that it has been instrumental in developing sound space in films.[67] The argument—particularly Kerins'—follows that digital technologies enabled more discrete channels of separate sounds. The discrete nature of these channels allowed sounds to be placed throughout the cinema (typically behind the audience, to their left and right, and in front in line with the screen). Sound could, therefore, quite literally be emitted from different parts of the auditorium, and allow for a more 'immersive' experience and spatialisation of sound. These channels also permitted a greater range of sounds, and of each sound. The move away from mono sound technologies meant that sounds no longer needed to be conflated and compressed into a single track. The introduction of the 5.1 system also enabled a Low-Frequency Effects (LFE) channel that provided 'the same range of volumes to low-frequency sounds as they do higher-frequency ones'.[68] Low-frequency effects are able to elicit a bodily response in the audience, and, therefore, affect the space between the audience and the film. This has obvious links back to theories surrounding the haptics, and a new synthesis of the two can be found in later chapters in which I endorse a sensory approach to understanding space.

Work by Kerins, Sergi and other theorists such as Randolph Jordan and James Lastra are important for the understanding of sonic space.[69] Kerins and Sergi, however, are not without issue. Both are guilty of using Dolby as a metonym for all sound technologies, particularly surround sound. Their arguments, therefore, lack the nuances that one might hope for when exploring sound technologies. Each technology makes available different options for filmmakers and sound technicians, by not exploring these, Kerins and Sergi have simplified a subject that, whilst useful, should be used with some caution. Another charge that may be levelled at their work, particularly Sergi's, is that they are theoretically very light; despite the focus on new technologies and the effect on film, their work does not lead to new ways of thinking about sound and film.

The Musical Spectrum

The musical genre is often discussed in terms of categories. While this taxonomy has its uses, it is reductive. The musical genre is not as different from other genres as at first glance it appears. It exists as a sliding scale; more a topology than a taxonomy. On this scale one can place the pop musical, the dance musical and operetta; once they are seen as part of a spectrum, part of the same entity, their complexities can be dealt with more appropriately. Indeed, on this scale one could place films that are not traditionally dealt with under the rubric of the musical; such films might include anything from *An Affair to Remember* (1957) to *The Red Shoes* (1948), *Gilda* (1946) or *The Big Sleep* (1946).[70] It is not my aim to dismiss the various difficulties of the sub-genres represented along the film musical spectrum, but rather to highlight the similarities and differences that are present. The musical as a genre should not be seen as inherently problematic, but perhaps rather only the musical numbers themselves, and it is these spaces that film theory has yet to deal with adequately. Likewise, one might again draw attention to the similarities existing across genres, bringing further support to the notion that methodologies and theories, in this case a reading of space, applied to the musical can just as fruitfully be applied to film more widely.

The most obvious similarity present across the musical spectrum is the existence of musical numbers or song sequences. Whatever the name given to them, they will undoubtedly take a number of different forms, from an Astaire and Rogers' dance number to an aria in an opera. These musical numbers are potentially the integral component of the musical genre, eclipsing the narrative and its long-held status as the primary mode of signification. The musical number represents the pinnacle, the space where, depending on where your theoretical ties lie, the truest expression of feeling can be exhibited, where Dyer's utopia can be experienced but not presented, or where music and sound come most overtly to the fore.[71] If one returns to Altman's musical number, it is a site where some form of an audio-dissolve takes place. Overarching all this discussion, however, is the understanding that music and sound become the integral components. For a musical number to be comprehended an audio-visual shift must take place. This shift may take place within the audience as well as within the very aesthetics of the film itself. The distinctive nature of the space of the musical number, that it marks a change from the 'rest' of the film, that it is the musical at its most visually and aurally spectacular; it is for these reasons amongst others that the musical number is the focus of my analysis. Other genres will have their equivalent moments—a chase sequence in an action film or the violent deaths of a horror—that demonstrate exaggerated spatial changes.

How to Analyse Space

My overarching aim is the promotion of a spatial methodology, understood through abstract aesthetics and achieved through a close adherence to forensic analysis. The term 'forensic' is defined by the *Oxford English Dictionary* as '*Noun* (**forensics**) scientific tests or techniques used in connection with the detection of crime' and 'Adjective relating to or denoting the application of scientific methods and techniques to the investigation of crime: *forensic evidence.*'[72]

In constructing this spatial methodology, I have made use of several different approaches to forensic analysis. These range from proxemic analysis and shot-by-shot tabulations to animated virtual reconstructions.[73] These are used throughout, each emphasising and documenting a different aspect of space. Proxemic analysis makes use of the aforementioned Edward T. Hall's theories as well as his forms of notations. These forms of notations offer the opportunity to explore different ways of 'drawing' space. A consequence of this is that new ways of understanding space emerge, a result of the different notation's various foci.

The shot-by-shot tabulations will be formed through the use of Yuri Tsivian's Cinemetrics software.[74] This software enables statistical data to be collected, tabulated and graphed depending upon the researcher's focus. It assists in the quantifying of aesthetic data, such as shot length and type. With regards to a study of the film *Intolerance* (1916), Yuri Tsivian has stated that

> One sometimes hears that statistical data are far-sighted, that if average numbers can show us something it is only a big average picture, while the whole interest about doing film history is in looking at individual films. I totally agree with the latter point and disagree with the former. Yes, the average shot length is a statistical index, but this does not mean that it binds

us to static data or average films. I tried it recently to examine a picture as off-beat as Griffith's *Intolerance* and it helped me to learn a few things about its editing style which I don't think I would have been able to find out by any other means.[75]

My use of the Cinemetrics software enables, as Tsivian suggests, new discoveries to be made about film language, particularly when divorced from narrative context and analyses with a view to exploring spatial relations. They can be taken further than their usual ocularcentric use and can reveal much about sound space.

This book marks my first attempt to make use of virtual reconstruction software to animate set musical numbers. The purpose of which is to create an innovative way of exploring spatial relations. The virtual reconstructions are synchronised with the respective sound tracks and provide a bird's-eye view of the scene as it unfolds, thus permitting a demonstration of the unfolding spatial representations. The move away from static images to aid in spatial analysis towards animated virtual reconstructions, enables a better understanding of how space changes thorough time; it best demonstrate the intrinsic relationship between the two.

My desire to use a range of types of close analysis stems from the need to break down the different aspects of film style to their constituent parts in order to best analyse the relationships and interactions between them. By using innovative approaches, as particularly demonstrated by the virtual reconstructions, new ways of understanding space can be found alongside the process of keeping film theory up to date. These approaches need continual testing and refining, however. Their usefulness and possible applications in a spatial methodology should be questioned and discussed and it is my hope that others will engage with these debates.

Whilst I make use of several different theoretical approaches, it is important to note at this juncture that my overarching theoretical approach is one based upon gestalt theory; the idea that the whole is more than the sum of its parts. Thus, though each chapter explores a specific aspect of filmic space: sound and visual, it is important to synthesise these in the final chapter, audio-visual space. Despite this separation and eventual synthesis, it is important to restate that both sound and visual space should be understood as following gestalt rules. Neither sound nor visual space are single elements, but rather created through many elements working together to create space that would be impossible without the constituent parts. Put simply, sound, image and more obviously audio-visual space, are created through more than putting together constitutive elements but rather through negotiated relationships. Gestalt theory offers a scientific approach to the understanding of perception.

Structure

This book is formed by five chapters, the latter four featuring examples of textual analysis. Chapter 2: Theoretical Approaches will focus on the theoretical underpinnings. It discusses both the broader theoretical concerns as well as how specific theories will be utilised. It does not attempt to overview every theory used, individual chapters will address those used within each specific section, but rather to introduce some of the newer and/or more obscure theories. The aim of which is to enable the reader to approach this book with the understanding needed to follow the methodology and analysis and to chart out how the methodological course was created. Whilst Chapter 2 provides an introduction, each subsequent chapter will go into more depth with regards to the relevant theories utilised, questioning the usefulness of the ideas and at times offering alternative ideas.

Chapter 3: Sound Space examines the role of sound in the representation of space. Sound is an integral part of the musical number and this chapter details the theories surrounding sound and argues that sound is able to (a) create a space that is separate from that created by the image and (b) provide cohesion to a fragmented visual space. It explores these theories in detail before demonstrating how they can be applied in an analysis of *Dancer in the Dark* (2000), which argues that sound provides coherence to the musical number, and furthermore, is the driving force behind it. Whereas other scholars have looked into the effect of sound technologies, I explore how sound can be used to create a negotiated space between audience and performer, one that forms a tangible space. It, therefore, blends theories that have previously never been put together and provides a new reading of sound: through space.

Chapter 4: Visual Space details how images can be used to manipulate the space of musical numbers. It looks at how visual space changes and can be interpreted by the audience. It argues that the uses of visual space are broadly twofold: firstly, that they provide sites for the performer to exhibit their skills, and secondly, that the visual space encourages readings that understand that the space extends from the frame of the screen. This chapter demonstrates how virtually reconstructed scenes can be used and animated in order to demonstrate the movement of the characters within the scene, as well as the camera. This introduces the reader to another new form of forensic analysis: virtual recreation. It then turns to an analysis of the RKO musicals of Astaire and Rogers.

Chapter 5: Audio-Visual Space explores the spatial relationships between images and sounds within musical numbers. It seeks to understand how the two negotiate the space at any given moment in order to discern if one dominates the other. The chapter looks at musicals that vary across the musical genre's spectrum in order to explore the space more fully. It transposes for the first time theories developed in Opera Studies onto the musical. It then turns to *Umbrellas of Cherbourg* (1964) and *Billy the Kid and the Green Baize Vampire* (1985) to demonstrate how some of these theories can be used in textual analysis.

NOTES

1. Rick Altman, *The American Film Musical* (Bloomington: Indiana University Press, 1989), p. 1.
2. Altman, *The American Film Musical*, p. 2.
3. Altman, *The American Film Musical*, p. 13.
4. Altman, *The American Film Musical*, p. 12.
5. Altman, *The American Film Musical*, p. 13.
6. Steven Cohan, (ed.), *The Sound of Musicals* (Basingstoke: Palgrave Macmillan, 2010).
7. Bill Marshall and Robynn Stilwell, (eds), *Musicals: Hollywood and Beyond* (Exeter: Intellect Books, 2000), p. 1. Marshall and Stilwell have essentially used Altman as a metonym for all genre theory studies of the musical.
8. Such musicals were popular in terms of box-office receipts, see 'The History of Film: 1940s', *Film Site*, www.filmsite.org/40sintro5.html [date accessed 19/12/2013].
9. See Michael Hammond and Linda Ruth Williams, (eds), *Contemporary American Cinema* (Maidenhead: Open University Press, 2006) for a discussion on the fall of the studio system and the rise of New Hollywood. Whilst not looking at the musical genre specifically, the book identifies the causal factors in the change of Hollywood's cinema more generally.

10. Though the trend of increased academic discourse into the musical seems to be steadily increasing, it should be noted that amongst a devout group of scholars discourse on the genre never ceased. See Rick Altman, Jane Feuer, Steven Cohan, K. J. Donnelly et.al. for examples.
11. Martin Rubin, *Showstoppers: Busby Berkeley and the Tradition of Spectacle* (New York: Columbia University Press, 1993); Rick Altman, *Film/Genre* (London: BFI, 1999).
12. Steven Cohan, (ed.), *Hollywood Musicals: The Film Reader* (London: Routledge, 2002), p. 3.
13. Claudia Gorbman, *Unheard Melodies* (London: BFI, 1998).
14. See Mark Kerins, *Beyond Dolby (Stereo): Cinema in the Digital Sound Age* (Bloomington: Indiana University Press, 2011); Daniel Goldmark, Lawrence Kramer, and Richard Leppert, (eds), *Beyond the Soundtrack: Representing Music in Cinema* (London: University of California Press, 2007); Alan Williams, "Is Sound Recording Like a Language?", *Yale French Studies*, 60 Cinema/Sound (1980), 51-66; Michel Chion, *Audio-Vision: Sound on Screen*, trans. Claudia Gorbman (New York: Columbia University Press, 1994); Jay Beck and Tony Grajeda, (eds), *Lowering the Boom* (Urbana: University of Illinois Press, 2008). et. al., for examples.
15. Marshall, p. 1.
16. J. D. Andrew, *Concepts in Film Theory* (Oxford: Oxford University Press, 1984). Quoted in: Rick Altman, *Film/Genre*, p. 14.
17. Altman, *Film/Genre*, p. 14.
18. Altman, *Film/Genre*, p. 15.
19. Altman, *Film/Genre*, p. 25.
20. Altman, *Film/Genre*, p. 25.
21. See Rick Altman, *Genre: The Musical* (London: Routledge, 1981).
22. See David Bordwell and Kristin Thompson, *Film Art: An Introduction*, 7th edn (New York: McGraw Hill, 2004).
23. See Altman, *Genre: The Musical*, pp. 1–7. in which Altman argues that early writers on the musical genre were more prone to criticising than analysing the genre. This book further explores the structural and formal properties of the musical genre.
24. Cohan, *Hollywood Musicals: The Film Reader*, p. 11.
25. Altman, *The American Film Musical*, p. 21.

26. See Altman, *The American Film Musical* and c.f. Rick Altman, "The American Film Musical as Dual-Focus Narrative", in Cohan, (ed.), *Hollywood Musicals: The Film Reader* (London: Routledge, 2002), pp. 41–52.
27. Tom Gunning, *The Silent Cinema Reader* (London: Routledge, 2003), pp. 41–50; Cohan, (ed.), *Hollywood Musicals: The Film Reader*, p. 18.
28. Marshall, p. 1.
29. Altman, *The American Film Musical*; Jane Feuer, *The Hollywood Musical* (London: Macmillan Press, 1993); K. J. Donnelly, *British Film Music and Film Musicals* (Basingstoke: Palgrave, 2007).
30. Altman, *The American Film Musical*, p. 21.
31. Altman, *The American Film Musical*, p. 69.
32. Gorbman, *Unheard Melodies*.
33. Feuer, *The Hollywood Musical*.
34. Adrienne McLean, *Being Rita Hayworth* (London: Rutgers University Press, 2004).
35. Cohan, *Hollywood Musicals: The Film Reader*.
36. Henri Lefebvre, *The Production of Space*. Trans. Donald Nicholson-Smith (Oxford: Blackwell, 1993).
37. For summaries and introductions to the work of these theorists and many others see: Phil Hubbard, Rob Kitchin, Gill Valentine, (eds), *Key Thinkers on Space and Place* (London: Sage Publications LTD, 2004).
38. Edward T. Hall, *The Silent Language* (New York: Premier Books, 1965); Edward T. Hall, "A System for the Notation of Proxemic Behaviour", *American Anthropologist*, 65 (1963), pp. 1003–1026.
39. Mark Baldassare, "Human Spatial Behavior", *Annual Review of Sociology* (1978), 29-56, (31).
40. Baldassare, p. 38.
41. C. S. Tashiro, *Pretty Pictures: Production Design and the History Film* (Austin: University of Texas Press, 1998), p. 18.
42. Léon Barsacq, *Caligari's Cabinet and Other Grand Illusions: A History of Film Design* (New York: New American Library, 1978).
43. Tashiro, p. 39.
44. David Bordwell, *Figures Traced in Light: On Cinematic Staging* (Berkeley: University of California Press, 2005).
45. Bordwell, *Figures Traced in Light: On Cinematic Staging*, p. 16.

46. Bordwell, *Figures Traced in Light: On Cinematic Staging*, p. 32.
47. For an understanding of different approaches and theories surrounding art and the senses see: Francesca Bacci, David Melcher, (eds), *Art and the Senses* (Oxford: Oxford University Press, 2011).
48. Giuliana Bruno, *Atlas of Emotion: Journeys in Art, Architecture and Film* (New York: Verso, 2002).
49. Yvette Hatwell, Arlette Streri and Édouard Gentaz, *Touching for Knowing: Cognitive Psychology of Haptic Manual Perception* (Philadelphia: John Benjamin's Publishing Company, 2003), p. 2.
50. Jennifer M. Barker, "Touch and the Cinematic Experience", in Francesca Bacci, David Melcher, (eds), *Art and the Senses* (Oxford: Oxford University Press, 2011).
51. Barker, p. 151.
52. Barker, p. 155.
53. Vivian Sobchack, *The Address of the Eye: A Phenomenology of Film Experience* (Princeton: Princeton University Press, 1991).
54. Antonia Lant, "Haptical Cinema", in *October*, vol. 74, Fall 1995, pp. 45–73.
55. Tim Bergfelder, Sue Harris, Sarah Street, (eds), *Film Architecture and The Transnational Imagination* (Amsterdam: Amsterdam University Press, 2007), p. 23.
56. The use of the term 'sound' is not without issue and debates around whether sound or music should be used can be found. See K. J. Donnelly, *Occult Aesthetics: Synchronisation in Sound Film* (Oxford: Oxford University Press, 2014), p. 2.
57. Alan Durant, "Review: *Unheard Melodies*", *Popular Music*, 7 (1988), pp. 339–342
58. Donnelly, *Occult Aesthetics: Synchronisation in Sound Film*, p. 12.
59. Donnelly, *Occult Aesthetics: Synchronisation in Sound Film*, p. 2.
60. Chion, p. 129.
61. Chion, p. 32.
62. Chion, p. 32.
63. Theories surrounding the haptic and perception suggest that describing film as audio-visual is still too limiting; films are felt and perceived with more senses than vision and hearing.
64. Geraldine P. Dilla, "Music-Drama: An Art Form in Four Dimensions", *Music Quarterly*, X (1924), p. 493.
65. Richard Wagner, *Opera and Drama* (Lincoln: University of Nebraska Press, 1995).

66. Mark Kerins, *Beyond Dolby (Stereo): Cinema in the Digital Sound Age*; Gianluca Sergi, *The Dolby Era* (New York: Manchester University Press, 2004).
67. Sergi traces the Dolby technology throughout its history rather than focusing solely on DSS technology, though this is an important theme of his book.
68. Kerins, p. 36.
69. Randolph Jordan, "The Visible Acousmêtre: Voice, Body and Space Across the Two Versions of *Donnie Darko*", *Music, Sound and the Moving Image* 3, no. 1 (Spring 2009), pp. 47–70; James Lastra, "Reading, Writing, and Representing Sound", in Rick Altman, (ed.), *Sound Theory: Sound Practice* (New York: Routledge, 1992), pp. 65–86
70. Other, more recent films would include, but are not limited to: *Kill Bill* (2003), *Volver* (2006), *Wild at Heart* (1990).
71. Richard Dyer, "Entertainment and Utopia", in Bill Nichols, (ed.), *Movies and Methods Volume 2: An Anthology* (Berkeley: University of California Press, 1985), pp. 220–232.
72. "Forensic", *Oxford Dictionaries* <http://oxforddictionaries.com/definition/english/forensic> [accessed 07/10/2013].
73. These virtual animations can be found on the accompanying website.
74. Details of which can be found here: "Movie Measurement and Study Tools Database", <http://www.cinemetrics.lv/index.php> [date accessed: 19/02/2014].
75. Yuri Tsivian, "*Intolerance* Study",<http://www.cinemetrics.lv/tsivian.php> [date accessed: 19/02/2014].

CHAPTER 2

Theoretical Approaches

This book will be synthesising and (re)introducing many, often new, theories to Film Studies and the study of the musical. As Chapter 1 outlined, a new approach for studying musical sequences has become necessary due to their inability to fit neatly into genre theory and their lack of reliance on narrative. Although it is not my aim to override previous theoretical approaches that have often yielded fruitful readings, I do, however, intend to promote an alternative theoretical approach; one based upon abstract aesthetics and spatial relations; and, as will become clear throughout the book, this has a strong phenomenological approach. This should not be seen as coming at the expense of more established theoretical bents, but rather supporting, questioning and offering an alternative mode of analysis. I do not want to throw the proverbial baby out with the bath water, but it is important that we stop to consider our approaches and do not use dominant modes unquestioningly. History has undoubtedly proven them academically useful but has also gone some way to making us blind to alternative approaches and their subsequent findings. This is not a one or the other approach to methodology, however. Indeed, the methodology I am promoting here, whilst in many respects an exaggerated form, could be integrated with already established modes, for instance with the reintegration of narrative readings or a consideration of gender. In order to first provide clarity on a spatial methodology it is important to introduce a number of the theories that will be dealt with and utilised. This chapter will outline some of the larger theories applied; its offering will, by necessity, be brief, with the theories expanded upon and applied in subsequent chapters. This chapter should be used as a reference point and supportive piece to the subsequent chapters; returned to when the key themes or theoretical ideas of later chapters need further grounding.

Gestalt Theory

Gestalt theory underpins this study, gives it cogency and permits abstract spatial relations to be the focus; it is a consequence of gestalt theory's work on perception that allows it to be so. Put simply, the central tenet of gestalt theory is that the whole is other than the sum of the parts. Though discussions of gestalt are often anything but simple, the central principle should be kept in mind throughout this book. Gestalt theory is thus important for this study as it provides an overarching approach to the exploration into musical numbers' spatiality. By utilising a gestalt approach I am not only able to offer an alternative to the more traditional Film Studies approaches, but I am also continuing the line of thinking that understands that one aspect of space affects another; they are all interrelated and cannot be looked at in isolation if a true understanding of the whole is to be achieved.

W. D. Ellis has echoed this view by describing how in gestalt, 'there are wholes, the behaviour of which is not determined by that of their individual elements, but where the part-processes are themselves determined by the intrinsic nature of the whole'.[1] The use of such terms as 'behaviour' and 'part-processes' begins to hint at the more scientific nature of gestalt theory, or gestalt psychology as it is often called.[2] It should be understood as a means of understanding rather than as the product of that understanding: gestalt theory is not what you get once analysis has occurred, but rather what you use in order to yield your results. Ellis states that it is

> [...] concrete research; it is not only an *outcome* but a *device*: not only a theory *about* results but a means towards further discoveries. This is not merely the proposal of one or more problems but an attempt to *see* what is really taking place in science.[3]

As outlined in Chapter 1, Film Studies has long been dominated by cognitive theory promoted by such seminal theorists as David Bordwell and Kristin Thompson.[4] Gestalt theory, comparatively, has been all but forgotten about.[5] One possible reason for this is that gestalt theory does not guarantee easy and useful results. It is a process that, when applied, may give you data that either does not correspond with your 'hypothesis' or very little can be extrapolated from. This is not to say that the data is wrong or incorrect, quite the opposite in fact, but rather that it may not easily fit well with established readings of films.

Gestalt theory arose as a reaction against atomistic psychology, which itself was adapted from the natural sciences. David Katz explains how 'the organism was represented as a combination of the smallest elements, namely cells; if one could achieve insight into the function of the single cell, comprehension of the work of the whole organism would come about automatically, to a certain extent, by summation'.[6] The aim was, therefore, to understand the parts that make up an organism in the hope of understanding the organism itself. This atomistic mode of thinking is often applied to Film Studies. Frequently multiple aspects will be looked at individually whilst analysing a film or sequence from a film, and through this the film is deemed understood. This method, however, pays little attention to the effect one aspect will have on another, and consequently what effect they will have when combined. Furthermore, they often overlook the fact that a film is frequently watched and perceived first as a whole, a complete 'film' rather than as a series of images and music or sounds that are independent of one another. It is here that gestalt theory can be used to redress this failing, through the gestalt theory of perception.

David Katz has stated that gestalt psychologists' reaction to atomistic psychology, which borrowed heavily from the natural sciences, is

> That all visual percepts are influenced by knowledge that comes with experience. But experience by no means plays the major role in forming objects into separate entities. Objects constitute themselves for other, more deep-seated reasons, and it is these which account for our ability to have experience with objects in the first place. The distinction is a vital one.[7]

A number of important features of gestalt perception can be taken from this statement. Firstly, that gestalt's chief emphasis, at least in terms of perception, is visual. The foremost and greatest volume of work by gestalt theorists has been around visual perception with the summation being the development of the 'laws of perception'. Secondly, that gestalt theory understands that experiences are one of the factors that can effect perception, but as Katz states, they are certainly not the key to understanding perception. Experiences are unique to the individual, therefore, if it is the main component of perception it is problematic, particularly if one is trying to understand perception on a larger scale than the individual. The components that make up visual perception have been dubbed the 'laws of perception'. These include:

1. The law of proximity
2. The law of similarity
3. The law of closed forms
4. The law of 'good' contour, or common density
5. The law of common movement
6. The law of experience

Katz argues that the first five laws 'are convincing evidence that environmental objects are seen exactly as they appear at the time of observation. Gestalt psychology maintains that the laws operate even in a consciousness that has had no opportunity to have experience with objects'.[8]

This book is not the first attempt at utilising gestalt theory in a Film or Media Studies context. Though it is true that cognitive theory has dominated Film Studies analysis, the Film theorist Rudolf Arnheim attempted to bring gestalt theory to a film and media context. 'A gestalt', Arnheim claimed, 'is not an array of self-contained elements, but a configuration of forces interacting in a field. Since this approach deals with structure, it eliminates a number of psuedodichotomies [...]'.[9] Arnheim's 'chief concern was how architectures of comparison, contour, line, and colour interact with a creative perceptual system'.[10] How, however, does this apply to film and media? One way that Arnheim suggests is through the often prevalent but bourgeois understanding of art as the creation of a single artist. Indeed if one takes the entire *oeuvre* of a filmmaker and understand that it takes place over a period of time with varying contexts, how can one read the individual films? 'To interpret an individual work means to deal with the structure of its style—a procedure no different from dealing with the style of a whole group of works or artists.'[11] 'Constancy and change' Arnheim states '[...] are incompatible only as long as the whole is defined as the sum of the parts; whereas gestalt theory can study the conditions that make a structure remain constant although the vehicle for it undergoes changes.'[12] Gestalt theory, Arnheim believed, therefore allows individual films to be seen as fitting into an artist's style.

This is but one way that gestalt theory can be applied to films. Gestalt theory's focus on the atomised units versus the whole is integral to its whole conception. 'The only reason why the individual is not equal to the sum of its ingredients is that the process of gestalt formation organises those ingredients in an entirely new structure.'[13] The 'ingredients' in the case of films can be interpreted in numerous ways; they can be the elements such as mise-en-scène, lighting, editing, and sound, or even within these they can be broken down further. Sound, for instance, can be divided into dialogue, sound effects and music, and even within these categories further splits can be made. This study continues Arnheim's attempt at transferring gestalt theory to a Film Studies context by studying all aspects of space, not in isolation, but with an understanding of how the constituent parts (sound, framing, proxemics, images, etc.) affect and are affected by the whole space of the musical number. Space, therefore, is the inherent focus of this book.

Through this book's discussion on sound, however, it challenges the visual emphasis that is frequently seen in gestalt theory. Perception is a vital component of gestalt theory, and perception of space is integral to the latter's invocation.

Space

As the central premise of this study is the understanding of spatial relationships in musical sequences, it would be remiss to omit discussion on what might be dubbed the 'grand theories of space', if only on a superficial level. Whilst an understanding of the following debated theories is important, their usefulness to this study is of varying degree. As previously detailed, theoretical discussions on space have undergone a variety of different approaches and foci, ranging from: culture, politics, gender, feminism, architecture, and tangible space amongst others. Space, as a concept and construct, can be both abstract and concrete; and furthermore, these terms are not mutually exclusive.

Henri Lefebvre's *The Production of Space* is a seminal example of spatial theorising.[14] Lefebvre's argument is that cultures produce and interact in a unique space. As something that is produced, frequently with political motivations and implications, space can be commodified; it is a social product that affects the way people interact and the manner in which things are perceived. The creation of this space commonly aids the ruling classes to meet their own ends and continue their power. In the Western world this is ordinarily capitalism. Lefebvre's theories, whilst seminal, are of little use to this study because of their broad cultural and political implications. Though these theories have influenced the comprehension of space in an almost all-encompassing way, they have little to make them applicable to a reading that focuses on abstract aesthetic representations of space. Lefebvre is not the only theorist who deals with political and cultural space. As with Lefebvre, however, these theorists provide background but are of little use to the present exploration of abstract aesthetics. These ideas have the potential to be applied once the 'actual' space of musical numbers has been established; it is this latter aspect on which I am focused.

More 'modest' theories of space are, however, of use. The film theorist C. S. Tashiro, for example, provides spatial analysis of film that is removed from the limitations that narrative places upon it.[15] Allowing film's narrative to take a secondary role permits a focus on alternative aspects that are also absorbed by audiences, no matter how (un)consciously; one of which includes the space of a scene. Tashiro develops the notion of 'circles of space' in which space is categorised by its distance from the site of action. This is undoubtedly problematic, not least in terms of how one characterises the focus of a scene. A musical number, for instance, may contain a single character standing alone, statically singing a song such as Deanna Durbin's performance of 'Danny Boy' in *Because of Him* (1946), or it might consist of several characters dancing in different parts of the scene such as the 'Barn Raising' in *Seven Brides for Seven Brothers* (1954). What, in the latter instance, counts as the epicentre of the scene in which the 'circles of space' emit from? Exploring this aspect is one way I will utilise and expand upon Tashiro's work.

C. S. Tashiro's circles of space, as adapted from the work of architect Christian Norberg-Schulz, are categorised as follows: space that is worn (i.e. costumes/makeup/jewellery), graspable objects, furniture, the house, the street, the landscape and cosmic space. Whilst these are not unproblematic, they are of use as they focus on *interaction*. Tashiro asks: 'Do I look at a film or do I participate in it?'[16] The answer to this question will be looked at in conjunction with theories surrounding haptic cinema. Tashiro's circles of space encompass both the diegetic and non-diegetic realm; but how are these spaces delimited?

DIEGESIS

Though the term 'diegesis' may well be one of the earliest terms we learn as students of film, it is not, however, as simple as it as first appears. Ontologically, it is a complex, amorphous concept, hard to delimit and easy to find filmic examples that contradict and complicate the notion. The use of the term diegetic, and its reverse counterpart non-diegetic are further complicated when applied to the musical genre including its use of sound.

Claudia Gorbman's book *Unheard Melodies* challenges the long-held assumptions regarding film music, such as its use in early film and development over time.[17] A central concept of Gorbman's work is the exploration into the term 'meta-diegetic', which, in terms of music and sound, may be described as the internally heard sounds by characters, whether it is in their dream, imagination or other such device. Gorbman's view of diegesis is not entirely unproblematic, however. Alessandro Cecchi, for example, has taken issue with Gorbman's conception of the term diegesis and meta-diegesis. Cecchi states that inference is a central tenet of the theory of diegesis as it is 'crucial in clarifying the strict connection that exists between diegesis and the ontological position of the narrated story within the fictional horizon of cinema'.[18] He expands on this idea by stating that inference (and induction) in terms of diegesis is implied to be a philosophically realist conception in that 'logical induction is able to guarantee a more reliable and complete knowledge than that deriving from sensible perception'.[19] When related to cinema the implication is that inference gives us knowledge of an 'objective and coherent world (diegesis), while what appears on screen (the narration) is merely a subjective and partial perspective on this'.[20] 'In other words', Cecchi states, 'the concept of diegesis contains a 'thetic' moment, implicitly instituting an ontology within the fictional representation.'[21] The consequence of this is that there should be a distinct difference between diegesis and narrative: diegesis 'in the sense of a reality established by inference starting from the data of perception, should remain separate from narration, or how such reality is presented on screen'.[22] Having a third category, as Gorbman promotes, is to Cecchi thus incompatible with the notion of diegesis.

Understood as two separate entities, the complications between diegetic and non-diegetic should be removed, making Claudia Gorbman's 'meta-diegetic' a moot point. Furthermore, Ben Winters argues that what is often considered non-diegetic music is actually playing a large role in the creation of narrative and cinematic space, thereby complicating the delineation of the diegetic realms still further.[23] These arguments notwithstanding, Gorbman is not the only theorist to contend for a 'meta-diegetic' space; though the concept may not maintain the same moniker. Rick Altman's 'audio-dissolve', whilst not explicitly stated as such by Altman, is concerned with the liminal space between diegetic and Gorbman's meta-diegetic.[24] Altman describes the audio-dissolve as the moment when there is a change in emphasis behind what is driving the scene, specifically in terms of sound. It is, put simply, that moment when the performer(s) start singing or dancing to the music that was, until that moment, considered either non-diegetic or lacking a visual source. Do the characters hear this music? Is it subjective and therefore meta-diegetic? And what happens when there is more than one character performing to the same accompanying music and sounds? Is this a shared space between audience and performer?

Another theorist that has focused on that ambiguous moment within the diegesis is Robynn Stilwell. Stilwell's article, 'The Fantastical Gap between Diegetic and Non-diegetic' recognises that the boundary between diegetic and non-diegetic is not as unambiguous as it at first appears. Indeed, the move between diegetic and non-diegetic happens frequently (and the musical provides prime examples of these traversings), but Stilwell claims the frequency does not negate the importance. Stilwell argues that because the 'boundary' between diegetic and non-diegetic is crossed so often, it emphasises the difference between them.[25] Stilwell refutes the crossing of the boundary being seen as an 'event', but rather claims it is a process: 'a trajectory, a vector, a gesture'.[26] Musical numbers are often prime examples of this 'fantastical gap'—as Stilwell dubs it—however, they often complicate the diegetic/non-diegetic dichotomy still further. Stilwell takes the example of a Busby Berkeley film and questions whether his great spectacular numbers are not 'far more "non-diegetic" than the music […]. The non-diegetic becomes a space of fantasy, at least in part because of anxiety over its "impossibility"'.[27] As the dichotomy is thus complicated further, Stilwell suggests refining Gorbman's concept of the meta-diegetic:

> As a kind of represented subjectivity, music clearly (through framing, dialogue, acting, lighting, sound design, or other cinematic process) situated in a character who forms a particularly strong point of identification/location for the audience. The character becomes the bridging mechanism between the audience and the diegesis as we enter into his or her subjectivity.[28]

The meta-diegetic then is, Stilwell contends, 'a kind of musical "direct address", threatening to breach the fourth wall that is the screen'.[29] This type of 'direct address' can be explored within the musical. Stilwell's argument for the direct address adds to the debate that is arguably at the heart of many discussions of the musical: how to delineate the musical number from that which surrounds it. The notion of direct address offers an opportunity to take discussion of the musical into new directions, by combining the notion with the theories of haptics and embodied spectatorship.

Proxemics

Proxemics is the term given by Edward T. Hall, the social anthropologist, to the study of spatial relations between humans and their environments.[30] It is an example of theorists attempting to understand and explore the unspoken interactions that exist between humans. An important aspect of proxemics is its cultural specificity; Hall argued that different cultures could not be relied upon to interpret proxemic behaviour if the example they were given came from outside of their own cultural group.[31] The application of proxemics and its use is, therefore, arguably very narrow. We might ask: what use can it have in a study of the representation of space in musical numbers? There are perhaps two main uses that make it relevant. Firstly, it can aid in the study of relations between audience and characters and set design—the film as a whole—and secondly, it can help interpret the space between characters within the diegesis. The former can be realised through the understanding of the camera as a metaphor for the audience and thus allows for an appreciation of a bridged and embodied space. The latter can assist in the comprehending of the use of space within the number itself: the way the set is used, how the characters travel and their movements with and between one another. Whilst the application of proxemics is looked at in more detail in Chapter 4, it is important here to outline the background and the general concepts of the theory as devised by Hall and developed by other theorists.

Hall argued that there are two aspects to proxemics; time and space.[32] 'Time talks' he claims,

> It speaks more plainly than words. The message it conveys comes loud and clear because it is manipulated less consciously, it is subject to less distortion than the spoken language. It can shout the truth where words lie [...] the silent language of time and space.[33]

Hall aligns both space and time, and indeed their interaction with one another, as a language to be read conveying meaning with more clarity than speech. Proxemics, therefore, while spatially motivated, can be transferred and employed in the study of speech also. This is still achieved through the study of space, one way is through the temporal space that exists between words or phrases, another through the changes in facial expressions. How is this 'silent' language to be understood, however? Hall details an example of a politician:

> A political figure makes a speech which is supposed to be reassuring. It has the opposite effect. When the words are read *they* are reassuring, yet the total message as delivered is not. Why? [...] sentences can be meaningless by themselves. Other signs may be much more eloquent. The significant components of a communication on the level of culture are characterised by their brevity as compared with other types of communication.[34]

What are these signs? Their brevity makes them more difficult to recognise; Hall's description also proposes that they are unconsciously read by the viewer, suggesting that they are understood on an emotional level, rather than a cognitive one. The viewer may not consciously know why the politician's speech is wrong, but they feel it. Hall, as Michael O. Watson claims, 'reminds us that man's culture transcends him in time and space and that much of his behaviour is rooted in his phylogenetic past'.[35] Proxemic behaviour and the ability to read it is therefore, in part, both culturally learnt and ingrained. Cultural specificity should, however, be understood as a caveat to proxemics. Mark Baldassare describes how, whilst Hall compared 'contact cultures' with 'noncontact cultures' (contact cultures being those that make frequent physical contact with other members of the group, noncontact cultures being the opposite) and felt that the former operated within smaller interaction distances than the latter, that there seems little agreement as to what explains the different variations.[36] The caveat then is largely one of an inability to understand the root course of the differences between cultures. This does not, however, come at the expense of any findings and observations. The reasons may remain unknown, but the observations remain consistent within cultural groups. Film enables repeated viewing and allows proxemic behaviour to be analysed in minute detail; the medium complements the theory.

Proxemics should be understood as a form of communication: 'the way in which one gains knowledge of the content of other's minds through judgements of behaviour patterns associated with varying degrees of proximity'.[37] Communication is an important aspect of space. Space communicates; it has the ability to relay any number of different ideas and meanings. Space is, however, more than its physical conception.[38] Michael O. Watson calls these the 'subjective' aspects of space: 'aspects that defy definition and measurement by "conventional yardsticks"' that are symbolic and expressive.[39] As such, I will utilise a number of these different aspects of space in particular.

In order to employ proxemics as a mode of analysis it is important to understand how it is configured. Watson describes how Robert Sommer has broken down proxemics into two categories: proximate space and the macro-environment. The former may be described as everything that is physically present to the individual at a given moment.[40] This category can also split further into personal space and more distant space. Personal space is that space that immediately surrounds the individual.[41] The macro-environment is everything not included in proximate space, everything outside the individual presence.[42] These are not the only proxemic categories. Edward T. Hall refutes Sommer's taxonomy and creates his own that he dubs fixed-feature, semi-fixed feature and dynamic space. Fixed feature, as one might expect, are those aspects of the environment that are materially fixed.[43] Examples might be the layout of a house or a village. Semi-fixed features are those aspects of the environment that have the potential to move, i.e. furniture arrangements in a home.[44] Dynamic space, finally, incorporates Sommer's use of micro space, and includes human's use of micro-space 'in his everyday encounters with others'.[45] Whilst Hall is one of the greatest proponents of proxemics, his taxonomy is not universally agreed with; aspects have been taken and additions made. Michael O. Watson, for instance, incorporates both Sommer and Hall's taxonomy and categories proxemics into macro-spatial, meso-spatial and micro-spatial.[46]

Rather than favour one taxonomy over another in an analysis, I will attempt to synthesise, as Watson has sought to do, the different categories created by the various theorists. In doing so, my aim is not to promote one over another, but rather demonstrate proxemics' usefulness to the study of space in films and musical sequences more specifically. Due to its limited use in Film Studies prior to this study, it would be unwise to restrict its use too prematurely. Edward T. Hall will, however, be the key proxemic theorist employed in the micro-analysis of key sequences and his various forms of notation, several of which I have used, can be found in his piece 'A System for the Notation of Proxemic Behaviour'. His extensive categorisation of space, up to and including how it can be read through the olfactory sense, offers the most practical and tangible approach to dealing with and understanding space. Though these will be expanded upon and their use justified in the relevant analysis, it is useful here to provide background to some of the categories that Hall has created to aid in the recording of spatial relations.

The SFP (Sociofugal-Sociopetal) Axis describes the movements that pull people apart and push them in from one another.[47] It allows an understanding of the relations of bodies to one another. Though, as Hall describes, there are theoretically endless variations; proxemic notation 'is interested in recording only those distinctions which are operationally relevant to the participant'.[48] Hall creates a form of notation that enables him to understand the different variations in interaction between people. It is important here to note that I will be adapting this to not only include the interactions between people, but also between the camera and the characters in the scene. If the camera represents the audience, reading a proxemic relationship between the audience and characters using the same notation should be possible.

Another model that Hall suggests is a voice loudness scale. Hall states that the loudness of the voice 'is modified to conform to culturally prescribed norms for a) distance, b) relationship between the parties involved, and c) the situation or subject being discussed'.[49] This model will be used to describe the sound levels throughout musical numbers, how they change and how they compare to other auditory cues. The senses are a key aspect of proxemics with regards to both how space is read and interpreted. Another way in which the senses can be seen as important to an understanding of space is through the theory of haptics.

Haptics

The haptic has been described by Hatwell, Streri and Gentaz as the 'tactilo-kinesthetic or active touch perception'.[50] How does the haptic, which places an emphasis on touch, appear in a medium that focuses largely on other senses? The possibility of haptic space within film is in part due to the nature of the medium. Stuart Hall has described how the cinema is as Grierson said, 'a physical medium. The experience of watching a film makes a direct impact on us—the darkened auditorium, the dominating screen, with its very large, moving figures, its very loud sound, its simultaneous appeal to the eyes and the ear'.[51] Whilst not discussing the haptic, Hall and Grierson's focus on the spectatorial experience, movement and cinema's ability to be both visual and aural hints at film's ability to be so; for they contribute towards some of the key aspects of the haptic. Touch, unlike vision and hearing, requires contact. Despite the sensory receptors being present all over the body, the effect is localised to the area that meets the object. Hatwell, Streri and Gentaz describe how 'passive tactile perception' (where touch is applied to a segment of the body), reduces the perceptual field considerably due to the lack of exploratory movement.[52] To compensate for the localised perceptual field, and in order to apprehend the entire object, movement must be made.[53] Movement is one of the key aspects of the haptic and a way in which film could be seen to offer a means of reading it. Musical numbers are often spaces of extreme movement, whether visual or sonic, and therefore are an ideal site to explore haptics.

'Like architecture', Tim Bergfelder, Sue Harris, and Sarah Street state, 'film is an art form that can be described as "tactile" or "haptic"', in the sense that Wollen explains: 'both require a kind of kinaesthetic habit-formation, the acquisition of a mode of moving through space in order to understand and inhabit it unconsciously'.[54] Walter Benjamin felt that audiences 'enter a space created onscreen' and it is this occupying or journeying through a space that likens cinema to architecture.[55] The focus on the kinaesthetic aspect of experiencing space is important due to, as Wollen has argued, audiences creating 'an internal diagram of the relationships between spaces'.[56]

Wollen is not alone in his belief that cinema and architecture are linked; both Juhani Pallasmaa and Giuliana Bruno believe the same. Pallasmaa suggests that both cinema and architecture imply a kinaesthetic way of experiencing space and images, which in our memory are embodied as haptic images as much as retinal pictures.[57] This creates a distinction between the haptic and the visual that Antonia Lant would agree with. Lant argues that the term 'haptic' predates cinema to ancient Egyptian art that has a refusal of depth and an emphasis on textured surfaces. As a result one could tell much about the object by touch alone.[58] This contrast between an 'optical' mode and 'haptic' mode of perception is the basis for Lant's objection to what she believes to be the misplaced use of the term 'haptic' in cinema. She suggests that at the beginning of cinema film was at its most haptic. With the discovery of depth of field, space and lighting techniques such as chiaroscuro, cinema moved more towards an optical form.[59] To discuss films that use such visual techniques Lant believes is inaccurate.

Bergfelder, Harris and Street, conversely, do not see this as an issue that prevents the use of the term haptic, though they do stress the importance of Lant's work. They believe that Lant's disagreement with the use of the term highlights an essential component of the haptic; namely, that it can be both a mode of artistic production and of spectatorial experience.[60] Bruno supports the latter evocation of the term and details the use of different elements of film language and technology of film, such as shots, editing, lighting and camera movement to further the connection to architecture. For these, she claims, offers 'the possibility of [...] a spectatorial voyage'.[61] Bergfelder, Harris and Street point out that this is an observation that accords with Tashiro's important point that 'static' images are never so because 'just as shots collide or flow, pieces of a design can work in harmony or dissonance'.[62] Bruno's desire is to move away 'from a concern with the object of the picture [towards a] critical concern [that] can move away from a focus on the pictorial object and towards "ways" of seeing sites and of considering the visual arts as agents in the making and mobilisation of space'.[63] In doing so, it would become clear that 'film's spectatorship is thus a *practice* of space that is dwelt in, as in the built environment'.[64] As before, an understanding of the haptic can be developed through a focus on movement and kinaesthetic images. As audiences journey through films they slowly begin to inhabit the space, and it is this embodiment that allows them a cognitive understanding of the place (re)presented to them. 'The inhabitation of space' Bruno continues, 'is achieved by tactile appropriation, and architecture and film are bound by this process.'[65] This understanding also involves emotion, as Bruno explains: 'the link between film and the architectural enterprise involves a montagist practice in which the realm of motion is never too far from the range of emotion'.[66] It can therefore be seen that haptic space, when considered a mode of spectatorial experience, can be found in films that allow great movement. The dancing films of Astaire and Rogers are very apt in this regard.

This movement is created in two ways; firstly, through the movement within the frame and secondly, with the use of film technology. Wollen describes cinema as existing within a tension that uses these two types of movement. 'Cinema', he claims, occupies 'a combination of "static", architectural space (the set) and "dynamic" narrative space (camera and editing).'[67] It is through both of these that space can be created in a haptic manner. This book, therefore, is in a unique position to synthesise both static and dynamic space in its discussion of the musical. Its gestalt-based approach enables a symbiotic understanding of the space. This evocation of the haptic omits sound, however. Or, rather, gives visual space primacy. This is not the case in this study. Sound and a haptic understanding of sound will be analysed. One important theoretical aspect of sound is the notion of the acousmêtre.

Chion's Acousmêtre

It is worth reiterating that this book endeavours to analyse sound and music within musical sequences to an equal degree with the image. It is, therefore, essential to examine and employ the work of one of the leading authorities on film sound: Michel Chion. As an influential theorist on sound, Chion's work enables a rather more nuanced understanding of this key element of film.

Chion devises a number of terms for the understanding of sound, its place in film and its relationship with the image. A key example being *added value*, which Chion describes as:

> The expressive and informative value with which a sound enriches a given image so as to create the definite impression, in the immediate or remembered experience one has of it, that this information or expression 'naturally' comes from what is seen, and is already contained in the image itself.[68]

There is undeniably an issue here with the very rhetoric used when discussing sound. Even Chion is still asserting to some degree that it is the image that comes first and that sound is a reaction to and/or against the image. 'Added value,' he claims, 'engages the very structuring of vision by rigorously framing it.'[69] It would be misleading to state that sound is solely in service of the image. Added value, as Chion describes, 'works reciprocally. Sound shows us the image differently than what the image shows alone, and the image likewise makes us hear the sound differently than if the sound were ringing in the dark'.[70] Whilst Chion believes that sound in film is vococentric, he also argues that music is used in two important ways: emphatically and anemphatically. The former is an example of music 'directly express[ing] its participation in the feeling of the scene', while the latter 'can exhibit conspicuous indifference to the situation'.[71] Anemphatic music, Chion claims, 'conjures up the mechanical texture of this tapestry of the emotions and senses'.[72] With regards to the senses, Chion argues that 'the eye perceives more slowly because it has more to do all at once; it must explore in space as well as follow along in time. The ear isolates a detail of its auditory field and follows this point or line in time'.[73] As a consequence of this, sound is able to temporalise the image through its ability to give images temporal linearization and vectorise or dramatise shots, 'orientating them toward a future'.[74]

Chion's acousmêtre is a central component of his work. It is the

> Character whose relationship to the screen involves a specific kind of ambiguity and oscillation [... it is] neither inside nor outside the image. It is not inside, because the image of the voice's source—the body, the mouth—is not included. Nor is it outside, since it is not clearly positioned offscreen in an imaginary 'wing', like a master of ceremonies or a witness, and it is implicated in the action, constantly about to be part of it.[75]

One reason why the acousmêtre holds added importance is a result of the latter's gestalt approach. As outlined previously, gestalt is inherently linked with perception and so too is Chion's acousmêtre. 'The question of listening with the ear,' Chion states, 'is inseparable from that of listening with the mind.'[76] Chion argues that perception is split between conscious and active perception. 'In the cinema to look is to explore, at once spatially and temporally, in a "given-to-see" (field of vision) that has limits contained by the screen.'[77] Listening, conversely, is not limited in the same manner; it is more exploratory as it does not have the same confinements. Sonic space, therefore, cannot be defined in the same manner as visual space.

Another important aspect Chion highlights is the *superfield* that may be found in multi-track films. It is composed of ambient sounds such as music, the noises of an urban environment and rustlings. The superfield is used to increase the physical boundaries of the screen.[78] This is achieved through multi-track's ability to place the speakers outside of the screen's limits. I will explore this notion of the superfield in conjunction with Mark Kerins' concept of the *ultrafield* in both Chapters 3 and 5.[79] In doing so, I will argue that gestalt theory provides the best understanding of the space: that there is a singular whole space of the musical number that is created as a result of the different spatial realms coming together to make a cohesive space.

As this chapter demonstrates, this book will utilise a substantial and varied theoretical corpus of work. The theories explicated here will be extended and expanded in subsequent chapters. They will be employed in a number of diverse ways so as to illustrate and comprehend how space is created in musical numbers sonically, visually and audio-visually. It should be restated, however, that I am using the musical genre as a case study to best demonstrate how a spatial methodology can be applied. The theories discussed, whilst adapted to the musical specifically, could be altered to reflect the concerns and peculiarities of any genre or film. Although certain theories are perhaps best exemplified by the musical, they are not unique to it. An understanding of Chion's acousmêtre, for example, is not restricted to the musical genre but could be applied more broadly.

Notes

1. W. D. Ellis, *A Source Book of Gestalt Psychology* (London: Routledge, 1950), p. 2.
2. Gestalt theory has been taken up over the years by a number of different disciplines including those in social sciences and humanities, as well as the sciences and thus has a few different names: gestalt psychology, gestalt theory and gestalt perception, amongst others. These should all be considered under the same rubric.
3. Ellis, p. 3.
4. David Bordwell, *Narration in the Fiction Film* (Madison: University of Wisconsin Press, 1985).
5. Rudolf Arnheim is a key exception to this. One aspect of his work was the application of gestalt theory to Media Studies. One such example is: Rudolf Arnheim, *Towards a Psychology of Art: Collected Essays* (Berkeley: University of California Press, 1992).
6. David Katz, *Gestalt Psychology: Its Nature and Significance* (New York: The Ronald Press Company, 1950), p. 4.
7. Katz, p. 22.
8. Katz, p. 27.
9. Rudolf Arnheim, *New Essays on the Psychology of Art* (London: University of California Press, 1986), p. 267.
10. Scott Higgins, (ed.), "Introduction" in, *Arnheim for Film and Media Studies* (New York: Routledge, 2011), p. 1.
11. Arnheim, *New Essays on the Psychology of Art*, p. 267.
12. Arnheim, *New Essays on the Psychology of Art*, p. 267.
13. Arnheim, *New Essays on the Psychology of Art*, p. 270.
14. Lefebvre, *The Production of Space*.
15. Tashiro, *Pretty Pictures: Production Design and the History Film*.
16. Tashiro, p. 17.

17. Gorbman, *Unheard Melodies*.
18. Alessandro Cecchi, "Diegetic Versus Nondiegetic: A Reconsideration of the Conceptual Opposition as a Contribution to the Theory of Audiovision", *Worlds of Audiovision*, (2010) <www-5.unipv.it/wav/pdf/WAV_Cecchi_2010_eng.pdf> [Accessed 04/06/2011 2011], p. 2.
19. Cecchi, p. 3.
20. Cecchi, p. 3.
21. Cecchi, pp. 3–4.
22. Cecchi, p. 4.
23. Ben Winters, "The Non-diegetic Fallacy: Film, Music, and Narrative Space," *Music & Letters*, Vol. 91, No. 2 (May 2010), pp. 224–244.
24. Altman, *The American Film Musical*, p. 69.
25. Stilwell, "The Fantastical Gap between Diegetic and Non-Diegetic", p. 184.
26. Stilwell, "The Fantastical Gap between Diegetic and Non-Diegetic", p. 184.
27. Stilwell, "The Fantastical Gap between Diegetic and Non-Diegetic", p. 188.
28. Stilwell, "The Fantastical Gap between Diegetic and Non-Diegetic", p. 196; Jeff Smith, "Bridging the Gap: Reconsidering the Border Between Diegetic and Nondiegetic Music", *Music and the Moving Image*, vol. 2, no. 1 (spring 2009), pp. 1–25. Smith's piece provides a compelling alternative to Stilwell; focusing in part on the relationship between music and narrative space, Smith argues that Stilwell has assumed an understanding of film's relation to theatre and an overemphasis of the audience's phenomenal experience of the 'fatastical gap' (p. 6). Smith advocates an approach that makes allowances for the awareness of narration.
29. Stilwell, "The Fantastical Gap between Diegetic and Non-Diegetic", p. 197.
30. Hall, *The Silent Language*.
31. Michael O. Watson, *Proxemic Behaviour: A Cross-Cultural Study* (Paris: The Hague, 1970), p. 16.
32. Heini Hediger, *Studies of the Psychology and Behaviour of Captive Animals in Zoos and Circuses* (London: Butterworth Co., 1955). Much of the work on spatial relationships focuses on animal behav-

iour. A key theorist is Heini Hediger, whose work has been used as a basis for forming an understanding of the meaning of possible interactions in particular contexts. The context in which his findings are based is always highlighted and informs Hall's understanding of culturally specific proxemics.
33. Hall, *The Silent Language*, p. 15.
34. Hall, *The Silent Language*, p. 94.
35. Watson, *Proxemic Behaviour: A Cross-Cultural Study*, p. 19.
36. Baldassare, pp. 33–34.
37. Michael O. Watson, "Symbolic and Expressive Uses of Space: An Introduction to Proxemic Behaviour", *Module in Anthropology*, 20 (1972), 1–18. (3).
38. Watson, "Symbolic and Expressive Uses of Space: An Introduction to Proxemic Behaviour", p. 1.
39. Watson, "Symbolic and Expressive Uses of Space: An Introduction to Proxemic Behaviour", p. 1.
40. Watson, "Symbolic and Expressive Uses of Space: An Introduction to Proxemic Behaviour", p. 3.
41. Watson, "Symbolic and Expressive Uses of Space: An Introduction to Proxemic Behaviour", p. 3.
42. Watson, "Symbolic and Expressive Uses of Space: An Introduction to Proxemic Behaviour", p. 3.
43. Watson, "Symbolic and Expressive Uses of Space: An Introduction to Proxemic Behaviour", p. 3.
44. Watson, "Symbolic and Expressive Uses of Space: An Introduction to Proxemic Behaviour", p. 3.
45. Watson, "Symbolic and Expressive Uses of Space: An Introduction to Proxemic Behaviour", p. 3.
46. Watson, "Symbolic and Expressive Uses of Space: An Introduction to Proxemic Behaviour", p. 3.
47. Hall, "A System for the Notation of Proxemic Behaviour", p. 1008.
48. Hall, "A System for the Notation of Proxemic Behaviour", p. 1009.
49. Hall, "A System for the Notation of Proxemic Behaviour", p. 1016.
50. Hatwell, p. 2.
51. Stuart Hall and Paddy Whannel, *The Popular Arts* (London: Hutchinson Educational LTD, 1964), p. 78.
52. Hatwell, p. 2.

53. Hatwell, p. 2.
54. Peter Wollen, *Paris Hollywood: Writings on Film* (New York: Verso, 2002), p. 201, quoted in Tim Bergfelder, Sue Harris, and Sarah Street, *Film Architecture and the Transnational Imagination* (Amsterdam: Amsterdam University Press, 2007), p. 22.
55. Walter Benjamin, "The Work of Art in the Age of Mechanical Reproduction", in *Illuminations* (New York: Schoken Books, 1969).
56. Wollen, p. 201.
57. Juhani Pallasmaa, *The Architecture of the Image: Existential Space in Cinema* (Helsinki: Building Information, Rakennustieto Oy Helsinki, 1991), p. 17.
58. Lant, pp. 45–73.
59. Bergfelder, p. 23.
60. Bergfelder, p. 24.
61. Bruno, p. 56.
62. Bergfelder, p. 25.
63. Bruno, p. 60.
64. Bruno, p. 62.
65. Bruno, p. 66.
66. Bruno, p. 60.
67. Bergfelder, p. 22.
68. Chion, p. 5.
69. Chion, p. 7.
70. Chion, p. 21.
71. Chion, p. 9.
72. Chion, p. 9.
73. Chion, p. 11.
74. Chion, p. 13.
75. Chion, p. 129.
76. Chion, p. 33.
77. Chion, p. 33.
78. Chion, p. 150.
79. Kerins, p. 87.

CHAPTER 3

Sound Space

INTRODUCTION

Whilst using an underlying gestalt approach to analysis, it is still important to understand the spatial qualities of sound as they apply to musical numbers, and their role when emancipated from the image's influence. Doing this allows one to see whether the understanding of sound differs when it is in a relationship with the image. Furthermore, such an approach can finally lay to rest subsequent arguments as to image's primacy. Sound can be read as a gestalt in itself, where the whole sonic sphere is more than the atomised parts that create it; an aural landscape formed from interrelated elements. An analysis of this sphere alone yields different results than both the subsequent chapters, highlighting and reinforcing the very nature of gestalt. This chapter analyses sound space: its construction and representation, how it is perceived and mediated, and uses *Dancer in the Dark*'s (2000) 'Cvalda' number as a textual example of how the theories can be employed. It posits that it is sound that is the source of a comprehensible space and the primary driving force behind the number. Furthermore, it explores the ways in which sound can create space and how it can then be utilised.

Soundtracks in film are a complex amalgamation of different sources and spaces. Within musical numbers, sound and music work to create soundscapes that provide independent sonic geographies—which can be read independently from the rest of the 'narrative'. Comprehending the differences between sound and image, though vital, is often difficult. Theo van Leeuwen has argued that whilst there are similarities between sound and image, they are inherently different media.[1] He writes that there is 'no equivalent of the "frontal" and "side on" angle in sound. Sound is a wraparound medium'.[2] Whilst van Leeuwen is highlighting the fact that images seemingly have the challenge of providing the appearance of spatiality on a 2D screen that sound does not have to overcome, he seems to pay little attention to the positioning of speakers, sound technologies and the effect that these can have. Does sound in actuality escape this limitation? Musical numbers often have a fraught relationship with the notion of diegetic, or, rather, they highlight the porosity of the distinction between the realms of the diegetic spaces. Although the frequent transgressing of the diegetic spaces will be dealt with later, it is worth noting that sound is often bound by the same spatial limitations as the image; though perhaps less directly so and in varying ways. When one discusses diegesis in terms of sound, it is often still the image that dominates and provides the reference point. Whilst fraught with ambiguities, a key example of this is the problematic 'meta-diegetic'. The meta-diegetic, with regards to sound, is the internally heard sounds by characters, whether it is in their dream, imagination or other such device. In other words, meta-diegetic sounds are sounds whose points of emission do not tangibly exist within the diegetic realm of the film. The term 'tangibly' may be used to cover a range of sources varying from an orchestra, to a television, radio or sounds from the urban environment. The meta-diegetic sound, therefore, is different from acousmatic sound in that the latter's source, whilst not seen, has the *potential* to exist within the diegesis. Though the two terms are not mutually exclusive and acousmatic sounds can also be meta-diegetic. For a point of emission to exist within the diegetic realm of the film it must have the potential to be seen; to be shot by the camera. Diegetic space, in the sonic as well as visual sense, is therefore communal. If one person can hear a diegetic sound, another person within the same location or scene of the film, should be able to hear it also. It is consequently bound by visual primacy.[3] Thus, to discuss sound in terms of the diegetic taxonomy is binding it to the same limitations as those of the image. A way of circumventing these limitations is not to entirely dismiss diegesis but to discuss sound in terms of audition, as this chapter will through its analysis of sound technologies and embodied spectatorship.

Van Leeuwen states that both sound and image create relationships between the subject and receiver: that which they represent and the audience that they address.[4] He asserts that this relationship is based upon distance in two ways: firstly, perspective (some sounds are in the foreground, others the middle ground, and so on), and secondly, social distance that, he argues, creates varying formalities between the relationship of listener and what is represented. Examples of these categorisations are intimacy, formality and informality.[5] Van Leeuwen is thus exemplifying a semiotician's approach to film. Although he has tacitly asserted the notion of sonic space, here described by the often-used spatial taxonomy of foreground, middle-ground and background, he has kept sound's effect largely to the screen. The two issues of perspective and social distance are, however, pivotal to the understanding of sound space that this chapter will examine. Whilst important, van Leeuwen has restricted filmic space (and by implication sound's space also), to functions rather than a/effects or aesthetics and is thereby propagating the dominance of narrative and sound's service to it.

Discussion of sound in musical numbers has been fairly limited—mainly to music. The historical dominance of semiotics and narrative within film theory (as exemplified by van Leeuwen), whilst having proven valuable for the development of multiple readings—Marxist, psychoanalytical or feminist amongst others—has, nevertheless, meant that sound has traditionally been placed as a device that leads to better understanding other issues, rather than as the primary focus itself. David Bordwell and Kristin Thompson's *Film Art: An Introduction* is a primary example of how an introductory text can deliver the tools for analysing and understanding sound, but puts them to use purely in order to better comprehend the narrative and its effect on the audience.[6] The musical genre more widely has also been given short shrift both in terms of its place within Film Studies and the readings it engenders. Musicals, despite the oft-stated adage, are not dead and nor have they ever been; they have historically been immensely popular. This notwithstanding, theoretical discussions about musicals appear to suffer the same aversion to sound as film theory more widely does; perhaps less forgivably so in the case of the musical. Over the years attempts have been made to rectify this omission utilising a variety of different approaches. Sounds, and studies of sound in film, are accompanied by several different difficulties inherent to the medium; sound in musicals also either introduces or exaggerates many of these.

As this book takes the musical number as its particular focus, as opposed to space in musicals more generally, the subsequent theoretical contextualisation concentrates on theories of sound and sound space that directly impact upon these sequences. It therefore, undoubtedly and by necessity, omits many theories that would prove fertile grounds for analysis in film more broadly. This chapter will first outline the theoretical foundations of sound and sound space before placing them within the context of a particular textual example; namely, the 'Cvalda' number from the notorious Danish director, Lars von Trier's *Dancer in the Dark*.

SOUND AS EVENT?

Before sound in musicals can be investigated with any level of detail, an understanding of sound more generally must be fully grasped. Like most terms that undergo academic scrutiny, an agreed definition is often sought but a long time coming. Alan Williams in his piece 'Is Sound Recording Like a Language?' has stated that:

> The difference commonly held to obtain between sound and image in film is generally reducible to terms much like the following: 'Whereas the image track *represents* the space-time accessible to the camera during shooting, the soundtrack *reproduces* the sonic material selected for inclusion in the film.'[7]

One can infer, therefore, that the very nature of recorded sound is contended; that it may be considered ontologically different to the image. Though Williams outlines this position, he does not conform to it. He suggests, conversely, that the two terms, 'represent' and 'reproduce' respectively, are misleading. Whilst the former does not denote a 'replica of the "real"', the latter does.[8] As such, it would be disingenuous, Williams argues, to posit recorded sound as a 'reproduction' of the sonic as a result of its spatial qualities. Williams stops prematurely, however, and fails to state that sound space is often not a 'real' space, furthering the redundancy of the application of the term 'reproduction'. Williams continues and states that:

> If sound is a three-dimensional, material event, if the notion of a sound-in-itself independent of its environment is not real but a construction of the subject that listens, then it follows that sound recording cannot by definition reproduce 'the sounds themselves'—since it is obligated by its nature to render a sound (as vibrating volume) as recorded *from one point* of the space in which and through which the sound exists.[9]

Such a statement illustrates several of the complexities of the issue. Although discussing sound as a 'three-dimensional, material event' highlights the spatial qualities of sound, the focus on the subject as perceiver, and arguably constructer, of sound challenges said spatial aspects by implying the imaginary and subjective nature of sound. If sound's locus is in the mind of the spectator where it is rendered by the individual, regardless of its initial point of audition (an issue that will be returned to in due course), then it follows that the perception of the sound is of more importance than an assumed 'original' version, for it signifies that the latter cannot be in existence. If each listener 'hears' a different sound—the creation of which will be dependent on the listener's hearing range, perception, understanding of music and the technology used to both transmit and create the music, amongst other aspects—then the existence and importance of the original must be called into question. This ontological debate at the heart of the notion of an original sound is vital for understanding sound's (perceived) spatiality. Can there exist a version of a sound that may be dubbed 'original'? And, what happens if there is no 'original'?[10] The very nature of sounds, as something that may be heard, means that the proportion of sounds that may be counted as *representations* rapidly increases. By which it is meant, as each person will perceive a sound differently (based upon the previously mentioned criteria among others) at every point of audition, then the concept of an original cannot exist in its most basic form—that of an 'accurate' rendering of the sounds. The perception of a piece of music performed live will be dependent on the surroundings as well as the position of the listener. An individual in the audience will get a different version of the music than the pianist situated in the orchestra. Can one be deemed more 'true' than the other? The environment within which the sounds are produced and heard (perhaps different locations more often than not in this technological age) are a vital aspect of the creation of a sonic space, for each locale will have its own unique nature that will affect echo and reverb, amongst other aspects of sound. Transposing this argument to recorded sounds would, at least superficially, appear to complicate the issue of an 'original' for surely the recording will demonstrate the music 'as it should be heard'. Even this is not so. Alan Williams summarises it thus: 'Microphones being more like ears than they are like rooms (they function as points and not as volume), it is never the literal, original "sound" that is reproduced in recording, but one perspective on it, a *sample*, a *reading* of it.'[11] What and how sound is recorded is entirely dependent on the placement of the microphone. An aesthetic decision has been made by the technician or artist, whether in dialogue with the musicians or not, and consequently what is achieved is no less than a version of a sound, as indeed all sounds are. Issues of embodiment should therefore be brought to the fore. The audience—as points of audition—thus become integral components in the creation of sound space for they hold power over their own interpretation. Put succinctly, if each listener hears the sound differently then the spatiality of said sound must too be in part dependent upon the listener's perception, and they thus become a source of meaning.

A point must be made here about post-production practices and mixing. Such processes can often be seen as attempts to create standardised sound across different auditory environments; where the space of the auditorium is not defined sonically but is uniform. The Theatre Alignment Program, for example, a subsidiary of George Lucas' THX sound technologies, requires that all theatrical sites of exhibition meet certain standards before they can be affiliated with THX.[12] Whilst ultimately unachievable in its purest form, each eventual point of audition—the ear—contains too many variables unique to the individual, the goal was to minimise sonic variation and representation. The achievement of this works largely on a basis of signal processing where a sound, regardless of its initial locus and source, is perceived in a specific way.[13] The audience, now many times removed from any concept of an 'original', obtains signals that are as close to the sound editor's desired form as possible. A consequence of this is that though each listener perceives sounds in subtle but unique ways, one can draw general understandings of the sound.[14]

The debates surrounding 'reproduction' verses 'representation' strike at the very heart of this issue. Put simply, those who support the notion of a sonic *reproduction* consider it a replica of the original; a version so similar that the listener would have difficulty, or even find it impossible, distinguishing it from the original. Those who favour sonic *representation*, conversely, argue that the representation becomes a version of the sound. Both call into question what becomes of the 'original' sound event. When discussing reproduction and representation it is crucial to highlight the technological aspects, and whilst this will be discussed in detail later, it is worth highlighting that for our purposes here, both depend upon technology transmitting sounds to listeners that are not present at the location of the initial sound occurrence.[15] This may be achieved through radio transmission, cassette or CD playback, or indeed film, amongst others. Alan Williams argues that emphasising sound recording as *reproduction* rather than *representation* implies that sound loses nothing through transmission. He states that:

> A three-dimensional event (or events, in the case of multiple tracks), is turned into a three-dimensional event in another medium (electricity or impressions on wax, versus air), then recreated as still another three-dimensional event in the original medium (but not necessarily the original acoustic environment) and all this without loss of essence or 'aura'.[16]

This he believes is a fallacy, and he utilises a psychological approach to his assertion that an argument that preferences the notion of reproduction over representation is flawed. This is achieved through an analysis of the placement of the listener, or in the place of film, the spectator.[17]

Before exploring in more detail the phenomenology of the viewing experience, it is important to move this present discussion towards the issues surrounding the medium of film. If the notion of the 'original' is called into question what does this mean for film where there is an 'original' copy—in the sense that a finished film is released—but where largely the sound has been recorded in post-production?[18] This of course exposes a number of complexities and assumptions about the medium of film and the concept of the original. Can the finished film be deemed an original? I have already claimed that there is no such object. It is important to note that not all films' sound has been done solely in post-production. The history of film sound is an increasingly theorised and discussed area of Film Studies. Mark Kerins has produced a good introduction to the sound technologies of film's early years in his chapter 'Cinema's Hidden Multi-channel History and the Origins of Digital Surround'.[19] Though it would be counter-productive to retrace Kerins' arguments in whole when a direction to his book would suffice, it is worth noting some key developments that he highlights.[20]

Sound Technology and Space

Dolby Surround Sound (DSS) has all but become metonymic for the whole range of surround-sound technologies. Although it is true that Dolby has long exerted a technological and aesthetic dominance in the film industry as well as in the minds of the spectators, there are and have been other multi-track technologies. Indeed, Kerins highlights Alexander Graham Bell's 1879 experiments with two-channel sound via telephone.[21]

This is not without irony, for Kerins' discussion on sound technologies seems to view DSS as exemplifying all sound technologies. This notwithstanding, the impact Dolby has had on the spatialisation of sound, both at the point of audition and the point of production cannot be overestimated. Despite sound's innate spatial qualities, the ability of musicians and technicians to use Dolby technology has greatly enhanced the soundscapes of films, and equally, the position sound plays. Important to note here is the fact that the move towards Dolby technology did not require a change in the construction of soundscapes by sound designers but rather enabled it. Kerins states how 'the advent of digital surround certainly did not *force* filmmakers to change their stylistic or technical approaches—anything that could be done in the Dolby Stereo or monophonic eras could still be done with DSS'.[22] When Digital surround sound was developed in the 1990s it enabled a higher level of control over the separation of sounds; the multiple channels enabled sounds to be independent of each other.[23] A result of this is that each track's sounds exist within their own space, whereas previous mono technologies had forced all sounds to be compressed into a single channel. Consequently, multi-channel technologies have enabled a wider soundscape with more distinguishable sounds. Sounds were thus given individuality. The sound space could, therefore, be more varied and complex, both aesthetically and in regards to the audience's experience of the music.

Detouring momentarily from sound technologies and returning to the issue of sonic space, there are a number of different aspects to consider in the creation of a filmic soundscape. A few of which may be described as follows: firstly, the diegetic space of the film; where the sound is fictionally created. The use of echo and reverb in such sounds may work to create and reflect the diegetic environment. Secondly, the non-diegetic space of the film; the complexities of which relate to its delineation. Thirdly, the space of audition; where the soundscape will be heard. This would traditionally be the cinema, the home or, increasingly, public spaces through the use of mobile viewing technologies. While the cinema provides the environment over which filmmakers and sound designers can exert the most control (take for example the Theatre Alignment Program), much like each individual perceiving a different version of the same sound, each individual environment will provide a different acoustic effect, different again at each viewing of the film. Any number of factors will affect the audition of sounds in these environments, such as: the number of people in the room, how closely packed they are together, items and number of furniture, the size of the room and where the sound is being emitted from. The problems this causes for the existence of an 'original' version of the soundtrack is wide ranging and reflects many of those previously stated. It is worth asking what effect this lack of original sound has on the acoustic intentions of the director and sound designer. Can their desired intentions still be achieved when there is no 'original' version?

At this point we return to the previously stated underlying and guiding theoretical principle of this book: that film is a gestalt. The fundamental outcome of the previous question, therefore, must be that the laws of perception are solid enough to allow for this subjectivity to remain in place whilst still maintaining the intended outcome of the director/sound designer. The gestalt laws of perception are hypotheses that have been scientifically tested. Thus a reading of the sonic space can be enabled despite, or rather because of, its existence in the body of the spectator. Although each person is interpreting the sounds with subtle differences, if one follows the gestalt laws of perception one can come to an understanding of the sound.

Returning now back to Dolby's audio channels, it is clear that there is a spatiality built into the technology, however malleable this may be (the speakers' placement will be dependent upon the size of the room). Dolby 5.1, which is now one of the most common systems found in cinemas and has also made the transition to the home entertainment system market, is so called due to its five full range channels and one Low-Frequency Effects (LFE) channel, which enables sounds at the lower end of the sonic spectrum (approximately between three and 120 hertz). Kerins asserts how the move to 5.1 (and indeed 7.1 in some cases) has affected filmic soundscapes:

> The combination of full-range channels with a discrete channel configuration means not only that any sound can be *placed* in any channel, but that sounds can smoothly be panned *from* one channel to another. While brief stereo 'fly-bys' across the front speakers have long been a staple of multi-channel soundtracks, digital surround sound represents the first commonplace system where sounds can move not just across the screen but all throughout the theatre.[24]

It is significant to note and reiterate the importance of the combination of space that is made up by both the diegetic and non-diegetic space of the screen, and that of the theatre itself. The emphasis on sound *movement* is a vital component in the creation of sound space and an embodied spectatorship. Vivian Sobchack has argued in *The Address of the Eye* that,

> When we sit in a movie theatre and perceive a film as sensible, as making sense, we (and the film before us) are immersed in a world and in an activity of visual being. The experience is as familiar as it is intense, and it is marked by the way in which significance and the act of signifying are *directly* felt, *sensuously* available to the viewer. The embodied activity of perception and expression—making sense and signifying it—are given as modalities of a single experience [...].[25]

Despite the emphasis on a visual form of spectatorship, much can be applied to sound. Sobchack is arguing for film spectatorship that is anchored in the senses; one that links the external audience with the onscreen images, characters and causes, in one sense, a single mode of viewing. The viewer is able to enter the cinematic space, and 'negotiate it'. Why then can the same not be achieved through sound? Robynn Stilwell has stated that,

> The experience of a film is still dislocated in space, split between the visual image projected on the screen at some distance from us, and the sound which envelops and even literally touches us as air vibrates in sympathy with the speakers to transmit the acoustic waves which give us 'sound'.[26]

The cinematic audience is by this logic forced into a tangible relationship with the sound. They are part of the cinematic experience; it may be felt on varying levels and very subjectively, but it opens a means of 'intense' immersion, of occupying the same space as the sound, and directly feeling the act of signifying that is suggested by Sobchack. Furthermore, Stilwell suggests that it is sound that enables a relationship with the screen and bridges the gap between audience and image. Consequently, the traditional privileging of image over sound in Film Studies must surely be called into question by the surround-sound technologies. It is not so far a leap, then, to state that sound can create a form of 'sonic being', the visual equivalent of which Sobchack champions.

The LFE channel is arguably the most effective channel, and the most important for an embodied form of spectatorship. The LFE channel has the biggest physical impact on the spectator's body. It causes those moments when sounds are so deep, and at such a low frequency, that they seem to send vibrations through the audience; when the audience can physically *feel* the sounds emitted from the film.[27] A. Grimani has described how the LFE channel is 'dedicated to high-volume bass sound effects that required a playback system capable of producing 115dB at the listening position'.[28] Furthermore, Grimani states that the LFE channel should not be thought of as a 'subwoofer channel', but rather 'as a path for super-loud base that would otherwise overload the main channels'.[29] The result is a physical effect on the audience as the LFE channel enables 10 dB of extra headroom otherwise lacking in the main channels. 'To get real chest-pounding bass', Grimani argues, 'we need to get up to 115dB. [...] With 10dB of extra headroom, [the LFE channel] can really get a person's body bouncing around in the seat.'[30]

Maurice Merleau-Ponty's ideas have become seminal to theorists of embodiment. His book *Phenomenology of Perception* is a key text for establishing a form of intentionality that is neither 'brute sensation' nor 'conceptual content'.[31] As Taylor Carman states, 'intentionality is', according to Merleau-Ponty, 'not mental representation at all, but skilful bodily responsiveness and spontaneity to direct engagement with the world. To perceive [...] is to be familiar with [...] and find our way around an environment. Perceiving means having a body, which in turn means *inhabiting* a world.'[32] The body thus becomes a central component of perception and experience and is, therefore, a central issue of embodiment. How, however, does this focus on the body enable a feeling of embodiment in a medium in which the audience is placed at a distance from the screen? Merleau-Ponty has highlighted how phenomenologically the body leans towards a tactile experience, where the skin is more than 'a biological object but also a mode of perception and expression'.[33] The skin, therefore, becomes the site where it meets other objects; as such, film itself can be said to have a skin, and through this skin, 'the film is caught up in a reciprocal, intimate, and fundamentally erotic intersubjectivity with its viewer'.[34] The skin of both the audience and film is the site where multiple spaces meet: the audience and the theatre, the theatre and the film, and the film and the spectator. The LFE channel enables the boundary between the film and the audience to be traversed, where the audience can feel the film, and thus allow an embodied experience with it. This does not mean, however, that a single synthesised space is created, but rather that the audience becomes, as Jennifer M. Barker describes, doubly situated: 'we exist in two places at once, even if we never literally leave our seats'.[35] Barker further describes how a film's style can reflect bodily movement, which may even be echoed by the audience itself:

> We and the film exhibit likeness in behaviour and comportment and in the way we use the muscular body as a means of perception and expression. Pushing, pulling, reaching, cowering, flinching, leaning forward, and pulling back, for example, all express in muscular terms one's 'attitudes' about one's relationship to the world and others in it. [...] In this way the film's body and the viewer's body are irrevocably related to one another, but neither identical nor completely divergent.[36]

For Barker, then, an embodied experience occurs through the emulation of effects between film and spectator. The LFE channel thus enables a haptic experience that is more than skin-deep. Barker describes how cinematic tactility works haptically, kinaesthetically, muscularly and viscerally; film can be felt in the murky recesses of the body.[37] Barker states how the different parts of the body: skin, musculature and viscera are not meant metaphorically, 'but they *are* stretched beyond their literal, biological meanings to encompass their phenomenological significance'.[38] Merleau-Ponty's claim, that the skin is a mode of perception and being in the world, is a key example of this stretching beyond literal meaning.[39] When one considers that both film and the body have a skin that negotiate a shared space, it follows that there must be a different mode of negotiation beyond the traditional readings of films. The 5.1 surround-sound system has enabled an understanding of this.

In a discussion regarding the 'passive' and 'active' space Kerins has stated how Dolby multitrack favours passive over active space whilst simultaneously challenging the primacy of the image over the soundtrack. He argues that the favouring of passive over active space means it

> Simultaneously offers the image a heretofore unparalleled degree of freedom. Relying on the soundtrack to function both as a frame of reference for the diegetic space *and* as a source of the stability and coherence that classical continuity practices [...] must traditionally provide, the image track is free to explore new patterns and constructions [...].[40]

Important for achieving this effect is the distinction between the *ultrafield* and the *superfield*. The superfield is a term coined by Michel Chion and includes the background sounds emitted from outside the screen; they are 'off-screen' sounds. In Chion's words the superfield is: 'the space created, in multi-track films, by ambient natural sounds, city noises, music, and all sorts of rustlings that surround the visual space and that can issue from loudspeakers outside the physical boundaries of the screen'.[41] These sounds, therefore, are clearly being emitted externally from the frame of the screen within the cinema itself; they are 'off-screen' sounds. The audience thus exists within a space that is essential to the creation of a filmic environment and soundscape. Their ability to negotiate the space, as suggested by Vivian Sobchack, is, therefore, not as unconvincing as it would at first seem. Central to this negotiation, however, is the affect sound can have on the individual. Whereas Chapter 4 demonstrates the role of the haptic in the formation of space and the admittance of the audience into it, previously we have seen how the theory can be applied to sound. Michel Chion argues that the superfield provides a more tangible and concrete 'continuous and constant consciousness of all the space surrounding the dramatic action' than traditional monaural films.[42] Chion is seemingly not entirely convinced by the tangibility of sound as evidenced by his statement that 'the image is bounded in space, but sound is not. Sound is mental, cannot be touched. An image can [...]'.[43] What he makes reference to, however, is an experiencing of sound. Chion's notion is problematic in that he is suggesting that sounds and images are *perceived* in different ways, something we shall return to shortly.

The superfield is of great significance for the construction of filmic space as a whole, not just sonic space. The foremost reasons for this are twofold (though interrelated): firstly, the superfield—as permitted by multi-track soundtracks—has challenged the hegemonic influence of the image (both in terms of film production and, increasingly, film theory). Secondly, it has provided a constant film sound; as Kerins' states, the superfield 'is the sensation of a complete space, produced by a multi-channel ambience'.[44] The former is due to the reduction in importance of specific camera shots, such as the long shot. The superfield enables 'a continuous and constant consciousness of all the space surrounding the dramatic action', thereby 'undermining the narrative importance of the long shot'.[45] Whereas the long shot traditionally was used to create an overall impression of the space—whether that is an understanding of the size of the location or what is contained in the scene—the superfield has often replaced it. The 'complete space' provided by the superfield is now achieved through the soundtrack's 'task of guiding the audience and creating a coherent narrative space'.[46]

Whilst Michel Chion's superfield is based upon Dolby Stereo multi-tracks, Mark Kerins has coined the term *ultrafield* to describe the evolution of the stereo superfield when under the reins of Dolby Surround Sound. Kerins explains how the two differ from one another in two key ways:

First, [the ultrafield] sacrifices the 'invisibility' of sound editing and mixing to embrace digital surround's aforementioned capabilities to exploit active and changing sounds. Where the superfield maintains a sonic continuity, the ultrafield constantly shifts sounds around the multi-channel environment. Second, it encompasses a much broader array of sonic elements than its predecessor. Where Chion limited the superfield to ambient sounds and noises, the ultrafield encompasses not just these background sounds but the *entire* aural world of the film, including sound effects, dialogue, and diegetic music.[47]

Kerins sees the difference between the superfield and the ultrafield as one of limitations. Whereas the former is suitable for the creation of a diegetic environment the 'responsibility for conveying that environment's literal *space* still lies with the image track'.[48] The ultrafield, conversely, removes the need for the image as the main supplier of a spatial environment, the 'ultrafield-based soundtrack', Kerins argues, 'accurately place[s] *all* the sounds of a space (ambient and otherwise) in their proper locations, taking the burden of explaining spatial relationships off the visuals'.[49] He suggests that the decline in the number of establishing shots since the Dolby Stereo era is evidence of this challenge to the hegemony of the image.[50] Consequently, the soundtrack is thus influencing the image track and has a claim for dominance in the creation of a filmic space in its entirety.

Just which of the two fields has the ability to 'influence' the image better than the other is a matter of contention. Whereas, as Kerins argues, the superfield has the ability to affect the visuals through its enabling the image track more freedom, the ultrafield 'cannot offer the visuals the same sort of stable "sound aquarium." Its fundamental emphasis on *coherence* between image and sound means that the soundtrack becomes as disjointed as the image track, with cuts in both being equally noticeable'.[51] The maintaining of a constant sonic environment by the superfield has limitations, as it cannot reveal the relationship between images within the environment. The ultrafield, conversely, locates the shots within a scene due to the ability to move sounds with greater flexibility and more discretion. Kerins states how each visual fragment of the superfield '"floats" on its own in the sonic aquarium, spatially unconnected to the shots before and after it'.[52] Alternatively, the ultrafield 'sacrifices continuity of the *soundtrack* for continuity of the *space*. Repeatedly reorienting itself [...] connecting each shot to the next through their implied relationship in the diegetic world'.[53] Though examining the various merits of both, Kerins ultimately, and rather unsurprisingly, deems the ultrafield the best for providing freedom to the image track. He claims that the superfield does not have the specificity of spatial relationships (such as between different shots, or explaining how they fit together) that the image track does and has done since the monophonic age. Consequently, visuals created in the superfield era maintain continuity editing practices. The image tracks 'of ultrafield-era films, in contrast, can disregard these conventions and cut freely from any viewpoint to another'.[54] A question should be asked here, however, about whether the soundtrack can ever be truly autonomous, particularly using Kerins' dichotomy between the superfield and ultrafield. Kerins' discussion of off-screen sounds hints at the issue being much more complicated than he would concede. After all, the term 'off-screen' sounds alone dictates a relationship with the image.[55]

What, therefore, does this mean for the space of the film, and more significantly, sound space? Three points can be taken from Kerins' discussion of the super and ultrafields. Firstly, that due to technological advancements, sound (or perhaps awareness of it) may be becoming increasingly important in the creation of filmic space. Secondly, that sound can create space separate from the image—they do not need to work together *actively* to achieve coherence. Thirdly, that a range of sounds are important for the creation of space—making full use of many and separate channels can provide a more detailed soundscape and sense of space. The creation of space sonically, as it is visually, is dependent upon audiences' perceptions and the manner in which sounds are perceived. Although subjectivity is unavoidable, there are perhaps universal constants durable enough for a filmmaker/sound designer to rely upon and it is for this reason that despite individual interpretations, an understanding of embodied spectatorship becomes possible.

Perceiving Sound

There are several aspects to reflect upon when considering the perception of sound. These include, though are not limited to: what is meant by sound perception, the process that is undergone in the perception of sound, how audiences hear, and how film sound works in tandem with the previous considerations. Whilst this book's concern is with the musical genre, and musical numbers much more specifically, there is little to no writing on the perception of film music with regards to it. This may be because it has as yet not been theorised, or it may be due to the increasing body of work on film sound (and sound more generally) providing a sufficient basis to be easily transposed onto the musical.

Robynn Stilwell in her discussion on 'Sound and Empathy' in *Film Music: Critical Approaches* has stated that listeners have the ability to learn how to hierarchise sounds.[56] It is dubbed the 'cocktail party' effect; where people in a dialogue with one another in an environment with multiple sound sources are able to choose to attend to some sounds more than others in order to maintain their focus—for instance, the conversation they are participating in at the expense of the other voices around them. Stilwell states that this 'allows us to interpret the cinematic soundtrack. Typically, we prioritise the dialogue, as a bearer of the narrative, but the occasional sound effect may catch our attention with new information. Music tends to remain a subliminal signal for most [...] audience members'.[57] Exceptions to the majority of audience members that Stilwell makes reference to may be understood to include such people as sound theorists such as Stilwell herself, fans of music, Film Studies students, cineastes and viewers of musicals. The musical genre typically has, arguably akin to the action and horror genre, more moments of music and sound coming to the fore than the average film. Consequently, the theoretical content of Stilwell's statement must be adjusted to accommodate the change in generic conventions. Thus, whilst the statement arguably holds true for the 'narrative' moments of the film, it would perhaps be better to state that for the duration of musical numbers the music has a privileged position both within the film and the audiences' perception.[58] This is not to say, however, that musical numbers are not sites of negotiation, and Chapter 5 demonstrates how the relationship between dialogue, music and visuals are traversed.

David Katz states how 'acoustic forms have had a special place in Gestalt theory [...]' and how 'a metronome may be used to demonstrate them'.[59] As previously stated, gestalt theory promotes the whole over the individual atomised parts that create it. Thus, Katz's suggestion that a metronome may be used to demonstrate how sound may be perceived as a gestalt is highly useful for it highlights how, '[...] it is practically impossible to think of each beat as isolated. Two, or several, always combine to form a rhythmic series'.[60] The rhythmic series is consequently what is perceived by the listener, rather than each sound. Such an understanding of sound is decidedly holistic, and Katz argues that 'all rhythmic processes, whether they occur in music, dancing, or everyday colloquial speech, can be treated scientifically only if regarded from a holistic viewpoint. No rhythmic experience is explainable on an atomistic basis'.[61] The rhythm is more important than the individual tones due to the gestalt 'law of proximity', which states that: 'Other things being equal, in a total stimulus situation those elements which are closest to each other tend to form groups.'[62] Thus the group is identified rather than the separate parts. In sound, and more importantly film sound, the spectator will consequently perceive rhythms and patterns first and foremost. In terms of space, it is therefore necessary for sounds to work together to increase the levels of perception within the audience. Chion's claim that sounds are perceived differently from images is consequently flawed; they both follow gestalt's laws of perception.

Kerins, conversely, suggests that:

> The human brain 'sorts' sounds in part by comparing the sounds coming from one ear to those coming from the other; if the two originate in different places—such as different speakers in a movie theatre—it is easier for the brain to separate them and hear them each individually.[63]

He argues that Dolby Surround Sound is thus more suited to hearing multiple sounds with more clarity than mono single-track soundtracks. Psychoacoustics, Kerins affirms, 'confirms that increasing the number of channels actually increases the number of individual sounds the audience can hear'.[64] Does this mean that gestalt theory is counterintuitive to Dolby Surround Sound and other multi-track sound systems that do so well in creating space through sound? Not when one considers that 'the auditory sense can do more than separate the forms of two simultaneous acoustic series, one of which is meaningful and the other meaningless'.[65] Indeed, Katz states that 'even under [the previously stated] circumstances it is possible to follow and comprehend any one of the four separately organised acoustic series at will'.[66] This is accomplished as a result of perception being a process that occurs in time, however subconsciously.

Space and time are thus intricately linked. One cannot exist without the other. Furthermore, 'Gestalt psychology does not deny that there are both psychological and physical relationships between the notes of a tune and that it is possible to discern them by means of appropriately directed analytical activity.'[67] Katz explores this notion further by asking: '[...] would the actual experience of hearing a tune have anything to do with understanding these relationships?'[68] He is thus drawing a distinction between perception and understanding, and suggesting that one does not necessarily follow the other.

Michel Chion believes that there is an essential difference between aural and visual perception in the cinema, and it is a distinction marked by the frame. He states:

> In the cinema to look is to explore, at once spatially and temporally, in a 'given-to-see' (field of vision) that has limits contained by the screen. But listening, for its part, explores in a field of audition that is given or even imposed on the ear; this aural field is much less limited or confined, its contours uncertain and changing.[69]

The limits of the spaces may indeed be different, but they are still delimited by the ability to be perceived and thus consequently share many of the same boundaries.

Sound Space

Now that we have discussed the ways that technology can influence how a sonic space can be created, and indeed perceived, it is essential to turn towards how sound more generally creates space.[70] Contemporary soundscapes are arguably demonstrative of the aforementioned challenge on the visual spatial hegemony. Whilst it is frequently said that films have never been silent, the role sound plays, and the extent to which it plays it, has altered.[71] The cultural theorist Slavoj Žižek has noted that 'it is now the soundtrack that functions as the elementary "frame of reference" enabling us to orient ourselves in the diegetic space'.[72] William Whittington has developed this argument and stated that a result of surround sound is that the image is now no longer necessary to the creation of diegetic space: 'cognitive geography is offered through echoes, reflections, and reverberations, which create spatial anchors or cues. Spaces, then, can exist without image-based referents. No image is necessary'.[73] The term 'cognitive geography' creates an immediate delineation of space. It is not the space one feels, but rather implies the space one's mind can discern from the information given.[74] Such a term is thus not without issue. Why has Whittington specifically used the adjective 'cognitive' to describe the geography, if not to make a distinction between the space formed from mental processes and the spaces formed through other means? If so, how does one create such a distinction, where does one space start and the other stop? Furthermore, Žižek's argument that the soundtrack is now the primary means of the audience being able to orient themselves in the diegetic space is also problematic. What of the non-diegetic spaces, or the meta-diegetic? How are audiences orientated in these?

This idea is further enhanced, or rather complicated, by Kerins who argues that the difference between 'active' and 'passive' space, as described by Michel Chion, is an important element of the construction of sonic space. This disparity is centred on Chion's conception of the 'acousmêtre', which is defined by Chion as

> The acousmatic character whose relationship to the screen involves a specific kind of ambiguity and oscillation [...]. We may define it as neither inside nor outside the image. It is not inside, because the image of the voice's source—the body, the mouth—is not included. Nor is it outside, since it is not clearly positioned offscreen in an imaginary 'wing', like a master of ceremonies or a witness, and it is implicated in the action, constantly about to be part of it.[75]

Chion continues his exploration of this ambiguous sonic space by stating that 'this voice that speaks over the images can see everything therein. This power arises from the notion that in a sense the acousmêtre is the very voice of what is called *primary identification* with the camera'.[76] A logical continuation of this statement would be that the primary identification with the camera—the primary space, therefore—exists outside of the confines of the screen. It is a sonic space rather than a visual one that has primacy. Moreover, as the chief source of off-screen sounds is more often than not the non-diegetic realm, does it not follow that it should create the primary space?

Dancer in the Dark (2000)

As this chapter has dealt with many of the theories of sound that are pertinent to the study of sonic space in musical numbers, it now seems appropriate to turn to a filmic example in order to demonstrate how both a forensic analysis and a synthesis of the aforementioned theories can be applied. The example in question is the infamous Danish director Lars von Trier's *Dancer in the Dark*. The film is undoubtedly a musical, but with the director's typical slant. It is an example of an integrated musical, which, whilst there is a musical production being rehearsed, takes place largely in the protagonist's mind; an interesting variation on embodied spectatorship. Set in 1964, a young Czech immigrant, Selma, played by Icelandic pop singer Björk, works in a factory whilst dreaming of musicals.

Musicals consume her, every moment is seemingly taken up either appreciating or daydreaming musicals; she appears to experience life as if she was in a musical.

Selma lives with a degenerative eye condition in a frugally appointed caravan. She is eventually arrested for shooting her landlord who has stolen the money she was saving to save her son from the same blindness-causing disease. Just before Selma is hanged for her crime, she learns from her friend Kathy (Catherine Deneuve), also known as 'Cvalda', that her son's operation was a success. Selma sings her last song on her way to the noose, and before reaching the end, is killed.

Dancer in the Dark then is clearly a happy tale, and one whose tone is not usually associated with the musical genre.[77] Throughout the film, as is perhaps expected from von Trier, the conventions of the musical genre are played with, for instance the audience's complicit relationship with Selma, but it is more particularly on the issue of sound space that this example focuses and specifically how the visuals from the 'Cvalda' number emanate from the music. The sound in the 'Cvalda' number of *Dancer in the Dark* is the driving force behind the representation of space. It is therefore important to return to one of the key arguments of this book as outlined in Chapter 1, that a traditional Film Studies analysis is insufficient when studying musical numbers as it too often privileges the visual and fails to understand the transformative power of sound. An approach based upon a gestalt reading of the musical numbers supported by forensic analysis is, therefore, preferable. It is important to outline why both this film and, in particular, the 'Cvalda' number have been chosen. The justification for the choice of the 'Cvalda' number over others within *Dancer in the Dark* is twofold: Firstly, the film's musical numbers are clearly shot differently from the rest of the film and err from the (often contradictory rules) of Dogme filmmaking that von Trier was so instrumental in developing. Indeed, Paul Théberge has noted a change in the use of different sound systems between the majority of *Dancer in the Dark*'s diegetic sound and the musical numbers, and argues that the former is played in mono, while the latter is in full stereo.[78] Mark Kerins believes this juxtaposition provides a narrative function: '[the] sharp contrast between the monotonous real life of its heroine Selma [...] and her exciting life-affirming fantasy world, in which the musical sequences, occur'.[79] Leaving aside the narrative driving force behind such aesthetic decisions by von Trier, the musical numbers within *Dancer in the Dark* stand out as aesthetically 'different' from the rest of the film. Though the spatial methodology explored in this book can be applied to all films, choosing an exaggerated example enables me to clearly highlight some of the issues that arise. Secondly, 'Cvalda' not only offers an opportunity to explore the concept of the audio-dissolve and ambiguous diegetic space (and all its variations thereof), but also provides an interesting environment sonically.

Throughout *Dancer in the Dark*, as indeed throughout many musicals, there is a complicated line that runs between the diegetic and non-diegetic; two seemingly separate spatial realms. The 'Cvalda' number takes place about a quarter of the way through the film and illustrates Selma's (Björk's) daydreaming tendencies as highlighted by Théberge.[80] The scene is an example of, using Claudia Gorbman's term, the meta-diegetic.[81] It is, however, more complicated than this. It is also a scene that represents hypnagogic and oneiric sound: the state of drifting away from reality and an alternated state of consciousness, respectively. These are key points to make in terms of the creation of a sonic space as, though they are not easily theorised, more often than not their creation is aided by sound. They are important states of sound that aid in the development of a reading based upon embodied spectatorship, which, whilst looked at in more detail Chapter 5, is a theme that runs throughout this book. Here it is important to note that this balance between hypnagogic and oneiric sound creates an embodied form of spectatorship in two ways. Firstly, by being hypnagogic, the sound in the 'Cvalda' number enables the audience to be doubly situated. The distinction between the 'reality' of the cinematic theatre and the 'reality' of the filmic space is blurred. The sound the audience experience is felt and heard in both locations simultaneously; they know the intention is that the music is coming from the film, but due to cinema sound technologies—such as 5.1 and 7.1 surround sound—the music is heard behind, to the side and in front of them, in short, in the space of the cinema. Secondly, oneiric sound also enables this double situation of the audience through their ability to alter the audiences' state of consciousness. This is achieved as a result of the space between audience and cinematic space being bridged. The audience have entered the 'immersive' space of the film that utilises the senses in much the same way as they are used outside of cinema going, and allows them to suspend their disbelief and alter their state of consciousness.

Carol Vernallis in her book *Experiencing Music Video* has suggested that music videos' important elements are their ability to withhold information by providing the audience with ambiguous depictions.[82] Traditional film theory often privileges narrative readings. This, alongside semiotics, has arguably been the hegemonic template for analysis, and such approaches have ultimately tried to 'tame' ambiguous depictions in film by placing them within narrative contexts to make them understood. Vernallis continues and explains how very few music videos could be seen to conform to conventional definitions of narrative, such as the events on screen being arranged by their causal relations, chronological order or spatial locations.[83] I contend that reading narrative through the audio-visual is misleading. It implies, and conventional film analysis would arguably accept, that they are subservient to the narrative, there to aid it, when it is just as likely that the audio-visual are in fact the focus, the very object of study, rather than tools in an analysis. Indeed, Vernallis argues

> Most videos tend to be non-narrative. An Aristotelian definition [...] describes only a small fraction of videos, perhaps one in fifty. Still fewer meet the criteria that David Bordwell and Kristin Thompson require in their *Film Art: An Introduction*: that all of the events we see and hear, plus those we infer or assume to have occurred, can be arranged according to their presumed casual relations, chronological order, duration, frequency, and spatial locations.[84]

Whilst often still at the centre of musical numbers, these elements are frequently subverted. One has only to return to the ontological debate surrounding the nature of the musical genre, as presented by theorists such as Rick Altman, to see that traditional notions such as chronology, duration and causal relations fit uneasily onto the musical genre.[85]

Although Vernallis is discussing music video, there are a number of points of intersection between the art form and musical numbers. Peter Doyle, in *Echo and Reverb*, has stated in his discussion on pop music that 'the combination of lyric content, vocal harmony, instrumentation and studio contrivance sets up a virtual geography, a coherent, highly specific sense of space and place'.[86] These are important aspects in understanding the spatiality of numbers in film musicals, and it is here that my analysis again moves away from conventional film analysis and towards one based upon film as gestalt: film is an audiovisual medium; the sound and images work together to form a dynamic relationship that is different from its constituent parts. It is arguably an isomorphic relationship whereby, as Carlos López Charles states:

> [The] promotional variations with which images and sounds change are there in the external world, but not the images and sounds as we experience

them. Indeed, a process of transduction takes place in which [...] space is transmitted via image and sound and through this process, transformed.⁸⁷

In terms of film theory, song sequences in musical films sit uncomfortably. One reason for this is due to many different types of media having to interact and constantly negotiate their positions; such as mise-en-scène, acting styles, cinematography, lighting, the theatre, the sound technology as well as the soundtrack itself. Film should be understood as a gestalt where the entirety of the pieces should be looked at in unity rather than as discrete parts. Within Film Studies there is a tradition of analysis that privileges the visual, such as camera and camera movement, framing, mise-en-scène, editing and lighting.⁸⁸ Though any analyses of these elements can provide interesting results, they will ultimately prove deficient as they fail to take into consideration the effect they will have on the whole, and what effect the whole will have on the reading of individual parts.

I am concerned here with the negotiation of sonic space. This being so, this chapter's specific focus is on sound and it would be misleading to suggest that sound can be simplified to a single atomised part of the whole; indeed sound itself, as has been discussed, should be seen as a gestalt. With this in mind, through the analysis of the 'Cvalda' number several arguments will be proposed: Firstly, on their own the images provide an incoherent space that the sound mediates. Secondly, that the images are emanations of the visual, thereby subverting their long-assumed dominance in film theory and holding with, what Kerins would argue, is a general trend that is a consequence of the surround-sound technologies. Thirdly, that the sound helps to create a tactile space that the audience can negotiate, thereby enabling a form of embodied spectatorship.

In order to better understand the spatiality of this scene and move away from conventional film analysis, 'Cvalda' was broken down to a 'micro' level and analysed using a number of different graphs and tables, thus demonstrating various forms of forensic analysis. Whilst expanding upon the methods used and the data found, it is necessary to outline some of the theoretical aspects of the scene in terms of sound and image.

Like with many music videos, the opening of 'Cvalda' positions the number in an ambiguous intermediate space where the diegetic boundaries are blurred and made imprecise, a theme of both musicals and *Dancer in the Dark*. Before the sonic space of the scene is analysed and the theoretical issues raised, it is worth illustrating how the visual space of 'Cvalda' is fragmented and all but incomprehensible, thus demonstrating the need for sound's intervention. In terms of visuals, the scene starts with a close-up of Björk centrally framed before the camera slowly zooms in towards her face. The shot lasts 11 seconds before there is a cut to a close-up image of two people using machines, which lasts for 5 seconds. After the opening shots, the pace of the subsequent edits speeds up considerably. Indeed, the musical number contains 199 individual shots and the average shot length is 1.2 seconds. The software used for this breakdown was Yuri Tsivian's Cinemetrics.[89] The graph shown in Fig. 3.1 is a visual representation of the data collected:

The graph depicts an example of the atomised parts (each shot) of the 'Cvalda' number and as atomised parts they convey little information on their own. Only when looked at as gestalt, as having an effect that is equal to more than the single shots, can they communicate information useful to an analysis of space. When the data is analysed the high number of shots can be clearly noted, each only lasting a short amount of time. The question thus becomes: how does the scene work? Or rather, how does the scene work spatially when the audience is assaulted with so many different images? How is coherence established and or maintained? I argue that it is the sonic sphere that underpins the scene, gives coherence and clarity to the space, and allows the audience to accept it.

After creating the graph, it is important to know what the different nodes coincide with sonically. In particular, it is essential to see if specific nodal groupings, such as that at 43 seconds, are indicative of anything. One way of achieving this is to overlay the different sections of the song onto the graph. *Dancer in the Dark*, despite toying with the musical genre's conventions in numerous ways, is also, paradoxically, very con-

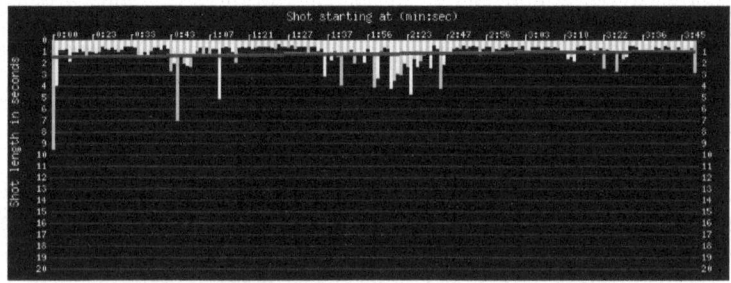

Fig. 3.1 Graph showing the number of shots within 'Cvalda', the time they occur, and the length of the shot in seconds

ventional. The music was written by the pop star and star of the film Björk, and despite being (increasingly) known for her alternative style, her music largely follows the musical form of popular song: introduction, verse, chorus, bridge, middle eight and so on. The graph shown in Fig. 3.2, therefore, is illustrative of where the different sections of the 'Cvalda' number, following the form of popular song, are found when overlaid on Fig. 3.1.

The first few nodes are shots of Björk and represent the moment of 'audio-dissolve', arguably the start of the musical number. The instance when the diegetic realms become more ambiguous. The editing in this section is at a fairly rapid rate (just over 1 second per shot), the justification for which is arguably to present a visual shift from the previously longer shots to indicate a change of space into the musical number. There is another grouping at roughly 43 seconds, the end of section 'B', which approximately corresponds to the first chorus of the song and a visual, often front on, focus on Björk, thus clearly linking the sonic realm with her character. The large grouping in the middle of longer shots, at almost 1 minute 37 seconds, occurs when the group of extras and Björk dance as an ensemble and Björk repeats, with variation, the chorus. Thus, one could argue that the structure of popular song: verse, chorus and middle 8, for instance, is driving the editing and visual space as each section of the song's structure offers a different type of image and editing rate. Consequently, rather than being subservient to the image of the musical

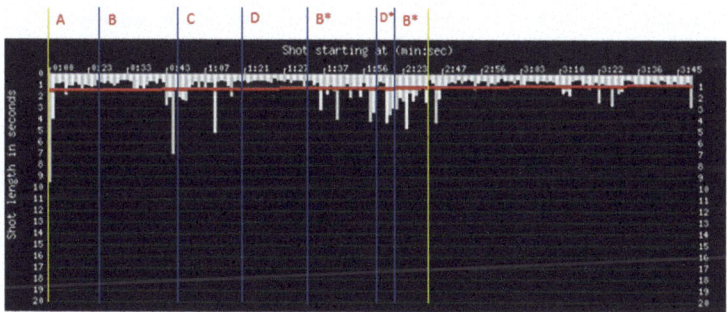

Fig. 3.2 Graph showing the different parts of the song overlaid onto Fig. 3.1 (length of time and shots in the 'Cvalda' number). Where an '*' is given next to the letter, it symbolises a variation on a previously heard musical section, indicated by the letter

number, the sound and music actually influences the visual space of the number. A traditional narrative framework for understanding the sonic space of the 'Cvalda' number fails as it would give precedence to a fragmented image track in an attempt to understand a narrative that, for all intents and purposes, has been put on hold throughout the duration of the musical number.

With 199 different shots, the 'Cvalda' number relies heavily on editing. Carol Vernallis has highlighted the importance of editing in music videos in creating a freedom where any element can be the focus at a given moment. She argues that this

> prevents powerful images from acquiring too much weight and stopping the flow of information. The editing thus preserves the video's momentum and keeps us in the present. A striking edit can allow one to move past a number of strange or disturbing images while neither worrying about them nor forgetting them completely.[90]

A number of important points can be taken from this. Firstly, one can infer that sound must be the primary source of information in such a context if a powerful image has the ability to stop the flow of information, one assumes by briefly being the dominant site of audience attention distracting from sound. Secondly, implicit here is also an acceptance on behalf of the audience that what they are watching might not be visually intelligible and this is the case for 'Cvalda'. The spatial intelligibility of the scene is clearly demonstrated by attempting the recreation of the musical number virtually. The aim of this was to create the set of the musical number using software and then track the movements of the camera and characters within it in time with the number, of which Fig. 3.3 is an example.

This basic virtual recreation was formed through the piecing together of the 199 shots, much as you would a jigsaw puzzle. The scene was re-watched several times with a view to placing every shot within the space of the set design to both have an understanding of where each shot took place, but also in an attempt to create the set used for the number.[91] Using this exercise on the 'Cvalda' number turned out to be more of an informative exercise than an accurate representation of the scene itself. Each different block represents the approximate location and scale of the various different pieces of machinery within the factory.[92] At this point it is important to restate the term 'approximate'; not once during the musical number is an establishing shot used that might enable the audience to

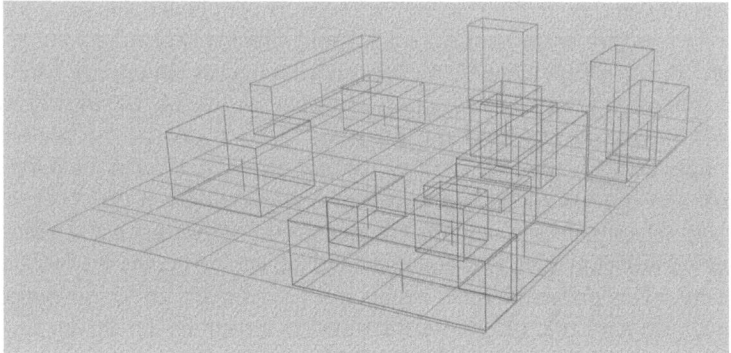

Fig. 3.3 A virtual recreation of the 'Cvalda' number from *Dancer in the Dark*

view the whole set and get a sense of spatial awareness—an interesting lack of spatial cohesion. When it came time to both virtually place the cameras in the scene and plot the sources of sound, it became clear that it was impossible. The visual space was too fragmented and a guess could not be hazarded as to where the majority of the sounds and shots were taking place in any given moment. This sort of virtual recreation is much easier to do, and much more rewarding in terms of producing helpful data, with numbers such as those in Astaire and Rogers' musicals where the numbers may consist of a single shot and a static orchestra. The reconstruction was thus kept as a static image rather than animated. The exercise, however, reinforces the view that the space in the 'Cvalda' number is visually fragmented. In terms of a gestalt reading, it demonstrates that the overall 'impression' of the scene is more important than the atomised single shots that create it; for whilst fragmented visually, the musical number is still accepted by the audience. Another element must, therefore, be added to grant spatial cohesion. The lack of continuity editing—as demonstrated both visually and through the virtual recreation—in the 'Cvalda' scene means that a standard point of reference for audiences has been lost; the preservation of the flow of time and the coherence of a visual space have been removed.[93] Lars von Trier achieves this by assaulting the viewer with a complete gamut of camera shots, a result of using many digital cameras—a technology that undoubtedly will have an effect on the visual space.

Theo van Leeuwen has suggested in *Speech, Music, Sound* that there is a 'three-stage plan' when it comes to film soundtracks, which splits sounds into different groups that then exist in a hierarchy. He states that what is important will change but it will always be seen as a signal the listener 'must attend to and/or react to and/or act upon, while background sounds are "heard but not listened to", disattended, treated as something listeners do not need to react to or act upon'.[94] Important here is the idea of 'distance', the notion of sound and the sonic realm as provider of spatiality. This links back to the theory of proxemics: the spatial relations between people and objects. What van Leeuwen is suggesting is a proxemic relationship whereby louder sounds are given more importance and reflect a closer relationship between audience and object or between object and character. This proxemic relationship and use of close-up sound suggests a spatial intimacy that often uses the singer as a conduit for the images. In this case it is Björk. It is important at this point to turn to an analysis of 'Cvalda' that has a more sonic focus.

Peter Doyle has stated in his description of Robert Johnson's recording of 'Come on in my Kitchen' (1936), that despite lacking a visual reference point to imagine the specific place invoked, the use of close-up sound through miking creates a sense of the listener being in a close proximity to the singer. 'The listener,' he states 'is afforded a kind of aural glimpse, a private sonic close-up of the singer in action'.[95] Unlike Doyle's example, the audience for *Dancer in the Dark* does have a pictorial reference point for Björk; however, the visual proximity to her changes throughout the number and so too does the audience's relationship with her voice. There is very little reverb on her voice that, as Altman has described, makes it a 'close-up sound, spoken by someone close to me, but it is also *towards* me rather than away from me'.[96] Having stated this, one might expect Björk's voice to be given aural precedence, but, as the number demonstrates and as illustrated in Fig. 3.4, her voice is often battling with the music that varies very little, at least in terms of volume. This can be demonstrated by the shift that takes place at the beginning of the second shot, whereby the machine's sounds contain even less reverb and continue in a similar manner throughout the number. Their timbre might well be described as rather harsh if it were not for their lack of reverb that causes their sound and duration to be dampened and therefore more staccato-like. There is, however, still intimacy between performer and audience, and it is through the combination of sound and image, an example of film as gestalt. Björk is an 'agent' for the music. She best represents the porous boundary between diegetic and non-diegetic, between sound and image, and, through doing so, is partially responsible for allowing the audience to accept the dynamic relationship between the two. She is a conduit for the

Fig. 3.4 Spectrograph showing changes in sound volume throughout the 'Cvalda' number

music, singing and dancing, visually representing the music. Björk's privileged role, which permits the boundary traversing of the different diegetic realms, is highlighted very clearly in the more 'melodic' moments of the number. At these moments, the reverb and echo of Björk's voice increases and brass instruments are introduced to the sonic landscape. These brass instruments follow a swing-like beat, which, coupled alongside their lack of visual grounding in the diegesis and the change in sound emanating from Björk, highlight the dream-like quality of the number. The audience is experiencing an intensely personal moment taking place in Björk's mind. Thus, a form of Film Studies that privileges the image proves deficient for it is the combination of sound and image that creates this version of Björk and allows the audience a spatial relationship with her.

The question that remains, however, is: Why does the audience move so easily from a proxemic relationship with the sound and image to one where the sound loses the sense of being rooted in the image? It is an example of what Rick Altman states in *Sound Theory, Sound Practice* with his description of a scene from *Union Pacific* (1939):

> The image displaces us incessantly, offering us diverse angles on objects located at radically different distances. Our voyeurism consists precisely in

this mobility. [...] Indeed, if we take the risk of flying about at all, it is certainly in large part because we know that our bodies are anchored by sound, and by the single continuous experience that it offers.[97]

The sound in the 'Cvalda' number therefore allows the audience to experience these fractured images due to its uniform and relatively unchanging nature, demonstrated in terms of volume in Fig. 3.4. Altman states that '[...] by holding the auditor at a fixed and thus stable distance from all sound sources [...] Hollywood uses the sound track to anchor the body to a single continuous experience'.[98] Yet how is this achieved in *Dancer in the Dark*'s 'Cvalda' number?

To understand the sonic space of the musical number and how it provides coherence to the visual realm, it is essential to analyse how the soundscape is created. As previously stated, the scene starts with a close-up of Björk and continues to favour close-ups and medium shots; there are few shots that actually establish the scene to any degree (Fig. 3.5) and no traditional establishing shots. How then does the soundtrack create a sonic space?

The first way this is achieved, as suggested earlier, is through a proxemics of sound. Proxemics, which in this specific case works closely with

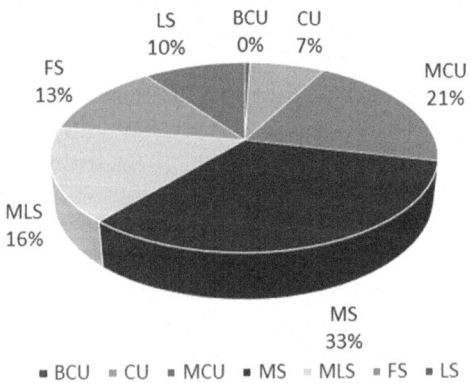

Fig. 3.5 Percentage of total shots in 'Cvalda' sequence as split between the different types of shot

a haptic experience, creates an embodied response in the viewer. The first sounds heard in the 'Cvalda' number are that of industrial sounds, which the audience can assume are taking place in the factory that Selma works and is situated throughout the course of the number. The machine sounds are delivered in a 4/4 time tempo (another similarity with popular song form) in a very rhythmic manner. The sound begins initially in the background before moving to the fore. The lack of any large movements by Björk, but rather her slight leaning forward in time with the music reinforces this movement of the sound towards being more centrally focused. The rhythms of the sounds are not, however, unchanging; before the edit into the second shot there is a change in rhythm but not tempo. One might assume that either the machinery making the noise has changed, or the place in its cycle has changed. As the sounds alter, so too does their volume (as seen in Fig. 3.5 at approximately the 35 second mark). As previously mentioned, by the second shot the sounds are considerably louder than before, implying that their source is getting nearer to the audience. This is the case in shot two when the audience is given a shot of a piece of machinery being operated by two people. It can be assumed based upon the movements of the characters and the machinery that it is this piece of machinery that is making the noise that has become louder. Thus, the closer the audience is to the machinery the louder it is; as the audience are shown the machinery in a close-up, they are indeed very close to it. Put simply, the spatial relation, or rather, the proxemic relationship with the noise of the machinery suggests a closeness matched by the image.

As the graphs and tables previously presented attest, the editing is very swift. Every shot at the beginning of the number is either of machines being worked by people or working autonomously. As each edit occurs, particularly each time a new piece of machinery is viewed, the sound changes: it is added to. The previous sound is still present, but the volume of the new piece of machinery gives the latter precedence. Therefore, whilst the sources of the sound have been located visually, this information swiftly disappears and only the sound remains to convey meaning: that of being in the same location at the same time. The sound is thus the primary signifier of the space of the number over a much longer period of time than that of the image.

Listening to the number, particularly the beginning when the music of the scene is first 'created', without the images provides an interesting point of comparison.[99] The nature of the sound changes very early on. There is a moment, which when watched back with the images one discovers occurs at the end of shot two, when all of the sounds increase in volume to a large degree, which acts as a sound bridge across the edit. Though present when the image is displayed, the distinction between individual sounds at any one moment—in this case when the image displays the piece of machinery making the sound—is far less obvious on a purely sonic level.[100] This chapter has already claimed that this has consequences for the proxemic relationship. The consequences, however, are not as problematic as at first they appear to be. Certainly, there is less variation than when the sound is accompanied by the image; however, this does not prevent a proxemic relationship. Rather, it merely means that the relationship is less varied than initial viewing suggests. The sounds are very 'close' to the viewer, by which it is meant that, as Peter Doyle suggests, there is little reverb. If the point of audition was conceived as far away from the audience, not only would verisimilitude suggest that the volume would be lower, but there would be more echo and reverb. The bigger the space, the more the sound can reverberate and echo; thus, the smaller the space, the smaller the reverb and echo. If, therefore, the space that the sounds are being emitted from is small, it follows that the proxemics between the audience and the sounds are equivalent; they are isomorphic.[101] The gap between audience and the sound of the 'Cvalda' number is thus minimal, or even non-existent. It is through this traversing of traditionally divergent spaces that an embodied form of spectatorship can be felt. I contend that the sound space of 'Cvalda' enables the audience to feel the scene in such a manner than enables comprehension of a space that is, in part, highly fragmented.

The regular 4/4 time signature of the sound, following the tradition of popular song has several effects on the audience; the first of which must surely be familiarity. The machine noises come close to replicating a percussive beat, and, in the absence of an obvious melody, the percussive rhythm becomes the focus of the song. An audience might find themselves tapping their feet to the rhythms presented by the machines, familiar with the predictable tempo. This immediate percussive familiarity is further heightened by the repetition, by Björk, of onomatopoeic words such as 'clatter', 'crash', and 'bang' to further heighten the use of individual sounds rather than a tune. As previously argued, gestalt laws state that, much like a metronome, these sounds, though individual, are heard in relation to one another; their sequence is more important for perception than any one individual noise. As such, although Björk emphasises particular sounds, they act as a palimpsest: each sound building upon the last.

This layering creates a more complex percussive sound, using both voice and machines in its creation. This amalgamated 4/4 sound can enable a trance-like state. The neurologist Oliver Sacks has argued that:

> One of the most dramatic effects of music's power is the induction of trance states, which have been described by ethnomusicologists in nearly every culture. Trance—ecstatic singing and dancing, wild movements and cries, perhaps, rhythmic rocking [...]—involves both motor and gross emotional, psychic and automatic effects, culminating in profoundly altered states of consciousness.[102]

He further goes on to state that 'whilst it can be achieved by a single individual, it often seems to be facilitated in a communal group'.[103] Thus, the repetitive percussive beat of the 'Cvalda' number can enable a trance-like state as it requires few mental processes to decode the music; the familiarity and repetitive nature of the beat means the audience is making little attempt to guess where the music will go next. This trance-like quality can have a social effect, one in which the participants are joined together by their experience. The audience, Björk, and the extras on screen are all participating with the music. The space between audience and performers has not only been bridged, but the music is having a physical effect upon the audience. This physical experience not only engenders an embodied experience, but also a haptic one, though the two should not be seen as mutually exclusive.

As suggested, the initial opening shots of the machines give the audience several of the sources of the percussive sounds. They are in close up, which not only enables a close proximity between audience and the space of the screen to be felt, but also the feeling of being able to reach out and touch said machines—much as the extras are doing. Though these close-up images of the machines do not continue throughout the number, they establish a precedent; the feeling is created in the audience at the very beginning. Furthermore, the use of instruments, and in the 'Cvalda' scene the machine percussion is joined by further musical (acousmatic) sounds seemingly coming from a source other than the machinery, requires a tangible relationship. Movement must be made for sound to emerge, whether this is the banging of a drum, the stroking of a harp or the workings of machinery. As the spatial relationship between audience and performer has been bridged and a tangible relationship with the music can be demonstrated in the 'Cvalda' number, it follows that the audience too has a physical relationship with the sound.

As *Dancer in the Dark* demonstrates, sound can play a vital role in the creation of space. Within the musical number, it is arguably the driving force behind the space as a whole. It enables the spectator to negotiate the space that is presented to them through perception. Whilst the theories of embodied spectatorship and haptics have focused predominantly on the visual realm, this analysis demonstrates that sound space can be perceived by several senses at once; it has more than an auditory function. Spectators can *feel* the sound space, and thus negotiate and comprehend it. Sound space should, therefore, be seen as more than fulfilling a narrative function or providing texture to the scene, but rather as a space that is created aesthetically. Visual primacy still remains in traditional Film Studies analysis, and like sound it can be used to create space. Chapter 4 thus explores ways the image can represent and create space.

Notes

1. Theo van Leeuwen, *Speech, Music, Sound* (London: Macmillan Press ltd, 1999), p. 14.
2. van Leeuwen, p. 14.
3. See Donnelly, *Occult Aesthetics* for more information on the wider issues of (a)synchronisation that exists outside of my remit here.
4. van Leeuwen, p. 14.
5. van Leeuwen, p. 14–15.
6. Bordwell, *Film Art: An Introduction*, p. 381. This book is interested in the 'effect' changes in space have upon the audience. This effect or impact can take a number of forms, such as emotional engagement with characters, the ability to sensually negotiate or the capacity to 'feel' the onscreen space.
7. Williams, "Is Sound Recording Like a Language?", p. 51.
8. Williams, "Is Sound Recording Like a Language?", p. 51.
9. Williams, "Is Sound Recording Like a Language?", p. 53.
10. A similar debate may also take place with regards to the image, especially if one considers that a viewer may not perceive all aspects of an image at any given moment, particularly if they are being directed to look elsewhere. Whether the viewer follows the cues or not, it follows that not all aspects of the image will be perceived, thus further questioning the nature of the 'original'.
11. Williams, "Is Sound Recording Like a Language?", p. 53.

12. "Recommended Guidelines for Presentation Quality and Theatre Performance for Indoor Theatres", 2000, www.film-tech.com/warehouse/manuals/TAPGUIDELINES.pdf [date accessed 10/09/12].
13. The specificity of the perceived sounds are of course dependent upon cultures being versed in the signals.
14. Whilst Staiger's "Reception Studies: The Death of the Reader" makes clear the issues with using the concept of an 'abstract audience', it is important for the argument here to first provide a new methodological approach. As such the abstract audience serves as a vehicle for demonstrating how such readings and approaches can be applied. Further studies into variations between specific audiences will be useful at a later date to develop the arguments further.
15. Randolph Jordan has written an interesting piece on the issue of 'authenticity' for audiophiles. He states that: 'the version of the audiophile ideal […] is that the best recordings are the ones that should never have been made in the first place. This seems like a contradiction, and of course it is'. He continues and describes how the issue is further complicated when any form of studio manipulation occurs; whilst mediation is necessary for a relationship between performer and listener, the latter, paradoxically, wants the 'equipment' to disappear. See Randolph Jordan, "Big Fun in My Living Room", *Squalid Infidelities 3*, 16th May 2005, www.synoptique.ca/core/en/articles/jordan_squalid3 [date accessed 24/02/ 2014].
16. Williams, "Is Sound Recording Like a Language?", pp. 53–54.
17. Williams, "Is Sound Recording Like a Language?", p. 56.
18. A further point could be made here with regards to embodied spectatorship, a key issue of this book, and the issues surrounding objectivity versus subjectivity.
19. Kerins, pp. 19–52. Whilst Kerins is concerned largely with tracking the history of surround-sound technology in the cinema, his chapter provides some key information on the developments of the medium in this area.
20. Though it is important to note the changes in technology, my argument here does not have a historical focus. I am more concerned with ideas of space and the aesthetics that produce them than the technology.

21. Kerins, p. 21.
22. Kerins, p. 54.
23. Kerins, p. 65.
24. Kerins, p. 79.
25. Sobchack, *The Address of the Eye: A Phenomenology of Film Experience*, p. 8.
26. Robynn J. Stilwell, "Sound and Empathy: Subjectivity, Gender and the Cinematic Soundscape" in K. J. Donnelly, (ed.), *Film Music: Critical Approaches* (New York: Continuum, 2001), p. 172.
27. For more information on the LFE channel, including details regarding bandwidth, see Tomlinson Holman, *Surround Sound: Up and Running* (London: Taylor and Francis, 2007).
28. A. Grimani, "Bass Management and the LFE Channel", *Sound and Vision* <http://www.soundandvision.com/content/bass-management-and-lfe-channel> [date accessed 24/02/2014], p. 1.
29. Grimani, p. 2.
30. Grimani, p. 2.
31. Taylor Carman, "Foreword", in Maurice Merleau-Ponty, *Phenomenology of Perception* (London: Routledge, 2013), pp. vii–xvi, (x).
32. Carman, p. x. Carman also usefully provides some historical background to Merleau-Ponty's ideas, for instance: the phenomenologist Edmund Husserl argued that to be conscious you must be conscious of something. Therefore, one can separate the act of thought with the intentional objects of thought, the latter of which becomes intentionality.
33. Barker, pp. 151–152.
34. Barker, p. 152.
35. Barker, p. 155.
36. Barker, p. 155.
37. Barker, p. 151.
38. Barker, p. 151.
39. Maurice Merleau-Ponty, *Phenemonology of Perception* (London: Routledge, 2012).
40. Kerins, p. 87.
41. Chion, p. 150.
42. Chion, p. 150.
43. Chion, p. 144.
44. Kerins, p. 86.

45. Chion, p. 151.
46. Kerins, p. 86.
47. Kerins, p. 92.
48. Kerins, p. 95.
49. Kerins, p. 95.
50. Kerins, p. 96.
51. Kerins, p. 96.
52. Kerins, p. 97.
53. Kerins, p. 97.
54. Kerins, p. 98.
55. A further point could be made about how the sounds and images are perceived and whether the latter can really ever be autonomous if they are synthesised in the head.
56. Stilwell, "Sound and Empathy: Subjectivity, Gender and the Cinematic Soundscape", p. 169.
57. Stilwell, "Sound and Empathy: Subjectivity, Gender and the Cinematic Soundscape", p. 169.
58. The term 'narrative' in this context, though not without issues, is taken to mean the moments within musicals that are not musical numbers.
59. Katz, p. 34.
60. Katz, p. 34.
61. Katz, p. 35.
62. Katz, p. 25.
63. Kerins, p. 66.
64. Kerins, p. 66.
65. Katz, p. 35.
66. Katz, p. 35.
67. Katz, p. 38.
68. Katz, p. 38.
69. Chion, p. 33.
70. Much of the discussion on sound technology and space can be transferred to sound space more generally.
71. See Ian Christie, "'Suitable Music': Accompaniment Practices in Early London Screen Exhibition from R. W. Paul to the Picture Palaces", in Julie Brown and Annette Davidson, (eds), *The Sounds of the Silents in Britain* (Oxford: Oxford University Press, 2012), pp. 95–110, for a discussion on sonic accompaniment to early cinema.

72. Slavoj Žižek, "Looking Awry", *October*, Vol. 50, (Autumn 1989), (pp. 30–55), MIT Press, p. 40.
73. William Whittington, *Sound Design and Science Fiction* (Texas: University of Texas Press, 2007), p. 126.
74. The Marxist theorist Fredric Jameson has discussed the issue of 'cognitive mapping', whereby he uses it to analyse the postmodern capitalism system in which the understanding of the 'self' is an increasingly difficult concept. Fredric Jameson, *Postmodernism or, The Cultural Logic of Late Capitalism* (London: Verso, 1991), pp. 409–418.
75. Chion, p. 129.
76. Chion, p. 130.
77. Critics of the musical genre often site it as being 'over the top', over-emotional and unrealistic. In reality, however, the genre is of course very multifaceted, ranging from realist to hyper-realist, and everything in between. In Dyer's "Entertainment and Utopia" he describes that the musical genre does not offer the audience images of utopia, but rather what it might feel like. Though this arguably lends itself to the thematically lighter-hearted musicals, this is not necessarily the case.
78. Paul Théberge, "Almost Silent: The Interplay of Sound and Silence in Contemporary Cinema and Television", in Jay Beck and Tony Grajeda, (eds), *Lowering the Boom* (Urbana: University of Illinois Press, 2008), pp. 61–62.
79. Kerins, p. 71.
80. Théberge, pp. 51–67.
81. Gorbman.
82. Carol Vernallis, *Experiencing Music Video: Aesthetics and Cultural Context* (New York: Colombia University Press, 2004), p. 4.
83. Vernallis, p. 3.
84. Vernallis, p. 3.
85. See Altman, *The American Film Musical*.
86. Peter Doyle, *Echo & Reverb: Fabricating Space in Popular Music Recording 1900–1960* (Middletown: Wesleyan University Press, 2005), pp. 1–2.
87. Carlos López Charles, *Transduction between Image and Sound in Compositional Processes*, (Mexico: Mexican Centre for Music and Sonic Arts) <http://www.ems-network.org/ems09/papers/charles.pdf> [accessed 08th May 2012], p. 1.

88. This dominance can be seen frequently in Film Studies; one must only look at David Bordwell and Kristin Thompson's seminal books such as *The Classical Hollywood Cinema* (London: Routledge, 1988). When one considers the position this book often has, as a core textbook for undergraduate students, it is not hard to see why semiotics and narrative continue to be the dominant theoretical modes of analysis.
89. <http://www.cinemetrics.lv/cinemetrics.php> [accessed 12/07/2012].
90. Vernallis, p. 27.
91. An attempt was made to contact Lars von Trier with the hope of being granted access to the original set designs, but there was no response.
92. Each block was kept as simple and detail-free as possible so that the visual information given in the reconstruction does not distract from the ability to explore the space.
93. Vernallis, p. 28.
94. van Leeuwen, p. 17.
95. Doyle, p. 3.
96. Rick Altman, "Sound Space", *Sound Theory, Sound Practice* (New York: Routledge, 1992), p. 61.
97. Altman, "Sound Space", p. 62.
98. Altman, "Sound Space", p. 62.
99. The term 'created' has been used in inverted commas as not only is the music compiled from sounds that are meant to already be present and heard, but it is also arguable that the music is taking place in Selma's mind; it is meta-diegetic.
100. The different sounds can be distinguished, but the obvious focus on one sound above another implied by the image, is less clear sonically.
101. Donnelly, *Occult Aesthetics* for more information on isomorphism.
102. Oliver Sacks, "The Power of Music", *Brain: A Journal of Neurology*, 129 (2006), 2528–2532, (p. 2528).
103. Sacks, p. 2528.

CHAPTER 4

Visual Space

INTRODUCTION

In this chapter, I focus specifically upon the visual space of musical numbers: their representation and perception. At first sight these two aspects may appear to be separate entities, however, they can be closely linked; their relationship can be in symbiosis with one another. This chapter analyses several different strands of visual space, including, but not limited to: the construction of the image, different ways of noting and recording space, interacting with space and the uses of space. It will consider the ways in which the construction and perception of space interact with one another and affect the outcome of the total visual space. To understand visual space one cannot simply analyse the images that are given, but must also explore the editing rate, the use of mise-en-scène, the way they affect the senses and the purposes they are put to amongst other elements. My focus here on visual space maintains gestalt theory's approach to analysis by understanding the holistic nature of its constituent parts, as mentioned in regards to the different strands of visual space that this chapter will address. The main positions championed here are therefore threefold: firstly, that 'forensic analysis' should be championed utilising a number of different methods; secondly, that visual space is perceived in a multi-sensory manner thereby challenging the ocularcentrism common in Film Studies; and thirdly, that the (visual) space can be extended from the frame of the scene. These are arguments that are made throughout the book, though they undergo slight changes in focus depending upon the relevant themes of the chapters concerned. The nature of Film Studies analysis over the years has meant that there is a better understanding of the role of the image than of sound. Thus, such visual primacy has meant that there are more theoretical ideas to cover in this chapter than Chapter 3, though one hopes that as Sound Studies develops this imbalance will be addressed.

This visual space chapter will draw upon forensic analysis in a number of different ways. The most prominent is through the use of virtual reconstructions, in which the chosen case studies are broken down, recreated via computer software and subsequently animated in order to illustrate the changes undergone in the space of the musical numbers. These reconstructions allow a closer analysis of the relationship between the various different characters, between the characters and the set design, and indeed between the characters, set design and audience. Another mode of forensic analysis that will be employed in this chapter is proxemic notation as developed by Edward T. Hall.[1] These will assist in the promotion of forensic analysis and will demonstrate the spatial variations and interactions between characters and their surroundings as well as between the characters and the audience. They are a fecund accompaniment to virtual reconstructions for they not only provide a means of annotating the space analysed within the virtual reconstruction, but also of understanding and reading it. Cinemetrics is another form of forensic analysis that shall again be explored in this chapter. This form of notation allows the recording of shot lengths, shot types, editing rates and other data to be compiled and presented in numerous ways.[2]

In order to analyse the visual space of musical numbers I take a number of examples from the Astaire and Rogers' RKO musicals from the 1930s. These have been chosen for numerous reasons, not least of which is that they provide fruitful opportunities for virtual reconstruction, an important mode of analysis. Due to the period of their release, the Astaire and Rogers' musicals frequently include a slower rate of editing. Although I am not exploring a particular era of musicals or seeking to isolate a country's musical genre output, I am arguing for a methodological approach of abstract aesthetic spatial analysis that can be applied to all musicals (and films more generally). The Astaire and Rogers' films, however, with their slower rate of editing, do allow the virtual reconstruction of the sequences to be expanded in more detail. This chapter will, therefore, outline the history surrounding the image and its place within visual space theories before detailing the different theories that will be utilised. These will then be applied to specific sequences to demonstrate how forensic analysis can be used to gain better understanding. A background to the Astaire and Rogers' musicals shall be given within a discussion of their use of set design to create space and allow movement.

THE IMAGE

The image, or rather 'image', is described by the *Oxford English Dictionary* (OED) as the following: 'an artificial imitation or representation of something', 'the aspect, appearance, or form of someone or something; semblance, likeness. Now only in allusions to, or uses derived from, biblical language [...]', 'A visual representation or counterpart of an object or scene, formed through the interaction of rays of light with a mirror, lens, etc.', and 'a mental representation of something (especially a visible object) created not by direct perception but by memory or imagination; a mental picture or impression; an idea, conception'.[3] What becomes clear from this is, rather paradoxically, that the image has taken on a number of meanings and inferences over time and varying contexts. It is both an artificial representation as well as the very appearance of the object/person itself. It is an integral aspect to cinema and the musical genre in both regards; the images depicted on screen are representations of previously filmed objects, people and surroundings, but they can become something more; original objects in and of themselves—experienced as such. The image is thus an important element of space perception as the audience develops a relationship with the image. When discussing space perception a number of different connotations are evoked that range from: an understanding of depth, locating oneself in the space, an understanding of surroundings, how space is perceived neurologically and the psychology of space perception amongst many others. These aspects, particularly the first three, could be described as 'visual data', whereas the latter two are means of interpreting said data. H. A. Sedgewick illustrates how important visual data is for living things in the following description:

> A typical environment is cluttered with objects. Various forms of visual information are available that help to specify the spatial relations between these objects. From a given point of observation only some surfaces are visible; others are hidden either by other objects or because they are facing away from the observer. When one surface only partially hides another, this *partial occlusion* provides information about the relative distance of surfaces from the observer. The surface that is partially occluded is necessarily farther away.[4]

Partial occlusion is a key aspect of visual space perception as it contributes towards the creation of distance, as is movement that enables spatial relations to develop. When spectators view a film they are essentially viewing the 3D world transferred to a 2D screen.[5] The image is in this case a representation. The notion of distance is therefore a fallacy and an illusion, however, partial occlusion works in the same manner. If the audience perceives a room in which characters stand in the foreground in front of a bar in the distance, then they may safely assume that the characters are 'closer' than the bar. This understanding of distance will change as the audience's location does. As the camera is often said to represent the eye of the audience, the camera's movement thus reflects the movement of the spectator.[6] Movement is an important aspect of human's lives, whether this is walking from 'a' to 'b' or the slight movement of one's head. Sedgewick describes how these movements 'serve many purposes, including gathering information about their environment. The transformations of the optic array produced by an animal's movements generate a variety of forms of useful information about the spatial layout of the environment'.[7] Sedgewick is illustrating how, as humans move, what was once far away becomes nearer, and what was once hidden becomes seen.[8] The cinema does not allow the audience to move, but this does not alter the effect, for after all, as Sedgewick argues, movement is relative and 'when we speak of the observer moving through the environment we might equally well speak of the environment as moving past a stationary observer'.[9] No difference is felt, however, as perception on the whole does not distinguish between the two.[10] 'Thus', Sedgewick states, 'rather than being uncertain about whether the observer or the environment is moving, the observer's perception is unambiguously of self-motion. The environment is perceived as the *stable framework* or background against which movement occurs.'[11] One could argue, therefore, that the set design and mise-en-scène of a film represents this stable framework and is thus of inherent importance to visual perception and indeed embodied spectatorship.

There are, however, minor differences that occur in the transferral of perception through different media. An important point to highlight in the case of cinema, for instance (and indeed this holds true for many other media, such as video games), is that the audience is also aware of their own environment, which, in the case of the cinema, is unmoving and static. The audience is consequently confronted with and viewing two different positions: the static cinema that they themselves exist within and the 2D screen in front of them. In such cases the feeling of movement evoked by the cinema is called *'simulated motion* of the environment'.[12] Sedgewick argues that such situations can be unsettling to the audience due to the double nature of their viewing position: 'these situations can produce instability in the perception of self-motion, with the perceptual choice of a reference frame being affected by a number of factors, such as which environment is perceived as being farther away'.[13] The motion in the cinema is therefore in large part a visual motion, which Maggie Shiffrar describes as consisting of 'a perceived change in optic information over space and time. Different changes in optical information are usually associated with different types of motion'.[14] The apparent differences between the cinema and unmediated perception (the term 'unmediated' is arguably fraught with contradictions and impossibilities due to both the nature of today's technology and the mental processes that are undergone. In this context it is taken to mean visual perception as seen through the eye rather than a screen) has been highlighted by E. Bruce Goldstein who has stated that 'pictures are flat but the depicted environment is usually three-dimensional. This obvious difference between pictures and the environment gives rise to the *dual reality of pictures*, the fact that "A picture is a surface that always specifies something other than what it is"'.[15] It does not necessarily follow, however, that the manner in which the images are perceived is different, that the visual space created through the camera and projected on the screen does not give the same data to the audience as they would perceive if seen without the screen. George Mather describes how important the notion of representation is to perception. He states that 'In the context of perception, representational states must correspond to brain states and [...] brain states correspond to particular patterns of neural activity evoked by sensory stimulation. So, specific patterns of neural activity actually represent specific states in the outside world.'[16] What happens, therefore, is that a representation is created regardless of the original source of the visual data. A famous example of how the image can be utilised to create and manipulate spatial perception is Alfred Hitchcock's 'Vertigo Shot' in which the camera moves away from an object whilst the lens zooms in (or vice versa).[17] What is demonstrated through this example is how quickly visual space can change, both in actual terms and with regards to perception. In terms of the former, both the camera's and lens' movement alters what can be viewed on screen as well as the framing. The latter, the perception of space, has been altered. The camera's position as the eye of the audience, and indeed Scottie (Jimmy Stewart) in this instance, has become more ambiguous. Despite the camera movement to create the effect, the audience and character are static and meant to be understood as such. Thus, it is clear that it is an apprehensive mental state that is evoked rather than actual movement on behalf of the character and audience.

Much as in Chapter 3, this concept of 'static movement' forces a return to theories of embodied spectatorship. Though I will deal with this in more detail subsequently, it is important to address the issue here, albeit briefly. Sedgewick's statement that, 'when we speak of the observer moving through the environment we might equally well speak of the environment as moving past a stationary observer', thus demonstrates that a feeling for the images is created. [18] The audience experiences no difference between themselves moving and the camera: 'the observer's perception is unambiguously of self-motion'.[19] A consequence of this is that the space represented on the screen is perceived by the audience and experienced as if they themselves existed within it.

Whilst an important concept in Chapter 5 will be the notion of 'cross-modal interaction', which may be briefly described as 'when different sensory modalities (vision, hearing, touch, balance, taste and smell) interact', here it is important to focus squarely upon vision.[20] In order to achieve this and an understanding of how the visual space represented on screen is actually perceived by the individual, neurologically speaking, one has first to explore the senses. George Mather describes how 'each sensory modality provides a cue about a specific object property, such as its size or location, and these different cues must be combined in some way in order for an experimental participant to report a single estimate of the object property'.[21] The object property discussed here is of course space. Mather continues to explain how the traditional view of perception is that a single sensory modality dominates over the others and creates the judgement on the specific object property; the sensory modality that dominates is generally considered to be vision.[22] Other, more recent theories have, however, been postulated. One that Mather describes is based upon Bayesian theory—an inference drawn by combining different sources of evidence according to a rigorous mathematical formula—that in a multi-sensory situation (which cinema indeed is) 'each sensory modality offers its own likelihood estimate for a particular object property'.[23] 'According to Bayesian theories', Mather continues:

> [T]he goal of cross-modal processing is to produce the most reliable and accurate single estimate from the multiple estimates that are available [...].

Bayesian inference predicts that the most reliable cues should have a greater influence on the final estimate, by virtue of their higher likelihood values.[24]

Consequently, it is not vision that is the default dominant sensory modality. Not only does this challenge the ocularcentrism found in Film Studies, for if vision is not by default the leading sense in terms of perception then it follows that the image cannot be claimed as the most important element of film language, but it also challenges the way one thinks about space, even visual space.

Returning to the perception of space, and how visual space is created, it is here necessary to revisit one of my main arguments: that visual space is perceived in a multi-sensory manner thereby challenging the ocularcentrism common in Film Studies. The preceding begins to hint at the challenge to the dominance of the image within Film Studies, but how does this fit hand in hand with the perceiving of visual space in a multi-sensory manner that I am advocating? An important aspect to the answering of this question is synaesthesia. All sensory pathways move from the periphery to the cortex, as George Mather describes. Along this route there are 'relay stations [that] offer side routes along which signals in one sensory modality can travel to interact with signals from another modality'.[25] An important destination is thought to be the superior colliculus, which is situated in the mid-brain as a mass of neurons. It is 'thought to be involved in integrating visual and auditory signals, and in directing visual attention'.[26] The reason for its perceived importance is that it contains cells responsive to a variety of different senses: visual, auditory and somatosensory (sensory activity that has an origin other than in the sense organs, for example the eyes and ears).[27] Mather states that 'some neurons show "superadditive" responses to multi-modal stimulation; their response to stimulation from multiple senses is much greater than the sum of their responses to each sense in isolation'.[28] Thus multi-sensory stimulation is more effective than a single sense being evoked.

This, however, is not the only way that neurologically speaking, multi-sensory stimulation is important. With regards to synaesthesia, the cinema demonstrates how a single sensory input can encourage multi-sensory perception. Mather describes synaesthesia as 'a multi-sensory perceptual phenomenon in which only a single sensory modality is stimulated, but it evokes a sensory experience in two or more modalities'.[29] An example might be seeing a picture of an apple and feeling as if you are able to taste it. A common form of synaesthesia is being able to see colours evoked by certain musical notes. Whilst as a phenomenon it is not yet entirely understood, George Mather believes that 'The most plausible account of synaesthesia is that it involves direct neural connections between uni-modal cortical areas [...]. These connections may be weak or absent in the majority of the population, but enhanced genetically in synesthetes.'[30] If true, this suggests that certain neurological regions can transmit and interpret multi-sensory data. It therefore follows that it is possible that any visual data can be interpreted in other sensory ways, thus yet again calling into question the dominance of the image and supporting the theory of embodied spectatorship.

The interpretation of visual space is thus a complicated issue, and not unproblematic. The dominance of the image within scholarly analysis must surely be called into question when one considers that the medium of film is multi-sensory, and therefore I can postulate that the multi-sensory perception that is undergone throughout the course of a film makes a haptic reading more than a possibility but a likelihood. One of the main proponents of reading films in a multi-sensory manner is Vivian Sobchack. Though focused largely on the effect that the image has on the body and the way that it can evoke a bodily response in the audience of a film, her work can extend into the aural realm.[31] Important to this chapter are Sobchack's core ideas on how the body reacts to the visual stimulus. Such ideas are pivotal for understanding the space of musical numbers as it directly addresses the space between the screen (both its diegetic and non-diegetic realm) and the audience in the auditorium. It is this space that has previously been described as the 'double nature of the viewing position': the conflict between the simulated movements on the screen with the static position of the observer. This is the space that is bridged, negotiated and indeed even entered by the audience through the theory of the haptic and an understanding of the multi-sensory nature of cinema and its effect on the audience.

Despite being a vociferous theorist on the body within cinema, Sobchack's work on the subject has remained largely outside the remit of traditional film theory. Over the years the liminal space it has existed in has been slowly eroded thanks to such theorists as Laura Marks, Yvette Hatwell, Arlette Streri, Giuliana Bruno and Jennifer M. Barker.

HAPTICS AND THE IMAGE

Theories surrounding the haptic are instrumental to this book and are implemented in a manner of ways. There are arguably two core threads to the theory of the haptic: namely, haptic images as described by Yvette

Hatwell, Arlette Streri and Édouard Gentaz, and, haptic modes of viewing advocated by Laura Marks and Jennifer M. Barker, both of which will be explored in this chapter.[32]

When dealing with the haptic and the wider work on the body's response to the cinema and film language, one has to ask why it has not been a more popular approach. Sobchack has argued that one of the reasons for theorists turning away from analysing the body in favour of the mind, semiotics or narrative analysis amongst others, is that the body is considered too 'base'.[33] A consequence of this is that such analysis becomes associated with 'low' genres, the likes of which traditionally include horror, melodrama and porn, as they produce in the audience involuntary actions hard to conceal.[34] Although it may be true that such reactions may be hard to control or indeed hide from others, it does not necessarily follow that they are any easier to understand or analyse. The focus on the mind and its ability to comprehend narrative often causes a separation between the theorist and the audience (however abstract or idealised). It is arguable that there is nothing more democratising than understanding the involuntary reactions of the body to film. Indeed one could see it as some of the most universal reactions. Whilst theoretically and hypothetically this is an appealing argument there is no guarantee of its truth, or that one person's bodily reaction will be identical to another's. A consequence of this is if the bodily response theories are to be followed one must still work with an ideal or abstract audience. Sobchack argues that 'scholarly interest has been focused less on the capacity of films to physically arouse us to meaning, than on what such sensory cinematic appeal reveals about the rise and fall of classical narrative' and other elements such as industry structure.[35] Furthermore, Sobchack finds that 'sensual reference in descriptions of cinema has been generally regarded as rhetorical or poetic excess—sensuality located, then, always less on the side of the body than on the side of language. This view is tautological'.[36] As has been previously demonstrated, bodily responses are not merely poetic, but the result of representations on the screen being processed neurologically and physically, thus to dismiss bodily analysis as too abstract, poetic (commonly used in a somewhat derisive manner) is to dismiss the science involved.

One of the many debates within Film Studies is the process that is undergone in order to understand a film. From these debates a number of different theories have arisen, such as cognitive theory and gestalt theory. Theories of the body, particularly Sobchack's work, exist within this debate also. Analysing the body's involvement in the process of spectatorship is as much concerned with understanding a film as the previously stated theories. It seeks to comprehend the affect and effect that film has on the individual as well as audiences as a whole. Traditional film theory, however, has largely attempted to understand the involvement of the senses in film spectatorship within the confines of the screen. Sobchack has argued that:

> [F]ilm theory has attempted (somewhat defensively, I think) to put the ambiguous and unruly, *subjectively* sensuous embodied experience of going to the movies back where it 'properly' belongs—that is, *objectively*—belongs: it locates the sensuous *on* screen as the semiotic effects of cinematic representation and the semantic property of cinematic objects or *off* the screen in the spectator's phantasmatic psychic formations, cognitive processes, and basic physiological reflexes that do not pose major questions of meaning.[37]

It is at this juncture that a number of important points arise from Sobchack's statement: firstly the issue of 'objectivity' versus 'subjectivity', and secondly the notion of meaning and how it can be found and/or sought. The first issue is a complex one. Often placed in binary opposition to one another and seen as mutually exclusive, the concepts of objectivity and subjectivity are open to debate. Perhaps, however, they are not as divided as at first they appear to be. Or, rather, in some situations they exist simultaneously with one another. There can be little argument in Sobchack's use of the terms in her statement presented earlier: '[…] to put the ambiguous and unruly, *subjectively* sensuous embodied experience of going to the movies back where it "properly" belongs—that is, *objectively*—belongs […]'.[38] Here Sobchack is highlighting film theory's attempts to deal with film analysis on an objective level, with the theorists distancing themselves from the material and thus critically engaging with the material and data without their subjectivity getting in the way; or, rather, minimising its impact. The problem is twofold: firstly, that there is an inherent negative judgement placed upon subjectivity as inferior to objectivity (for the reasons that Sobchack outlined previously), and secondly, that it dismisses the inherent problem of the unavoidable subject of the theorists themselves.

Here we return to the notion of the abstract audience. As mentioned earlier, discussions on the body (arguably the most 'subjective' of discussions as a consequence of being an analysis of the very 'subject' itself) and its reactions to film cannot ignore the neurological and physical processes that are undergone not just by the individual, but by every individual viewing the film. Thus to discuss the body is not just to be subjective, but to discuss a universal truth. This may be done as objectively as any other form of theorising and one can use an abstract audience to do it. The difficulty arises, and perhaps herein lies the inherent negative judgement that is attached to bodily analysis, in the language that is sometimes utilised. Sobchack herself states that 'sensual reference in descriptions of cinema has been generally regarded as rhetorical or poetic excess—sensuality located, then, always less on the side of the body than on the side of language'.[39] Such language is perhaps one of the core problems and at the root of the objectivity/subjectivity issue. Theorists who discuss the body often do so from a traditionally 'subjective' viewpoint; discussing their own feelings, reactions and senses triggered by the films they watch. It does not necessarily follow, however, that they could not just as successfully discuss the reactions invoked in terms of an abstract audience and thus deal much more objectively with both their analysis and language used. Furthermore, this notwithstanding, though such an approach is a possibility, it does not necessarily follow that theorists *should* promote it. Subjective analysis can be dealt with in absolutes. There is no denying the personal reaction that the theorist has to the film, nor is there any reason to discount it. Theoretical discourse may be both subjective and objective simultaneously: whilst discussing personal reactions they are also examining (whether consciously or unconsciously, overtly or covertly) the way the aesthetic data is dealt with neurologically—something that almost every audience member will experience to degrees. Thus a haptic reading should be considered not only a likely possibility, but also a possibility that should be promoted and encouraged more into the mainstream of film scholarship.

As the history of the theories surrounding the haptic have been explained, and so too the basic neurological basis behind it, it is important to turn to how it can be utilised in order to better understand visual space in musical numbers. It should by now be clear that though this chapter is concerned with visual space, discussions surrounding the haptic are not restricted to a single sensory input. Indeed, at the heart of haptic images, and haptic spectatorship, is the basic idea that through one sense another can be evoked: synaesthesia, as previously mentioned. Sobchack argues that although film is an audio-visual medium (and arguably the visual and aural senses are the primary ones invoked by film), attending the cinema utilises more of the senses than would at first appear to be the case. 'Whatever its specific structure, capacities and sensual discriminations', Sobchack states,

> vision is only one modality of my lived body's access to the world and only one means of making the world of objects and others sensible—that is, meaningful—to me. Vision may be the sense most privileged in the culture and the cinema, with hearing a close second; nonetheless, I do not leave my capacity to touch or to smell or to taste at the door, nor, once in the theatre, do I devote these senses to my popcorn.[40]

Let us now look at different forms of sensory analysis within the context of the Astaire and Rogers' examples. Set musical numbers will be examined from their films, each seeking to understand a particular aspect of visual space: tangible, symbolic, proxemic. Whereas Chapter 3 provided methodological approaches to analysing the representation of sound space in a general manner, I will here offer a more specific focus, namely one based upon Ginger Rogers' use of space. The aim here is to demonstrate that a methodological approach based upon understanding space through the lens of abstract aesthetics can be used in a multitude of ways, in this case through a particular star.

Tangible Space in 'Fancy Free'

Astaire is often credited as the more dominant member of the Astaire–Rogers' partnership: creatively, with regards to talent, as well as in terms of onscreen time. Indeed, it is a common trope found within the rhetoric surrounding the RKO musicals. Though it is undeniable that Astaire has more solo performances than Rogers, it does not always follow that he is the sole orchestrator of the space constructed within these musical numbers. Certainly, traditional Film Studies analysis that may analyse a particular star, in this case an auteur such as Fred Astaire, can create a dominant narrative in which Astaire is the primary focus and creative force behind the films. Questions of the validity of these readings aside, it is clear that an alternative reading, one based upon the construction of space within musical numbers, can offer alternative data. Hannah Hyam has stated how 'Astaire excels […] while [Rogers] is listening with varying degrees of pleasure, sorrow, acquiescence or resistance, quietly [contributing] to the impact of each number.'[41] Though Hyam's assessment refers only to those numbers in which Rogers is present in some capacity, she makes an important point. Namely, that in the numbers in which Rogers is present, though not always directly involved in the musical number she has a relationship with their representation of space. Such instances are not uncommon; many of Astaire's solos, Hyam notes, are frequently about Rogers' character and some even performed for her benefit, whether knowingly or not.[42] Whilst Hyam takes an underlying narrative approach to understanding in this instance, there are important aspects of space to be discerned from such a reading of musical numbers. 'Fancy Free' from *Top Hat* is one such example and it will be analysed with a view to understanding both its use and construction of space.

When discussing space, set design becomes a key element; it is often what is primarily identified as one of space's more tangible qualities. It is one of the main constituent parts of the larger category of mise-en-scène. Pinning down and discerning exactly what set design is, however, is not as easy as it at first appears. Throughout the 1930s, as Tim Bergfelder, Sue Harris and Sarah Street have described in *Film Architecture and the Transnational Imagination*, it grew in importance.[43] As an understanding of the qualities a set could bring to a film was realised, a name was finally conferred on those in charge, namely 'Production Designer'. Van Nest Polglase was in command of designing the sets for eight out of the nine films Astaire and Rogers made at RKO during the 1930s.[44] Whilst Polglase was the production designer, Carroll Clark was the Art Director, responsible for dressing the scenes and perhaps more directly involved in the working of the sets. As Steven Cohan has stated, 'the production staff at the studio maintained a consistent style of photography, editing, costuming, set designing, with artists and technicians going from one musical to the next'.[45] The frequent re-use of certain practitioners suggests that this is partly responsible for the RKO musicals' traceable style. Though the analysis of 'Fancy Free' should not be seen to illustrate the construction of space in all the Astaire–Rogers' numbers, it does demonstrate a number of spatial aspects prevalent throughout the series; thus, though an attempt is made to avoid the rhetoric of absolutes, examination of 'Fancy Free' does give a greater insight into other numbers in the series.

One reason why sets became a key element was because they 'aid in identifying characters, fleshing out and concretising their psychology, and often in conjunction with other contributing elements such as lighting and music, they help in creating a sense of place in terms of "mood" and "atmosphere"'.[46] Two important aspects can thus be taken from this. Firstly, that the psychology of the characters or the atmosphere that the sets evoke can aid the narrative and secondly, that though not necessarily working contrapuntally with the narrative, sets can create a sense of place separate from and without narrative involvement. Also of significance is the reference to other contributing elements. Bergfelder, Harris and Street expand upon this and argue that:

> Sets on their own do not create space on screen. Designed sets are realised cinematically only in conjunction with the work of the cinematographer, who through framing and lighting devices animates the fragmentary construction and imbues it with an imaginary wholeness, and the editor, who during post-production adds a temporal dimension to spatial relationships, and thereby anchors them in constructed reality.[47]

Other elements, such as framing, lighting and cinematography will therefore also have to be looked at when discussing 'Fancy Free'. Furthermore, this highlights film's collaborative nature and the importance of contributors that are not always directly concerned with the development of narrative.

The theorist C. S. Tashiro has argued that attempts should be made 'to try to isolate design from its narrative purpose in order to understand the image's impact beyond the story'.[48] C. S. Tashiro's work is important for promoting spatial analysis removed from the confines of narrative. Allowing film's narrative to take a secondary role permits a focus on alternative aspects that are also absorbed by audiences, no matter how (un)consciously.

Top Hat's 'Fancy Free' utilises and creates space in interesting ways. One example is through the use of the haptic. There are several different interpretations and prerequisites of and for haptic space within film, both of which can be seen in 'Fancy Free'. 'Like architecture', Bergfelder, Harris and Street state, 'film is an art form that can be described as 'tactile' or 'haptic', in the sense that Wollen explains: "both require a kind of kinaesthetic habit-formation, the acquisition of a mode of moving through space in order to understand and inhabit it unconsciously"'.[49] Haptic space, when considered a mode of spectatorial experience, can be found in films that allow great movement. The dancing films of Astaire and Rogers are very apt in this regard.

This movement is created in two ways; firstly, through the movement within the frame and secondly, with the use of film technology. Wollen describes cinema as existing within a tension that uses these two types of movement. 'Cinema', he claims, occupies 'a combination of "static", architectural space (the set) and "dynamic" narrative space (camera and editing).'[50] It is through both of these that space can be created in a haptic manner.

The importance of movement is clear in the Astaire–Rogers' musicals, particularly, though not exclusively, in the dancing numbers. 'Fancy Free', as a dancing number, contains much well-choreographed movement both of the characters and the camera. As a number, it can be seen to exemplify the tension that Wollen discusses. Edward Gallafent, in *Astaire and Rogers*, almost immediately describes the Astaire–Rogers' musicals in terms of movement:

> [...] endlessly presented in motion, whether they are embarking on a number, dancing through it or bringing it to its triumphant conclusion, this star couple seems to exude a sense of ease, or accessibility, even an intimacy—we can feel at home with them.[51]

Though not the purpose of his book, Gallafent has shown how the use of movement can be associated with the creation of emotion, much like Bruno has suggested. 'Fancy Free', like many of the numbers, uses movement to incite an emotional involvement between the audience and the film. It therefore follows that this can be achieved quite separately from narrative.

There are several different aspects of movement to be considered in 'Fancy Free', many of which contribute to the creation of a haptic space, and they shall be looked at under the two groups of space that Wollen describes: static and dynamic. Such terms are perhaps misleading, for even the static space allows for movement in and around the set. Notwithstanding this, 'Fancy Free' shows that both Astaire and Rogers construct space through movement. Two forms of close analysis will be looked at here, Virtual Reconstruction 1 (VR1) and Appendix 1. VR1 is a virtual reconstruction of the 'Fancy Free' number from *Top Hat* utilising a static 'birds-eye-view' shot so as to enable the movement of the camera and characters in the scene to be constantly viewable. Appendix 1, conversely, details a shot-by-shot analysis of the scene in question and the second column in particular is of interest here. From almost the very beginning of the sequence Astaire begins the movements that will become key to the scene as demonstrated in VR1. Shot 'b' of Appendix 1 shows that Astaire begins quickly to incorporate the set design into his performance. He is initially holding a cigarette that is kept in his hand whilst he moves the latter in time to the music before he throws the cigarette into a dish after he stands; this is highlighted as red to show the interaction in VR1. This is an example of interaction with set design, and more specifically, props.

C. S. Tashiro in his book *Pretty Pictures* incorporates the theory of the architect Christian Norberg-Schulz into a form of analysing set design. He uses Norberg-Schulz's five categorical circles to describe architectural space, starting from the individual human subject and spanning outwards, and adds two more of his own creation.[52] Though almost all categories are useful to an analysis of 'Fancy Free', it is the second category of 'Objects' that is particularly pertinent. 'Objects', which forms the second circle outside the human subject, after 'Costume, Makeup and Jewellery', consist of graspable objects that are close to us in space. 'Apprehensible objects', Tashiro describes, 'overlooked in order to privilege narrative, ground the viewer in a set of details easily understood because of their comforting smallness. Implicit in this description, however, is the possibility of picking up the object if we desire'.[53] This particular aspect of the haptic demonstrates the underlying notion of the audience's inhabitation of the onscreen space and subsequently permits them the potential feeling of control. Furthermore, the tactile element to the object, and in this case the cigarette, is an example of the building of a haptic space, and as previously stated, the haptic has roots in ancient Egyptian art work that had an emphasis on textured surfaces.

The use of the cigarette in the number is one of a myriad of examples of how movement and set design complement one another in 'Fancy Free' to create space, more specifically haptic space. Another example can be seen in the next shot. Shot 'c' sees Astaire pick up a glass bottle and pour drinks in time to the music, and highlighted red at 0:52 in VR1. Tashiro argues that film can give only the impression of real objects, such as the decanter Astaire holds.[54] By focusing on these objects, however, film can attempt to compensate for cinema's inherent inability to provide solid objects. Emphasis on these objects suggests their tangible qualities, and in an act akin to synaesthesia, 'the visual appeal is a substitute'.[55] By allowing such objects 'inordinate emphasis', Tashiro claims, it throws the story 'off balance and [reverses] traditional narrative values, levelling actors and objects to the same significance'.[56] Consequently, though not working contrapuntally, Astaire's use of props such as the cigarette, the decanter and, later in shot 'q', the statue (3:54 in VR1), allow the objects to exceed the narrative. Tashiro states that 'such magnifications are frequently based on visual fascination *apart from* narrative [...] a temporary roadblock [is placed] on the narrative's forward journey'.[57]

Such emphasis on objects affects the space of 'Fancy Free', for it diverts the audience's attention towards another plane of space that is tactile, optical and haptic. Existing simultaneously is not only the space of the set acting as a form of 'denotation', as outlined by the Affrons in *Sets in Motion*, to support the narrative, but a space that privileges objects and accessories that do not further the plot development.[58]

One potential reason for the ability of 'Fancy Free' to allow an emphasis on objects and accessories is its use of Art Deco, which in turn can work towards the creation of a haptic space, for as Bergfelder, Harris and Street state: 'Art Deco's emphasis on texture, smoothness and form, does indeed invite a tactile response: we want to touch the perfect surfaces.'[59]

Art Deco was an international trend with many different artistic influences that arose between 1910 and 1935. Lucy Fischer's work on Art Deco set design is particularly interesting and explains how it was a term coined retrospectively in the 1960s as an abbreviation of the hallmark exposition *International des Arts Décoratifs et Industriels Modernes* (staged in Paris between April–October 1925).[60] The importance of Art Deco within 'Fancy Free' and the Astaire–Rogers' RKO musicals cannot be underestimated and this is illustrated by Fischer who states that the 'Art Deco sensibility informs the spaces in which the characters reside, work, and perform'.[61] Astaire and Rogers' very actions in the 'Fancy Free' number can thus be seen to be dictated to a certain degree by their Art Deco surroundings; the space, which they inhabit, affects their emotions and actions.

Horace and Jerry's hotel suite in the 'Fancy Free' number reveals a set that is heavily influenced by Art Deco. Camera angles, for instance shot 'e', allow the audience to take in the accessories that punctuate the room's décor, many of which, such as the ashtray that becomes prominent in shot 'n2', can be seen to be examples of standardised products. Bergfelder, Harris and Street describe how 'the style used geometric forms and symmetrical patterns for a wealth of designs that were often made from materials such as chrome, plastic, glass or Bakelite that were in keeping with Deco's revolt against Victorian embellishment and clutter'.[62] The ashtray typifies this style; it is chrome, simple, placed in an isolated area and is unadorned. Fischer states how 'Art Deco's attitude towards technology contrasts strongly with that of its predecessor, Art Nouveau (1890–1914), that was highly identified with nature, [it was an] oppositional stance to the Industrial Revolution'.[63] The ashtray can thus be seen as a consumer product that emphasises its standardised nature; only the result of being machine built.

In a discussion of the film *Evergreen* (1934) Bergfelder, Harris and Street describe how 'the set has a typical Art Deco mixture of curves and vertical lines and in Tommy's room its furniture and fittings are very obviously displayed for an admiring gaze'.[64] Art Deco's emphasis on vertical lines can be seen to be epitomised by the ashtray, particularly when one sees how it is originally situated before Astaire brings it into his suite. Shot 'p2' demonstrates how the ashtray is a long cylindrical shape that creates a strong vertical line. It is placed directly alongside a strong vertical line on the wall, making it appear as if one line runs into the other. Next to the ashtray is a large lift door, again creating strong vertical lines, these are particularly emphasised by the vertical strip of four circular faux Greek faces placed in a line running the length of the lift. The sparse surroundings outside the hotel suite mean that these strong lines are stressed. Subsequently, the set, despite its simplicity, becomes a focus of the eye. The same appears true of *Evergreen*; Bergfelder, Harris and Street explain how 'the hard clean lines of the décor provide a contrast with her free-flowing movements, forcing us to notice the set as an entity in itself'.[65] A similar example can be found in shot 'o', which shows Astaire dance and kick a coffee table in time with the music, whilst seen through a mirror (3:30 in VR1). As before, this shot places emphasis on the set dressing, this not only creates a haptic space but also allows the props to exceed their narrative function. Astaire's movements make use of a large amount of the set, frequently incorporating the props into his dance. He is thus blurring the boundaries between the static set and the dynamic movements of both himself and the camera. Additionally, as can be seen in *Evergreen*, this movement creates a contrast with the strict lines of the set, thereby drawing attention to it.

Another aspect of 'Fancy Free', which is important with regards to the construction of space, is the issue of space as performance. If we return momentarily to Hyam's assertion that 'Astaire excels [...] while she [Rogers] is listening with varying degrees of pleasure, sorrow, acquiescence or resistance, quietly contributes to the impact of each number', the issue of audience or diegetic reception is raised.[66] Within 'Fancy Free' the audience is presented with this at several different levels, or rather, Astaire inhabits several different levels of performative space within the number. The character Horace represents the first. Though 'Fancy Free' is not a public performance, nor is it performed in a typical dance setting such as a stage or a theatre, Horace's presence ensures that it is a performance for more than the audience. Rubin has described how in the Astaire–Rogers' musicals 'performance space [is] not confined to a separate, compartmentalised domain such as a theatrical stage. Any place is a potential performance space'.[67] In 'Fancy Free' Astaire performs an impromptu song and dance of which, for the most part, Horace is the sole diegetic audience member. As Bergfelder, Harris and Street state 'the obtrusiveness of the sets invites an element of self-reflexivity—this is not live theatre, but a film'.[68] Horace's position within the number, as typified by shot 'e', exemplifies this. The camera is not positioned as a point-of-view shot that one might experience in the cinema, but rather the audience is given a unique position to the internal audience (as demonstrated by the camera positions shown in VR1); they are occupying a different part of the space to Horace, one that cannot be found in the theatre.

The importance of this self-reflexivity can also be seen in the way space exists within and beyond the frame throughout 'Fancy Free' and Rogers plays a role in this. Bergfelder, Harris and Street describe how

> C. S. Tashiro is interested in images and frames that invite the spectator to look outwards, to suggest meaning that cannot be contained within the frame: whole 'closed images' operate 'centripetally', 'open images', encouraged by camera movement away from the centre of the frame suggest designed space beyond the frame.[69]

As Appendix 1 demonstrates, and as typified by Astaire's movement in such shots as 'g' and 'i', the movement within the number creates an 'open' image. Tashiro draws on a number of different theorists, such as Arnheim, Leo Braudy and Heinrich Wölfflin to explain his theory. Tashiro uses Wölfflin's work in particular to detail how 'open form emphasizes movement, and suggests that we can equate camera stasis with closed (framed) film and camera movement with open (window) form'.[70] The camera movement alone throughout 'Fancy Free' is not enough to suggest the window form. Combined with Astaire's own movement, however, the scene suggests depth, which is a requirement of the open, window form; this depth can be seen in VR1 through Astaire's moving between the three grounds: foreground, middle ground and background as well as lateral movement. 'The "window" metaphor', Tashiro explains, 'stresses the film image's illusion of depth by using compositions that move *away* from the centre of the image and towards the edges of the field'.[71] The use of Rogers throughout the number is a large part of this movement away from the centre and suggestion of life, and space, outside of the frame. These cut-away 'Rogers' moments are shown in VR1 by a darkening of the scene.

At the end of shot 'e' the camera tracks down to a new space directly below, shot 'f'. It is revealed to be Rogers' bedroom; the camera tracks towards her, revealing her looking upwards and out of shot. This is an example of Rogers being used as means of connecting the two, previously distinct, spaces. Her looking off screen also implies a continuation of space outside the confines of the frame; that the diegetic space is boundless. 'The window metaphor', Tashiro states, 'suggests that the camera's selection of material is arbitrary, that the world on-screen is merely what *is* shown, not all that could be shown'.[72] One way that Rogers is used to create space, despite not being directly involved in Astaire's solo number, is to create open images that connect multiple spaces. Bergfelder, Harris and Street describe how

> the use of stars within sets recalls Tashiro's ideas concerning the mobility of the performer within the frame, especially from the centre to the edges. This constellation, for Tashiro, invites an 'open' reading of a scene that promotes contemplation [...] of designed space beyond the frame.[73]

Although this is more directly related to Astaire's movement whilst dancing, shots 'a2' to 'm2' show the same type of movement by Rogers, and it is this movement, created by both the performer and the camera that is important in the creation of space for it suggests its endless nature. The space presented onscreen is endless, unable to be confined by the film itself and thus could be seen to blend seamlessly with and incorporate the space that is inhabited by the external cinematic audience, thereby creating a relationship between audience and performer that will be looked at subsequently.

Another way that Rogers is pivotal to the connection of spaces is through the use of music. Whilst this chapter focuses on visual space, a point should be made here about how image and sound can work together in a cohesive manner. Claudia Gorbman describes how 'film music follows seven principles; one of which is 'inaudibility'. Music is not meant to be heard consciously. It should subordinate itself to dialogue, or visuals; to the primary vehicles of the narrative'.[74] Though this is not argued with musicals in mind the scene does contain some musical leitmotifs that arguably work subconsciously on the audience. Altman attests that the musical follows a different narrative structure from other genres, namely one based upon a dual focus narrative and simultaneity.[75] This dual focus extends to the music that, he argues, 'even when the musical style is not so prominently displayed it makes its presence felt, sometimes as a simple accompaniment (e.g. strings for one, brass for another)'.[76] This can be seen in 'Fancy Free'.

Though the same musical rhythm present whilst Astaire is onscreen continues as the camera cuts away to Rogers in such shots such as 'f' and 'h', there is a slight change in emphasis. Whereas there had been a strong use of strings in the previous shots of Astaire dancing, the shots of Rogers experience a subtle shift in favour of woodwind instruments, though both are present in each scene. Though the use of the same rhythm works to link the two spaces—Astaire's hotel suite and Rogers' bedroom—together, the subtle shift in music creates a separate musical space for each actor. The continuation of the same rhythm, however, could be seen to follow Altman's argument that 'pairing off is the natural impulse in the musical, whether it be in the presentation of the plot, the splitting of the screen, the choreography of the dance, or even the repetition of the melody'.[77] If a focus were to be placed on narrative, the repetition of the melody between Astaire and Rogers could therefore be seen to illustrate their future romantic relationship.

Not only are the two different spaces of the set linked together in 'Fancy Free', but so too are the larger visual and aural spaces. Astaire's tapping is the most overt example of how the two spaces are connected; it does not merely repeat the music, but rather works to complement it in an almost syncopated rhythm. It creates the illusion that the two are knowingly working together despite the impossibility of this being so due to the non-diegetic nature of the music. The tapping, along with the performative actions in time with the music, such as the kicking of the table and the pouring of the decanter in shot 'c', work to remove boundaries between distinct spaces.

'Fancy Free' constructs and utilises various different levels of space that are equally independent and complementary to the narrative of the film. The creation of a haptic space enables the audience to inhabit the diegetic world of the film through motion and an emphasis on specific aspects of the set; a tangible space is created that is quite uninhibited by the confines of narrative. Additional levels of space are created musically and through the use of Art Deco. 'Fancy Free' also offers an example of a performance that takes place in a domestic, private space unlike several other numbers in the Astaire–Rogers' musicals and of which 'The Yam' is an example.

Symbolic Space in 'The Yam'

Set design, and its relationship with various other elements of film language such as editing, framing and camera movement, is one means of constructing and understanding the space of a musical number. As demonstrated in 'Fancy Free', it is in part responsible for the creation of the haptic, but this could be considered a tangible space; a tactile space that invites an appeal to the senses, particularly that of touch and permits a feeling of inhabitation of the on-screen images. Such inhabitation brings with it a measure of control to the audience, or rather the appearance of it. If the audience can 'feel' the objects and the larger mise-en-scène then they can choose what to touch and explore, as illusionary as this may be in reality. This is not, however, the only space. Another more abstract level of space exists within films and particularly numbers, namely the space between audience and performer. This level of space is just as important for it allows 'immersion' in the number and conditions the audience into a different way of viewing; one that permits a shift in register from narrative to number. These characterise three key elements of the relationship between audience and performer: control, immersion and modes of viewing. In short, embodied spectatorship and a focus will therefore be placed on these aspects.

Michael Wood describes how 'many musicals [...] present the moment of breaking into song and dance as a literal break, a sharp change of gear from the prosaic speech of dull motions or ordinary existence [...], a clear separation of music and life'.[78] Suggested by such a statement is the implicit notion that this shift in register can occur when the musical moves from narrative to number. This shift is not merely an alteration in emphasis—from 'non-musical' moments to a break out in song and/or dance—but one also of a change in space; more particularly, the change in space that contains the relationship between the audience and performer. For this to be achieved a variety of techniques are utilised, many of which are demonstrated in Rogers' 'The Yam' solo from *Carefree* (1938).

Carefree is an example of 'the fairy tale musical', a sub-genre created by Altman in order to explain the different Broadway-Hollywood relationships. Altman claims that this particular sub-genre can be seen as encompassing a more continuous development from its stage origins; taking up 'where the stage operetta (all but) left off'.[79] The early days of sound film had a focus on music, and speech was used as a 'support mechanism for song', to introduce, justify, explain and complete them.[80] The musical elements of the sub-genre are thus its key aspects. It was borne out of a tradition of early film's synchronised musical soundtrack and, as Altman describes, '"live" music performed by characters portrayed within the film'.[81] There is consequently a long-established viewing tradition present, even for contemporaneous audiences, and to a certain extent this informs the relationship between audience and performer.

Unlike 'Fancy Free', which was a private performance (a private performance for Horace in the hotel suite, Rogers in the hallway and simultaneously for the external audience), 'The Yam' is delivered with support of a full orchestra amidst an onlooking internal audience. This audience changes the dynamic of the number. Jane Feuer states how 'in order to get a direct response from the film audience, Hollywood musical-makers had to place in their path another, spectral audience'.[82] The use of an internal audience could be read as another of film's manipulative techniques, used to ignite a particular reaction through the formation of a connection been audience and performer. There are numerous reasons why internal audiences in numbers became important, many of which are connected with issues surrounding the inherent nature of the musical genre and furthermore, its association with theatre and the revue format.

'One could say', Feuer argues, 'that the internal audience in the musicals, like the studio audience and canned laughter on television, are latter-day versions of the old theatrical claque'.[83] This reference to theatre is important as it highlights issues surrounding the different nature of spectatorship between theatre and cinema; the first of which is the matter of spontaneity or immediacy. Feuer maintains that 'live entertainment seems to be a "first-person" form, a performance which assumes an active and present spectator. The typical story film, [conversely], is more like a third-person narration the audience eavesdrops on. It is not a direct dialogue between performer and audience'.[84] This issue of a direct dialogue or address is reiterated by Cohan who claims that in musicals the 'narrative follows general conventions, but when singing stars typically face the camera to sing or dance, [they are] readjusting the film's register to a more direct address'.[85] This direct address is one that acknowledges a present audience, such as that of the theatre, often through a subtle breaking of the fourth wall; this can be demonstrated by the lining up of the performers to face the camera, as can be seen in 'The Piccolino' in *Top Hat* and in

VR1 where Astaire faces the camera whilst singing. One could argue that Hollywood narratives do not require an active spectator; techniques were developed whose sole aim was to hide the filmic mechanisms that were necessary in order to encourage a willing suspension of disbelief, and arguably allow the unconscious absorption of particular hegemonic ideologies. Thus, audience members' passivity was often sought. A direct address, conversely, is recognition of the audience's presence.

A direct address is desirable for several reasons, one is that it permits the illusion that audiences inhabit the same space as the performer, and thus allows them a sense of participation in the number; and consequently, control. In the theatre, it is a result of the nature of theatrical architecture that both the audience and performers are present within the same area. Though watching a theatrical performance the audience, through necessity, must occupy the same space as the entertainment at the same time. Cinema, conversely, allows for the entertainment to be transported to different locations, and, at the point of its consumption, the moment of its creation has passed; it is no longer live as in the theatre. The temporal dislocation notwithstanding, as Hall points out, 'in the cinema, in TV, in radio, a great deal depends upon the impact and 'immediacy' of the performance'.[86] This is an issue that Stanley Cavell addresses and argues that 'the audience in a theatre can be defined as those to whom the actors are present while they are not present to the actors'.[87] Unlike pantomime, theatre frequently makes no conscious overt allusions to the present audience, a fact that is further enforced by cinema that allows the audience to be 'mechanically absent'.[88] In viewing a film, Cavell states, 'my helplessness is mechanically assured: I am present not at something happening, which I must confirm, but at something that has happened, which I absorb (like a memory)'.[89] Cinematic audiences are thus dissimilar to their theatrical counterparts due to not inhabiting the same space as the actors, despite the fact that their presence may be felt to a larger degree due to a film's close-ups and editing techniques. This suggests film's problematic and contradictory relationship with the present and subsequently, audience's inhabitation of onscreen space. If as Cavell suggests, external cinematic audiences relinquish control upon entering the cinema where does this leave the control that results from the creation of haptic space? In truth, it is an illusion; audiences willingly suspend their disbelief and relinquish control, the cinema seeks to cushion this transfer of power by disguising it as much as possible. It does not necessarily follow, however, that the illusion holds less power over the audience than their actual cinema viewing position.

As a result of this, film musicals often go to great lengths to recreate theatre's live quality; one consequence of this being the creation of the backstage musical. This sub-genre is renamed by Altman 'The Show Musical' so that it may include films that are not restricted to a Broadway theatre and includes musicals whose plots concern the creation of a show.[90] Whilst *Carefree* is not encompassed under the sub-genre, for it does not seek to incorporate any of its musical numbers into a plot concerned with professional performance, 'The Yam' contains elements that benefit from analysing it as such; for instance the internal audience. In the backstage musical the internal audience would be one of several ways for a film to establish the number's context, it would give the filmmakers leave to direct action towards the camera, which is often positioned as an audience member, and it would also allow the internal audience to dictate the external audience's reaction to the numbers. In *Down to Earth* (1947) for instance, the external audience is told to read the 'Greek Ballet' as an exaggerated and pretentious performance because the internal audience does. This connection between the internal and external audience is one means in which the illusion of inhabiting the space of the numbers, and thus the same space as the performer, is utilised.

Jane Feuer has described how 'the musical developed a filmic vocabulary to create [an] almost kinetic sense of participation in the film audiences'.[91] Though this kinetic participation could suggest a haptic space, it could also refer to an audience—performer interaction. This is possible due to the notion of audience immersion. Laura Mulvey's work on the fetish is an interesting way of approaching an analysis of the external audience's position within the musical number. Mulvey discusses the two varieties of the fetish, namely Marx's commodity fetishism (an abstract value placed upon an imaginary investment beyond its worth) and Freud's sexual fetish (displacement of sexual repression) and places them within the context of feminist criticism.[92] She states that 'the fetish very often attracts the gaze'.[93] A fetish does not want to be overlooked 'but to be gloried in'; it is a consequence of this that the close up is often employed.[94] The close-up raises to the surface interesting issues with regards to audience immersion and the space of numbers; it can be seen as a form of fetishisation that places emphasis on areas giving them excessive value, and aiding in the creation of haptic images. The close-up is perhaps most famously seen in numbers in Busby Berkeley scenes, for instance the 'By a Waterfall' number from *Footlight Parade* (1933). Berkeley gives undue attention to faces and limbs of the (women) filmed, but frequently without giving the audience the means of distinguishing the different performers. Mulvey argues that the fetishisation of women is a means of spreading the hegemonic ideology, one that places Woman as an object of the gaze. This ideology is spread both through narrative and film technique, such as the close-up.[95] Béla Balász argues that

> close-ups radiate a tender human attitude [...] and are often dramatic revelations [...] that show the faces of things and those expressions on them are significant because they are reflected expressions of our own subconscious feeling.[96]

With such an argument, the possibility for audience immersion stems from the emotions created by the use of close-ups. Does it therefore follow that the lack of close-ups in 'The Yam', and indeed all of the Astaire–Rogers' dancing numbers, resists emotional involvement and immersion by the audience? If so, do the musical numbers that take the form of a tableau create (emotional) distance from what is viewed? Mulvey has argued that during the development of filmic conventions such as continuity editing there was also a focus on movement and excitement, both developed through the focus on modern movement, for instance trains, and camera movement.[97] The close-up, however, Mulvey believes, develops a rhetoric of stasis, 'holding back the excitement of movement into a moment of eroticised visual pleasures'.[98] 'The Yam' is neither infused with camera movement, nor close-ups; the movement from the number comes predominantly from Rogers herself.

Another aspect of the filmic vocabulary that Feuer suggests includes the recreation of a stage setting, or as Feuer states, a proscenium arch. These position the number in an acceptable performance space, one that carries with it certain expectations derived from the theatre; it would not be out of place to see a musical performance on a stage. Appendix 2 details how a stage is created despite there being no theatre. Shot 'p', for instance, works as a means of establishing Rogers' performance in an appropriate setting. She begins facing the camera in the middle-ground with the orchestra in the foreground and the seated audience members in the background. Behind her is a large wall that arches the length of the room and creates a secondary frame to that of the camera. It acts like stage dressing and works to position Rogers as the central focus, both of the camera and the internal audience.

The recreation of a stage-like environment does two things. Firstly, it enables the external audience to occupy a space they are accustomed to and, therefore, do not rebel against; accepting what they see presented to them. Secondly, it allows for a feeling of spontaneity, in spite of how problematic this may be. Despite the recreation of a stage, Rogers is not performing in a theatre. This enables Rogers to give a performance that is natural, unplanned and 'spur-of-the-moment', something that many musicals strive for. The setting of 'The Yam', and in particular the stone arch that frames Rogers' performance, is not entirely necessary for the creation of the stage. Indeed, as Feuer states 'whenever a number commences in any musical, the world does become a stage'.[99] Implicit in this is the notion that the space of the stage is a psychological one rather than merely tangible. The stage is a (transferable) concept and can thus be recreated outside of a theatre, such as in 'The Yam', and often this is beneficial. The concept of the stage is developed through a series of expectations; firstly that the characters of the stage are different from those of film, and secondly, that there is a variation in the style of acting. The two, however, are not mutually exclusive. Cavell has argued that 'in a theatre we are in the presence of an actor, in a movie house we are not'.[100] Like Edgar Morin's analysis of stars, Cavell declares that in the theatre the character is timeless rather than the actor; in film, the medium's permanence necessitates the opposite.[101] Panofsky has stated how 'stage work is continuous but transitory; film work is discontinuous but permanent'.[102] The character of Hamlet in a theatrical production of Shakespeare's play will remain the focus, over the years many different actors shall play the role, each seeking to bring the character to life. In film 'the character lives and dies with the actor'; there is often a traceable persona imbued by the actor's own persona. In the case of Astaire and Rogers, throughout the RKO films the different characters they play are all connected by the pair's persona; the characters are of secondary focus to Astaire and Rogers, but merely act as an interchangeable skin. The difference in acting style between the two media, Leo Braudy argues, is an essential element of this. He claims that 'the stage actor [projects] a sense of holding back, discipline and understanding, the influence of head over feelings, while the film actor projects effortlessness, nonchalance, immediacy, the seemingly unpremeditated response'.[103] It is this immediacy and unpremeditated style that is of importance. A theatrical performance is rehearsed before being performed in chronological order to a waiting audience; film, conversely, is often filmed out of order with the feelings exhibited on the screen having the appearance of stemming from the moment, of genuine response. The actors are frequently said to be 'playing themselves', giving the performance a sense of spontaneity and the appearance of being less studied.[104] Film therefore arguably offers an immediacy and spontaneity that theatre cannot offer, despite it being a recorded past event, and not being performed in the present.

This tension with the theatre is shown in the idea of a transferable proscenium arch, which Feuer claims is layered with ambiguity in the musical. This is due to its perception as a barrier whose distance must be bridged in the backstage musical. 'But', she claims, 'when performance is taken outside the theatre, the proscenium is reborn out of ordinary space and the world is a stage'.[105]

Though still referring to the backstage musical, Feuer's assessment of the difficulties the proscenium arch, or theatre, can be seen to represent is an accurate one. They can prevent a suitable audience—performer relationship as it reminds the audience of the performer's status as a professional and consequently, the audience's role as a consumer. When audiences pay to see an Astaire and Rogers' musical they are accepting a series of preconditions; firstly, that they are consumers and Astaire and Rogers the professionals, and secondly, that as a result of this the numbers will be highly rehearsed, perfected and enacted by specialists. A number of filmic techniques are used in an attempt to negate the relationship between audience and performer that such preconditions create.

One way to lessen the audience's awareness of their status as a consumer is through the aforementioned feeling of spontaneity that a created proscenium arch can produce. Hall highlights the importance of this:

> Most cinema goers will remember with pleasure the barn dance in *Seven Brides*... [...] The quality of these and other sequences in good musicals is only achieved through sheer professional skill based on hours of rigorous training and rehearsal. But this by itself does not account for our pleasure. What we respond to is the sense of spontaneity in the performances. The dancers seem to be spontaneously expressing their feelings. The quality of these feelings is an element in our pleasure.[106]

Hall's argument that spontaneity and feeling are linked is a compelling one and gives motive for many of the numbers in films. In 'The Yam', Rogers' performance is impulsively given, with no prior indication that performing was what she intended to do, as a result of her unfulfilled feelings towards Astaire. She wants him to dance with her, as evidenced in shot 'd', and her dance is motivated by feelings of frustration, desire and cunning in equal measure. The spontaneous nature of the dance is further enforced when Rogers is finally able to get Astaire to dance with her. Shot 'u' demonstrates how Astaire must copy Rogers' dance moves in order to learn the performance. The result is that he briefly remains a beat behind Rogers. This build-up of spontaneity, both Rogers giving an impromptu performance and Astaire having to learn the steps whilst dancing, is important with regard to the audience-performer relationship for it allows a willing suspension of disbelief by the external cinematic audience; the audience is aware that these are two professional performers, but are watching them learn and perform songs with the appearance of a lack of practice. 'The Yam' allows Astaire and Rogers to connect with the audience; Braudy states how the film actor in 'playing themselves' is interpreting 'what is most successful and appealing in one's own nature [...]. Film actors play their roles the way we play ourselves in the world'.[107]

Feuer describes how 'for a movie genre which itself represents professional entertainment and which is also frequently about professional entertainers, there seems to be a remarkable emphasis on the joys of being an amateur'.[108] Emphasis on amateurism is therefore a key element of this and often encourages a feeling of spontaneity. In *Carefree* Rogers plays a character who is a singer on the radio and is used frequently in advertisements, she is not, however, a professional performer who is used to encompassing dance and physical performance into her routines. 'The Yam' is such a routine. Rogers begins her performance when the orchestra conductor agrees to play a song only if Rogers is willing to sing it; Rogers reluctantly agrees to this after she has realised that she can use the situation to her benefit. Rogers begins her performance by humming a few bars of the 'The Yam' rhythm. The camera, shot 'p', is positioned behind the orchestra looking out onto the internal audience. Rogers is standing between the orchestra and the audience in the middle ground on the dance floor facing towards the camera. There is a clear creation of a proscenium arch behind Rogers where the orchestra is separated from the dance floor by a large stone archway. Though such devices make the country house they are frequenting into a stage, it is a much more interesting use of space than at first it appears. The framing of the shot not only positions the cinema audience as a member of the orchestra—a privileged position to be in during a number—but places the internal audience as one of the objects of the gaze under the proscenium arch. It is not as simple, therefore, as watching Rogers perform under a constructed stage. When the camera cuts away and repositions itself in a point of view shot of one of the internal audience members it breaks the 180-degree rule and reinstates Rogers as the object of the internal audience's gaze, and subsequently the cinematic audience's.

One possible explanation for this is that by offering the cinematic audience the privileged position behind the orchestra the number is enabling them a more conspiratory relationship with Rogers. The cinematic audience is aligned with Rogers through inhabiting the same space. Consequently it removes the appearance of the cinematic audience as consumers, for they are no longer aligned solely with the internal audience, but also with Rogers. The anthropologist Brad Shore has argued that a discourse on human play is important for understanding the connection between athletes and spectators, and this can be translated to the audience/performer dynamic. In his discussion on baseball he states how emphatic engagement between spectators and players can develop throughout the course of a game.[109] It is called 'emphatic' because it suggests sports' (and a musical number's) ability to arouse powerful identifications in spectators. 'Spectators', he argues, 'not only "engage" as loyal fans, but also experience powerful physical empathy, a kinesthetic resonance with the play itself'.[110] Spectator sports, and cinematic performances of musical numbers, establish constitutive boundaries between players/performers and spectators/audiences and this boundary is marked by a kind of 'magic' circle or square where spectators are confined to marginal areas, thus shaping their relative 'experience—distant perspective', especially when compared to that of the players.[111] A consequence of this distance is that spectators are afforded a reflexive self-awareness.[112] Spectators are aware of their position outside of the play area, yet still become involved in the game. This kinaesthetic involvement, (kinaesthetic as the spectators often feel a physical participation in the sport) can lead spectators to easily forget that they are merely viewing the game and experience 'emphatic engagement'.[113] This is a form of proxemics. There is a distance between the spectator and player, and in the case of 'The Yam', the audience and Rogers, both due to the nature of the medium—the external audience is in an auditorium whilst Rogers is a projection on a screen—and the internal audience positioning which is placed in an arch around the dance floor, thus enabling Rogers, like the baseball players on the field, to be the centre of attention. This distance is surmounted in part due to the audience's emphatic engagement in her performance.

Feuer explains how a musical number can sometimes demonstrate how the stage world is a community that involved mass co-operation, co-operation that includes the film's audience. The film's audience thus feel's participation, that, she argues, '[cancels] out the alienation inherent in the viewing situation'.[114]

This demonstrates another means in which the distance between audience and performer is reduced. The prevention of alienation in 'The Yam' is achieved through a shifting audience position. Shot 'q' sees the camera track right as Rogers moves across the dance floor; she remains centrally framed and the camera is positioned behind the heads of some internal audience members. This removes the static audience view that is found in the theatre. Shot 'r' illustrates a return to the angle shown in shot 'p', but the camera has moved in front of the orchestra looking out onto the internal audience directly in front of the stage. Rogers again looks at the camera, creating a sense of space that gives the constructed stage the appearance of being visible from all 360 degrees. Again, this is unlike the theatre. Feuer has argued that

> through shot transitions (rather than through any particular shot) the spectator may be included in the internal audience; or he/she may replace the internal audience or both. In each case it's the intrusion of the internal audience between us and the performance which, paradoxically, gives the effect of a lived—and more significantly—a *shared* experience.[115]

Though Feuer's emphasis on the importance of the spectatorial audience is important, 'The Yam' makes it clear that an alignment *with* the internal audience is not required. Though 'The Yam' does include an internal audience, the cinematic audience does not maintain a position as one of the audience members, or indeed, replace them; the cinematic audience shares a space with Rogers. Nor is the shifting cinematic audience's position in 'The Yam' merely an opportunity to offer a better view of Rogers as Feuer suggests, though this is perhaps one motive for it. She argues that camera shots that show the internal audience are not used alone. The reason for this is due to the alignment of film audience with the internal audience and our desire to see what they do. As such, shots that demonstrate the theatre audience's point of view of the performer, whilst eliminating the audience from the frame, become common. The result is that the 'in [the] second shot (or more properly in the effect of the cut to this shot) the spectator replaces the internal audience'.[116]

In 'The Yam', as evidenced at the end of shot 'q', the cinematic audience is shown Rogers through the heads of the internal audience, preventing a clear view of her feet as she dances. They are therefore not offered a clearer view of what the internal audience is able to see. Yet, as Feuer also claims:

> in a literal sense, these rapid shift of viewpoints do splinter our identification during a proscenium performance. Our view of the show is like that of a Cubist painting compared to the fixed positioning and fixed identification of the audience in the film.[117]

This splintering of identification is a more beneficial means of viewing the cinematic audience's positioning as it suggests how they can occupy a number of spaces at any given time: the space of the cinema, that of the performer as well as the internal audience.

By changing the cinematic audience's position from those found in theatres, filmmakers can combat some of the issues a constructed proscenium arch can create. Feuer details how the proscenium arch can restrict direct communication. Understanding this leads to attempts to 'overcome this barrier', for instance, 'by turning the stage into a nightclub, by dispensing with the stage altogether, by putting on shows in barns, and so forth'.[118]

The barrier to direct communication that Feuer is referring to is the inability of performers to communicate directly with audience members when there is the professional—consumer dichotomy at work. 'The Yam' demonstrates how Rogers is placed as the focus of both the internal and external audience's attention; she remains centrally framed despite the shifting camera positions. Furthermore, the mise-en-scène seeks to recreate a proscenium arch that problematises the audience/performer dynamic. This is not true of all the musical numbers, however. In *Carefree*'s 'Since They Turned "Loch Lomond" Into Swing' a different form of stage is created in which Astaire dances and sings whilst swinging his golf club, one that sees Rogers placed above Astaire looking down on his performance, again changing the viewing position. 'The Yam' uses the concept of the proscenium arch to create a space that allows the seamless movement from narrative into song, thereby concealing the shift in space. In order to combat the negative associations connected with the theatre that the proscenium arch brings with it, 'The Yam' relies upon the creation of the illusion of spontaneity and the immersion of the audience, in this case, emphatic engagement.

Metaphorical and Proxemic Space in 'Waltz in Swing Time'

Both 'Fancy Free' and 'The Yam' have demonstrated the ability of numbers to create space for specific purposes: as a means for the audience to inhabit the musical number or as a way of creating a unified space for audience and performer to occupy. These are not the only representations of, or reasons for, constructing space. Indeed, even the Art Deco set design, that was important for the creation of the haptic, has a part to play in the construction of a metaphorical space. This metaphorical space is better understood if one highlights its relationship with the haptic. Through the formation of a haptic space there also arises the creation of a more abstract realm; a space where meaning is created that is intangible, and though not necessarily contrapuntal to the narrative, exists in its own right. The abstract space has a connection with the haptic due to the latter's tendency to place emphasis on specific objects and thus draw attention to their design. In the case of the Astaire–Rogers' films, these objects are frequently Art Deco and an understanding of this aspect of space may aid in the analysis of the musical number 'Waltz in Swing Time' from *Swing Time*. Although Art Deco was a design movement that was named retrospectively, it consisted of a number of works and influenced numerous designers who shared some common ideologies. Though there are several of the latter, of particular interest here is the conception of the Woman. An understanding of this aspect of Art Deco provides an opportunity to comprehend the space created during 'Waltz in Swing Time', using Rogers as a means of negotiating the space.

Lucy Fischer's *Designing Women* describes how the Art Deco woman had cultural power.[119] She claims that 'a discourse on sexual difference (either literal or metaphoric) informs the entire Art Deco aesthetic'.[120] This sexual difference occurs on two levels, firstly sexual difference between Art Deco's conception of the Woman and that of its predecessor Art Nouveau; and secondly, male/female sexual difference. Fischer describes how Katharine McClinton believes that

> Deco can be divided into two broad stylistic schools that might be imagined along traditional gender lines. The 'feminine' curvilinear mode favours such

saccharine imagery [rose garlands, baskets of flowers, doves, nudes, deer]. On the other hand, in the 'masculine' geometric pole, 'Curves gave way to angularity and motifs of design tended to be...dynamic'.[121]

The two, however, should not be seen as mutually exclusive. Indeed, Appendix 3 demonstrates how in shots 'a' and 'g' a large white statue of a woman appears clearly in the background. It is a nude that is wearing a shroud with flowers at its base. Though it is the only statue visible in the number, its considerable size gives it significance and is, by McClinton's taxonomy, a subject of the feminine school of Art Deco. Victor Arwas felt that Art Deco sculptures fell into four categories: *hieratic, naturalistic, erotic* and *stylised*. The 'naturalistic' statuettes portrayed 'female athletes, nudes, dancers', and the white statue adorning the set of 'Waltz in Swing Time' fits this category.[122] This is of particular significance when placed within the context of the scene, namely a dancing number. Such a statue could add to the representation of Rogers due to her status as a dancer and her white costume that acts as a mirror to that of the statue. The general representation of women in the Art Deco movement, in part typified by the statue, is therefore important with regards to forming an understanding of Rogers' relationship with the abstract space of 'Waltz in Swing Time'.

Fischer describes how 'it was not only the statuettes that were modern [...] but the look of the women represented in them, [...] these works generally depict women who were "slender and boyish in shape, hair bobbed, dressed in fashionably floppy pyjamas or as...Amazons"'.[123] This is a contrast to the ubiquitous woman of Art Nouveau, endowed with a sense of primal nature. The Art Deco female is more synthetic, austere, high-tech and neutral.[124] This shift in representation is arguably a means of both conquering the fear of Woman, or rather the power they maintain through the ability to give birth, and a revolt against the New Woman who had access to contraception and was thus enabled more freedom; a freedom also experienced in the work place. The Art Deco female, particularly as established in the musical, is malleable and manageable, unlike in the 'Art Deco film melodrama [where] the heroine's association with modernity signals her status as risqué and dangerous'.[125] Fischer assesses this fear thus, 'as conceived by men (who are, after all, the authors of Art Deco), Woman has often been viewed on a cultural level, with a modicum of masculine fear. This is, certainly, another way of comprehending why her sexuality has to be romanticised or demonised'.[126]

The Silver Sandal, the club in which 'Waltz in Swing Time' takes place, is typical of the Art Deco style, and by existing within this space so comfortably, Rogers is associated with this Art Deco representation of the Woman. A point that Fischer makes with reference to the plots of the Astaire–Rogers' films:

> While the characters Rogers plays are spunky and plucky—sophisticated and independent working women with their feet on the ground—they are not threatening, a fact that seems signalled by the prim and ubiquitous bows at Rogers' collars in so many of her screen outfits.[127]

The Silver Sandal is what, Cohan has dubbed, a 'Big White Set'; 'the architectural set piece designed and photographed to take advantage of the rich contrasts of black and white film and to which the largest part of the budget for the physical production was devoted'.[128] Fischer sees The Silver Sandal as the peak of *Swing Time's* Art Deco influence and claims that

> the film's Art Deco promise [...] is not fully realised until Penny and Lucky arrive at The Silver Sandal Café where they are to perform, [...] the night club looks quite modern and beautiful, with its glossy white floors and luxuriously tufted walls. As Penny and Lucky dance, their dark shadows are projected on the floor and move abstractly alongside them.[129]

Another important aspect of the Art Deco mise-en-scène, which aids in the formation of an abstract space, is costume. Hyam illustrates the importance of Rogers' outfits in particular:

> [Astaire] is the constant, the perfect foil for the exquisitely variable Rogers, and it is to her that our eyes are drawn for the greatest part of the performances together [...] Rogers' dresses and hairstyles are different on each occasion and our image of each dance is individually shaped by the way she looks.[130]

If one leaves aside the question of the male gaze and the objectification of Rogers—which are both problematic issues in the musical—and looks solely at the inferences that can be drawn from her costumes, then a further understanding of the space can emerge. Rogers' costumes throughout the Astaire–Rogers' musicals, and typified by the one worn during 'Waltz in Swing Time', are classic examples of Art Deco and illustrate some of its inherent symbolism. Katharine McClinton has described how typical Art

Deco statues had dancing girls in tunics or bikinis and turbans balanced on one leg with outstretched arms. Others had long weighted dresses with bateau or 'V' necklines, full circular skirts longer in the back and trimmed with several rows of ruffles, bowknots or ostrich feathers.[131] The latter is a particularly apt description of Rogers' dress, which has thick ruffles running the entire rim of the skirt and sleeves as well as a bateau neckline. The similarities between Rogers' dress and the statues that McClinton describes, further reinforces Rogers' connection to the aforementioned white statue in 'Waltz in Swing Time'; whilst it is a nude, it still typifies the Art Deco style. The use of the bateau neckline demonstrates Mark Winokur's point that the Art Deco's female figure was a vision of Woman 'as apparently free but literally hobbled to prevent menace', for its wide neck still reveals Rogers' feminine shape, yet simultaneously keeps her covered.[132]

An important figure in Art Deco fashion design was Erté. Though the French designer was not responsible for Rogers' dress, his designs are important for they inform an understanding of Art Deco's style. Erté's female design creations focused upon androgyny and eschewed the mythological symbolism of Art Nouveau.[133] Furthermore, Erté's designs focused upon the outline of the female form rather than its specifics. This is a common trope in Art Deco and is clear in 'Waltz in Swing Time', which makes great use of shadows. Throughout Astaire and Rogers' dance a spotlight is focused upon them allowing them to stand out. A long shadow is cast of both Astaire and Rogers as they move across the dance floor making it appear as if four and not two are dancing. This silhouetting makes it difficult at times to distinguish between Astaire's and Rogers' shadow, thereby adding a sense of androgyny to the dancers' shadowed counterparts; an androgyny that is not present in the dancers themselves. Frequently the shadows merge giving the appearance of Astaire and Rogers dancing as one. This blending is seen between the dancers themselves, who appear to negotiate their personal space.

Personal space is an important aspect of dancing, and particularly duets. Proxemics is the title given to the study of measurable distances between people, and through forming an understanding of the reasons and meanings of these shifts in personal space one can better comprehend 'Waltz in Swing Time'. Edward T. Hall is an important theorist and he argues that there are two aspects: time and space.[134] 'Time talks' he claims,

> It speaks more plainly than words. The message it conveys comes loud and clear because it is manipulated less consciously, it is subject to less distortion

than the spoken language. It can shout the truth where words lie [...] the silent language of time and space.[135]

Hall aligns both space and time, and indeed their interaction with one another, as a language to be read and convey meaning with more clarity than speech. How, however, is this language to be understood? He details an example of a politician:

> A political figure makes a speech which is supposed to be reassuring. It has the opposite effect. When the words are read *they* are reassuring, yet the total message as delivered is not. Why? [...] sentences can be meaningless by themselves. Other signs may be much more eloquent. The significant components of a communication on the level of culture are characterised by their brevity as compared with other types of communication.[136]

The brevity of these signs makes them more difficult to recognise; Hall's description also implies that they are unconsciously read, suggesting that they are understood on an emotional level, rather than a cognitive one. We may not consciously know why the politician's speech is wrong, but we feel it.

A secondary difficulty with this overlooked language is that it is culture specific. One cultural group may read the analogous politician's speech as problematic, another as reassuring. 'Literally thousands of experiences', Hall argues, 'teach us unconsciously that space communicates. Yet this fact would probably never have been brought to the level of consciousness if it had not been realised that space is organised differently in each culture'.[137] This reading of space is an approach based upon anthropology rather than psychology and thus represents a shift away from the more established mode of analysis and into new, somewhat untested territory. Despite this language being culturally specific, there will inevitably be variations even at this level. Indeed, the communication that Hall is suggesting, namely, body language and the shift in the space between people interacting, is strongest at an individual level. He describes how 'as one leaves the cultural part of the spectrum and proceeds to the personality portion, the wave length increases. The analytic building blocks, instead of being sounds and the like, are whole interactions between people'.[138] This level of personality, though determined to a degree by cultural codes, allows for greater awareness of this understanding of space. Space, such as Hall is outlining, is a personal space that he dubs 'territory'.

Every living thing has a physical boundary that separates it from its external environment [...] a short distance up the phylogenetic [evolutionary development of a species] scale, however, another, non-physical boundary appears that exists outside the physical one. This new boundary is harder to delimit than the first but is just as real. We call this the "organism's territory". The act of laying claim to and defending territory is termed territoriality.[139]

Allowed changes in our territory can reveal much about relationships and communication between people. Hall claims that 'spatial changes give a tone to a communication, accent it, and at times even override the spoken word. The flow and shift of distance between people as they interact with each other is part and parcel of the communication process'.[140] Hall is reiterating the importance of space by emphasising its importance in comparison to the more widely recognised communication: speech.

Hall has established a set of notations to analyse the proxemics of a situation; each notation correlates to a particular dimension of proxemic behaviour, of which there are eight: Postural—sex identifiers, Sociofugal—sociopetal orientation, kinaesthetic factors, touch code, retinal combinations, thermal code, olfaction code, voice loudness scale.[141] Despite the usefulness of these distinctive elements (four of which are beneficial for analysing the space of 'Waltz in Swing Time': Postural–sex identifiers, Sociofugal–sociopetal orientation, kinaesthetic factors, and touch code), Hall does not give reasons for the changes of space identified through the use of such dimensions due to his understandable unwillingness to make generalisations without a cultural context to work from. Postural–sex identifiers are the means of establishing the gender and basic posture of the individuals interacting. Hall's postural categories are, however, restricted to vertical movement: prone, squatting and standing. Astaire and Rogers undergo several changes in postural category throughout their dance; in shot 'g' for instance Astaire executes a series of leaps assisted by Rogers, thereby changing their positions along the vertical axis. Sociofugal–sociopetal orientation is used to describe the 'arrangements that push people apart and pull them in'.[142] Though this suggests a more horizontal movement, they are still constrained by a fixed central point.[143] The two most common orientations found between Rogers and Astaire in 'Waltz in Swing Time' are '0' and '4'; facing one another and side by side, respectively. Hall describes how '0' is used in direct communication in order to convey maximum intensity.[144] Position '4' conveys an informal air used in a transitory manner. The frequent use of positions '0' and '4' throughout the dance could demonstrate the couple's strong relationship. They are intimately acquainted and their body positions illustrate the passionate feelings towards one another. The kinaesthetic factors are based upon Hediger's assertion that they are the basic forms of relating in space.[145] The kinaesthetic factors are assessed through the inherent potential in a situation for bodily contact; it is based on what people can do with their arms, legs and bodies.[146] This relates closely to the fourth relevant category: touching. Touching, as a dimension of proxemic space, will vary greatly between cultures. Astaire and Rogers appear to enact almost all variations of Hall's touch code within their dance—nothing in their dance is accidental—a consequence of this is that though helpful with note taking, Hall's shorthand offers little in the way of insight. Astaire and Rogers may hold hands for prolonged periods of time, even dance separately, but to what purpose? Hall's system can allow us to understand the changes in space, but not the motives behind them; a point he himself is keen to make through his repetition of the need to employ them in culturally specific contexts.

The spatial changes should be read culture specifically. 'Waltz in Swing Time' could therefore be read through American culture's sense of space due to its status as a Hollywood film; though this would not mean that all audience members would interpret the images as such. Americans, Hall believes, have a culture that discourages touching except in moments of intimacy.[147] This tendency is part of 'an underlying hidden level of culture that is highly patterned—a set of unspoken, implicit rules of behaviour and thought that controls everything we do, "hidden cultural grammar"'.[148] Subsequently, most Americans will subconsciously interpret a reduction in personal space as a sign of growing intimacy. These reactions to the changes in space are paradigms of Primary Level Culture (PLC) for they occur subconsciously.[149] 'Waltz in Swing Time' begins with Astaire, shot 'a', grasping Rogers' hand and directing her towards Romero (Georges Metaxa), the conductor. The ease with which Rogers' hand is taken, and her lack of reaction to the breach in her personal space suggests an easy familiarity between the two. When talking with Metaxa there is a clear divide between the three; Rogers and Astaire stand closely together left of centre frame, and Metaxa remains further away on the right of the frame. The gestures made by both Rogers and Astaire appears to encroach on the others' personal space. At the beginning of the dance, shot 'f', Astaire helps Rogers remove her cloak, and so starts the beginning of the pair's physical contact. Throughout the dance Rogers and Astaire move steadily closer. Although they are frequently poised together dancing in the ballroom style as Astaire leads Rogers around the dance floor, there is frequently space between them. Their arms are touching, but the spotlight emphasises the distance between them. They also frequently split from one another, dancing separately for brief interludes, before re-joining one another. As the dance continues, Rogers and Astaire begin to spin more frequently; Rogers spins from one of Astaire's arms to the other and back again. This illustrates a growing sense of the two characters sharing the same space, much as their shadows are doing. As the dance progresses the couple do not move more than a few feet away from each other at any one time. The moments when Astaire and Rogers dance together, though not increasing in regularity, do show a developing closeness between the pair. Whereas at the beginning of the dance when they would dance together there was once space between them, towards the end they are dancing as if one. The boundaries of personal space and territory have been eroded.

The other aspect important to Hall's work on understanding the hidden cultural grammar is time, which he claims 'is not just as immutable constant [...] but a cluster of concepts, events, and rhythms covering an extremely wide range of phenomena'.[150] One of these phenomena is personal time that differs from biological time due to the former being dependant on the individual. Hall explains it so:

> Is there anyone who has not had the experience of time 'crawling' or 'flying'. Although biological time is relatively fixed and regular and personal time more subjective, there do seem to be environmental and psychological factors which help explain these great shifts in the way in which time is experienced.[151]

Thus, everybody has an individual sense of personal time and their behaviour is a direct result of their inbuilt personal rhythm. He argues that individuals 'are dominated in their behaviour by complex hierarchies of interlocking rhythms. Furthermore, these same interlocking rhythms are comparable to fundamental themes in a symphonic score [...], rhythm is the very essence of time, since equal intervals of time define a sequence of events as rhythmic'.[152] Such interlocking rhythms originate from a synthesis of the rhythms of others, of business, media and many other aspects of culture.

An understanding of personal time and rhythm is important for comprehending how people occupy the same space, because time is treated as a language [another means of communication], as primary organisers for all activities, a synthesiser and integrator...a feedback mechanism for how things are going, a measuring rod...as well as a special message system revealing how people really feel about each other and whether or not they can get along.[153]

In order to establish whether people can positively occupy the same space, William Condon has claimed that 'when people are talking the two central nervous systems drive each other [...] in most cases they don't even know it' [sic].[154] Hall goes further and argues that for everyone 'there is [one] kind of person: the one who is always in sync, who is such a joy, who seems to sense what move you will make next. Anything you do with him or her is like a dance'.[155] Hall likens two people's synchronised rhythms to love and states that 'as one might suspect, there is a relationship between rhythm and love: they are closely linked. People in general don't sync well with those they don't like and they do with those they love. Both love and rhythms have so many dimensions' [sic].[156] The synchronising of two people's rhythms Condon has titled 'entrainment', which is the process that occurs when two or more people become engaged in each other's rhythms.[157] 'Waltz in Swing Time' is a clear example of Condon's conception of entrainment. Rogers and Astaire are able to dance in sync with one another through a range of different dance steps. This is demonstrated in several ways. One of which is through a decrescendo in the music that places emphasis upon the sounds of the pair tapping in perfect rhythm with one another, and another is through a complex series of turns that the pair execute that requires them to alternate steps that demonstrates how the pair are able to share the same rhythm, occupy the same space, and dance as if they are a single dancer.

Astaire and Rogers' ability to synchronise to the music imbues Irving Berlin's 'Waltz in Swing Time' music with an unspoiled and flawless quality that gives the appearance that the music is symbolic of Astaire and Rogers' characters' internal world; they are driving the music. An idea that Hall would certainly consider possible, for, as he states,

> no matter where one looks on the face of the earth, wherever there are people, they can be observed syncing when music is played. There is a popular misconception about music: because there is a beat to music, the generally accepted belief is that the rhythm originates in the music, not that music is a highly specialised releaser of rhythms already in the individual. Music can

also be viewed as a rather remarkable extension of the rhythms generated in human beings.[158]

'Waltz in Swing Time' could thus be seen to represent the internal rhythms of Astaire and Rogers' characters and the subsequent entrainment that occurs when the two dance. Hyam has described how the music is 'the perfect complement to a dance that is both brilliantly virtuosic and raptly intimate'; intimate because it perfectly reflects the rhythms of the two characters.[159] The audience has displayed before them a space that is driven by Astaire and Rogers' internal rhythms that are in tune with one another to such a degree that it creates a mutual, singular space.

Hyam has described 'Waltz in Swing Time' as a 'magnificent creation that is pure dance, the most virtuosic and choreographically complex of all the Astaire—Rogers' duets'.[160] This choreographically complex dance Lucy Fischer believes 'functioned as a substitute for lovemaking'.[161] Such rhetoric is demonstrating dance's ability to communicate; a fact reiterated by Feuer who describes it as a 'danced dialogue' that leads us to 'forget that we are observing a carefully planned, executed and filmed performance'.[162] The repeated references to the expression of emotions through dance in the Astaire–Rogers' musicals further suggest that there exists a level of symbolic space within the musical numbers. Hyam, when looking at the entire group, discusses how the twenty-two dance duets all exhibit, as a group, the five defining elements of the Fred and Ginger series. First three of these elements—complementarity, or the rapport and emotional richness of the relationship between Astaire and Rogers; humour; and romance—are not specific to dance; they are central both to the non-musical scenes and to the songs that Astaire and Rogers perform together. The fourth element, drama in dance, is closely related to romance, for romance is at the heart of all the dance duets in which a drama is played out, whatever the mood or the circumstances. The fifth and final defining element is intimately related to the first; the manifestation in dance of the emotional richness of their relationship.[163]

Who, however, was in control over this symbolic space? Ethan Mordden asks:

> Who exactly choreographed these films? [...] A dance director laid out the ensemble numbers, but Astaire did his own choreography, improvising with pianist Hal Borne and Hermes Pan [...] for the duets Pan learned Rogers' part then taught it to her. Astaire was a perfectionist and a three minute rou-

tine took weeks of creation and rehearsal before it was ready to shoot and then it was [done in a] whole take until they had a clean one.[164]

Such statements would undoubtedly support the idea that Astaire was the person who was responsible for the construction of the space of the musical numbers; however, does this rely too heavily upon extra-filmic knowledge? Must the audience be aware of who had choreographed the dance to appreciate Astaire and Rogers' role in its construction?

Steven Cohan has described how the musical is a star-driven genre above all else. The affiliation of stars with certain studios helped to establish a company brand name for product differentiation. Whenever musical performers '"do a number" they usually shift their identities from being actors in a drama to entertainers addressing the audience directly'.[165] This shift in identity is a vital factor in the construction of space for it leads to a degree of self-reflexivity. Edward Gallafent has noted how the names Astaire and Rogers' characters are given 'seem to mimic the syllabification of Fred and Ginger', for instance Bake and Sherry in *Follow the Fleet* (1936) and Huck and Lizzie in *Roberta* (1935).[166] He goes on to state that 'the rhyming is more than just a kind of fun, or play. It acknowledges the connection of the screen roles with one another, giving the hint that the parts played by the pair are variations of a concealed root—Fred and Ginger'.[167] Through these references to other films the audience is reminded of what connects them all: Astaire and Rogers. The style in which the musical numbers are shot also works as a reminder of the performers dancing. Hyam describes how 'in the Astaire—Rogers' duets the dancers themselves, and the relationship between them, are the whole point of the dance and the unobtrusive camera work allows the two dancers to take centre stage throughout'.[168] As Astaire became increasingly responsible for the choreography of the numbers he had a considerable influence over the cinematography and his guiding principle, as John Mueller observes, was 'to let the dance speak for itself and to keep the camera work observant but not unobtrusive'.[169] Astaire himself has stated that

> You can concentrate your action on the dance; the audience can follow the intricate steps that were all but lost behind the footlights, and each person in the audience sees the dance from the same perspective. In consequence, I think that the audience can get a bigger reaction watching a dance on screen than behind a fixed proscenium arch—probably because they get a larger, clearer and better focused view and so desire a larger emotional response.[170]

The musical numbers are characterised by long takes, slow-paced editing, long shots and a relatively static camera that enabled the intricate dance steps to be seen in their entirety.[171] Rogers illustrates the complexity of the dances in the following statement:

> Just try and keep up with those feet of his sometime! Try and look graceful while thinking where your right hand should be, and how your head should be held, and which foot you end the next eight bars on [...] and not to mention those Astaire rhythms. Did you ever count the different tempos he can think up in three minutes?[172]

The intricacy of these dances and the manner in which they are shot—to highlight their difficulty—have been emphasised so as to draw attention to the self-reflexivity that this can cause. Adrienne McLean, in her book *Being Rita Hayworth*, has made a convincing argument that during the dance the performers have an element of control over the space in which they are dancing. In her description of Hayworth she states:

> She is a dancing, whirling, twirling, active and alive force...running down from above in a dancing attack, smiling, laughing with young men dancing to meet her. Hayworth, in other words, is no stationary cover girl. She is a living, breathing talent. She is also free and unleashed, in control of her dance, the centre of the universe.[173]

Through dance, Hayworth (and Rogers) have the ability to take momentary control over their representation and the space they inhabit. In doing so they offer the promotion of a new reading that has the potential to negate that of the Art Deco Woman, as well as arguably a narrative reading of these films. McLean states how 'the Rita Hayworth [she recognises] in films is so often a dancing, sweating, and moving body, whose training as a dancer was obviously extensive'.[174] Whilst watching these numbers McLean has evidentially temporarily removed herself from the narrative and is appreciating Hayworth for her abilities as a dancer, which as she asserts, film cannot completely recreate; 'dance cannot be a fictional treatment of itself in performance. To dance, one has to be able to do it, not merely to suggest it'.[175] 'Waltz in Swing Time' is perhaps the most virtuoso Astaire and Rogers' performance in their entire RKO output and as such it is possible that a self-reflexive space is created that reminds the audience that who they are watching is Fred and Ginger.

'Waltz in Swing Time' demonstrates how several different realms of space can be present within any one number. The space created can be symbolic and carry meaning that encourages particular readings of the performers, or it can be culturally specific. The space of 'Waltz in Swing Time' needs no knowledge of the narrative to be analysed affectively. The spatial relationship between the pair as they move across the dance floor demonstrates a passion and familiarity; their willingness to allow a close proximity and the ease with which they accommodate it, is as keen an illustration of the abstract emotions conveyed by the dance than if it were to be told by the narrative.

The musical numbers discussed in this chapter are, however, ultimately audio-visual with a reliance on the audience to be able to connect the singing and dancing of Astaire and Rogers to the sound track. Though there are many different forms of visual space represented in these musical sequences, it is important to understand how sound and image work together in an audio-visual relationship; this will be the focus of the subsequent chapter.

Notes

1. Hall, "A System for the Notation of Proxemic Behaviour", p. 1008.
2. "Cinemetrics", <http://www.cinemetrics.lv/cinemetrics.php> [date accessed 18/12/2012].
3. "The Image", *Oxford English Dictionary* <http://www.oed.com/view/Entry/91618?rskey=4fYlie&result=1&isAdvanced=false#eid>[accessed 07/02/2013]. Other definitions are given ranging from the image within a computing context to an electrical one.
4. H. A. Sedgewick, "Visual Space Perception" in E. Bruce Goldstein, (ed.), *Blackwell Handbook of Sensation and Perception* (Oxford: Blackwell Publishing, 2005), p. 135.
5. This book only looks at 2D films. Analysing the 3D representation of space will be achieved through subsequent research.
6. Traditional feminist readings position the camera as inherently male. See, Laura Mulvey, "Visual Pleasure and Narrative Cinema", *Screen*, 16.3, Autumn, (1975), pp. 6–18.
7. Sedgewick, p. 140.
8. Sedgewick, p. 140.
9. Sedgewick, p. 144.

10. This raises the issue of embodied spectatorship, which will be dealt with subsequently. If there is no discernible difference felt by the audience, as suggested by Sedgewick, then film scholars should begin to take more seriously the physical and sensual reactions felt by the audience.
11. Sedgewick, p. 144.
12. Sedgewick, pp. 144–145. The double viewing position is also discussed in Chapter 3: Sound Space.
13. Sedgewick, pp. 144–145.
14. Maggie Shiffrar, "Movement and Event Perception" in E. Bruce Goldstein, (ed.), *Blackwell Handbook of Sensation and Perception* (Oxford: Blackwell Publishing, 2005), p. 238.
15. James J. Gibson, quoted in, E. Bruce Goldstein, "Pictorial Perception and Art", in E. Bruce Goldstein, ed., *Blackwell Handbook of Sensation and Perception* (Oxford: Blackwell Publishing, 2005), p. 344.
16. George Mather, *Essentials of Sensation and Perception* (London: Routledge, 2011), p. 82.
17. In Steven Spielberg's film *Jaws* (1975), an example of the latter can be seen when Brody is sitting on the beach.
18. Sedgewick, p. 144.
19. Sedgewick, p. 144.
20. Mather, pp. 129–130.
21. Mather, p. 134.
22. Mather, p. 134.
23. Mather, p. 134.
24. Mather, p. 134.
25. Mather, p. 137.
26. Mather, p. 137.
27. Mather, p. 137.
28. Mather, p. 137.
29. Mather, p. 139.
30. Mather, p. 140.
31. See Vivian Sobchack, *Carnal Thoughts: Embodiment and Moving Image Culture* (London: University of California Press, 2004).
32. Hatwell, p. 2; Bruno, *Atlas of Emotion: Journeys in Art, Architecture and Film*; Barker, "Touch and the Cinematic Experience".
33. Sobchack, *Carnal Thoughts: Embodiment and Moving Image Culture*, pp. 56–57.

34. Sobchack, *Carnal Thoughts: Embodiment and Moving Image Culture*, pp. 56–57.
35. Sobchack, *Carnal Thoughts: Embodiment and Moving Image Culture*, p. 57.
36. Sobchack, *Carnal Thoughts: Embodiment and Moving Image Culture*, p. 58.
37. Sobchack, *Carnal Thoughts: Embodiment and Moving Image Culture*, pp. 59–60.
38. Sobchack, *Carnal Thoughts: Embodiment and Moving Image Culture*, pp. 59–60.
39. Sobchack, *Carnal Thoughts: Embodiment and Moving Image Culture*, p. 58.
40. Sobchack, *Carnal Thoughts: Embodiment and Moving Image Culture*, p. 65.
41. Hannah Hyam, *Fred and Ginger: The Astaire—Rogers Partnership 1934–1938* (Great Britain: Pen Press Publishers, 2007), p. 107.
42. Hyam, p. 101.
43. Bergfelder, p. 11.
44. Cohan, *Hollywood Musicals: The Film Reader*, p. 8.
45. Cohan, *Hollywood Musicals: The Film Reader*, p. 8.
46. Bergfelder, p. 11.
47. Bergfelder, p. 15.
48. Tashiro, p. 18.
49. Wollen, p. 201.
50. Bergfelder, p. 22.
51. Edward Gallafent, *Astaire and Rogers* (New York: Columbia University Press, 2002), p. 6.
52. Tashiro, p. 18.
53. Tashiro, pp. 19–20.
54. Tashiro, p. 20.
55. Tashiro, p. 20.
56. Tashiro, pp. 20–21.
57. Tashiro, p. 21.
58. Charles Affron, *Sets in Motion* (New Brunswick: Rutgers University Press, 1995).
59. Bergfelder, p. 263.
60. Lucy Fischer, *Designing Women: Cinema, Art Deco and The Female Form* (New York: Columbia University Press, 2003), p. 11.
61. Fischer, p. 12.

62. Bergfelder, p. 254.
63. Fischer, p. 12.
64. Bergfelder, p. 256.
65. Bergfelder, p. 256.
66. Hyam, p. 107.
67. Rubin, p. 59.
68. Bergfelder, p. 20.
69. Bergfelder, p. 21.
70. Tashiro, p. 41.
71. Tashiro, p. 39.
72. Tashiro, p. 40.
73. Bergfelder, p. 28.
74. Pauline Reay, *Music in Film* (London: Wallflower, 2004), p. 33.
75. Altman, *The American Film Musical*, p. 19.
76. Altman, *The American Film Musical*, p. 44.
77. Altman, *The American Film Musical*, p. 32.
78. Michael Wood, *America In The Movies* (New York: Columbia University Press, 1989), p. 147.
79. Altman, *The American Film Musical*, p. 131.
80. Altman, *The American Film Musical*, p. 132.
81. Altman, *The American Film Musical*, p. 131.
82. Feuer, p. 26.
83. Feuer, p. 26.
84. Feuer, p. 23.
85. Cohan, *Hollywood Musicals: The Film Reader*, p. 13.
86. Hall and Whannel, p. 60.
87. Stanley Cavell, "Audience, Actor, and Star", in Leo Braudy, Marshall Cohen, (eds), *Film Theory and Criticism*, 6th edition (Oxford: Oxford University Press, 2004), p. 345.
88. Cavell, p. 345.
89. Cavell, p. 345.
90. Altman, *The American Film Musical*, p. 200.
91. Feuer, p. 15.
92. Laura Mulvey, *Fetishism and Curiosity* (London: BFI, 1996), p. xi.
93. Mulvey, *Fetishism and Curiosity*, p. 6.
94. Mulvey, *Fetishism and Curiosity*, p. xiv.
95. Mulvey, *Fetishism and Curiosity*, p. 41.

96. Bela Balász, "The Close up", in Leo Braudy, Marshall Cohen, (eds), *Film Theory and Criticism*, 6th edition (Oxford: Oxford University Press, 2004), p. 315.
97. Mulvey, *Fetishism and Curiosity*, p. 41.
98. Mulvey, *Fetishism and Curiosity*, p. 41.
99. Feuer, p. 24.
100. Cavell, p. 345.
101. Edgar Morin, *The Stars* (Minneapolis: University of Minnesota, 2005).
102. Erwin Panofsky, "Style and Medium in the Motion Pictures", in Leo Braudy, Marshall Cohen, (eds), *Film Theory and Criticism*, 6th edition (Oxford: Oxford University Press, 2004), p. 299.
103. Leo Braudy, "Acting: Stage Vs. Screen", in Leo Braudy, Marshall Cohen, (eds), *Film Theory and Criticism*, 6th edition (Oxford: Oxford University Press, 2004), p. 433.
104. Braudy, "Acting: Stage Vs. Screen", p. 434.
105. Feuer, p. 24.
106. Hall and Whannel, p. 32.
107. Braudy, "Acting: Stage Vs. Screen", p. 434.
108. Feuer, p. 13.
109. Brad Shore, *Culture in Mind: Cognition, Culture and the Problem of Meaning* (Oxford: Oxford University Press, 1998), p. 109.
110. Shore, p. 109.
111. Shore, p. 109.
112. Shore, p. 109.
113. Shore, pp. 109–110.
114. Feuer, p. 17.
115. Feuer, p. 17.
116. Feuer, p. 28.
117. Feuer, p. 29.
118. Feuer, p. 23.
119. Fischer, p. 27.
120. Fischer, p. 27.
121. Fischer, p. 27.
122. Fischer, pp. 30–31.
123. Fischer, p. 31.
124. Fischer, p. 29.
125. Fischer, p. 127.
126. Fischer, p. 32.

127. Fischer, p. 127.
128. Cohan, *Hollywood Musicals: The Film Reader*, p. 9.
129. Fischer, p. 126.
130. Hyam, p. 194.
131. Katharine Morrison McClinton, *Art Deco: A Guide for Collectors* (New York: Clarkson N. Potter, 1986), p. 193.
132. Mark Winokur, *American Laughter: immigrants, Ethnicity, and the 1930s Hollywood Film Comedy* (New York: St Martin's, 1996), p. 196.
133. Fischer, p. 36.
134. Hediger; Much of the work on spatial relationships focuses on animal behaviour. A key theorist is Heini Hediger, whose work has been used as a basis for forming an understanding of the meaning of possible interactions in particular contexts. The context in which his findings are based is always highlighted and informs Hall's understanding of culturally specific proxemics.
135. Hall, *The Silent Language*, p. 15.
136. Hall, *The Silent Language*, p. 94.
137. Hall, *The Silent Language*, pp. 148–149.
138. Hall, *The Silent Language*, p. 95.
139. Hall, *The Silent Language*, p. 146.
140. Hall, *The Silent Language*, p. 160.
141. Hall, "A System for the Notation of Proxemic Behaviour", pp. 1003–1026.
142. Hall, "A System for the Notation of Proxemic Behaviour", p. 1008.
143. See Hall, "A System for the Notation of Proxemic Behaviour" for examples of his notations.
144. Hall, "A System for the Notation of Proxemic Behaviour", p. 1009.
145. Hall, "A System for the Notation of Proxemic Behaviour", p. 1009.
146. Hall, "A System for the Notation of Proxemic Behaviour", p. 1009.
147. Hall, *The Silent Language*, p. 149.
148. Hall, *The Silent Language*, p. 6.
149. Hall, *The Silent Language*, p. 6.
150. Hall, *The Silent Language*, p. 13.
151. Hall, *The Silent Language*, pp. 19–20.

152. Edward Hall, *The Dance of Life* (New York: Doubleday, 1989), p. 153.
153. Hall, *The Dance of Life*, p. 3.
154. William S. Condon, "Neonatal Entrainment and Enculturation", in M. Bullowa, (ed.), *Before Speech: The Beginning of Interpersonal Communication* (New York: Cambridge University Press, 1979).
155. Hall, *The Dance of Life*, p. 163.
156. Hall, *The Dance of Life*, p. 165.
157. Hall, *The Dance of Life*, p. 177.
158. Hall, *The Dance of Life*, p. 178.
159. Hyam, p. 98.
160. Hyam, p. 216.
161. Fischer, p. 127.
162. Feuer, p. 11.
163. Hyam, p. 134.
164. Ethan Mordden, *The Hollywood Musical* (New York: St Martin's Press, 1981), p. 115.
165. Cohan, *Hollywood Musicals: The Film Reader*, p. 12.
166. Gallafent, p.11.
167. Gallafent, p.11.
168. Hyam, p. 138.
169. Hyam, p. 137.
170. Bruce Babington, Peter William Evans, *Blue Skies and Silver Linings: Aspects of the Hollywood Musical* (Manchester: Manchester University Press, 1985), pp. 93–94.
171. Babington, p. 94.
172. Hyam, p. 142.
173. McLean, p. 120.
174. McLean, p. 123.
175. McLean, p. 127.

CHAPTER 5

Audio-Visual Space

Introduction

The previous two chapters have dealt with the issues of audio space and visual space, respectively. In them I argue that the construction and representation of space in musical numbers can be analysed independently of the constraints of narrative and with a focus on aesthetics. Whilst these aesthetic elements are read in an abstract manner (free from narrative and representational concern), not as a means of understanding a theoretical framework through the lens of representation (such as in a Marxist or a Feminist reading of a narrative), there is a focus on space. Furthermore, they seek to understand how the audience comprehends the different spaces with the aim of furthering an analysis of both spatial representation and perception. I argue in Chapter 3 that sound, and thus its space, can be felt in a multi-sensory manner enabling the audience to enter and negotiate it. In Chapter 4, conversely, I argue that, like sound, visual space can be felt in a multi-sensory manner, but additionally that the traditional notion of the visual space, restricted to the frame of the screen, should be questioned. The overarching theory of this book is that film should be understood as a gestalt, in which the whole is more than the sum of its parts. Consequently, this chapter will explore how both sound space and visual space work together in a symbiotic relationship, each enhancing and subtly changing the overall spatiality of the musical numbers. As such it is important to address how the construction and representation of space changes and is negotiated in new ways when the two realms are considered simultaneously: when the negotiable audio-visual relationship of musical numbers is acknowledged and gestalt theory's primary tenet (the whole being other than the sum of its parts) is investigated fully.

This chapter thus explores how spatial relationships within song sequences are created and represented in musical numbers in audio-visual contexts. It acknowledges that the musical genre, and musical numbers more specifically, are in many respects defined by their interaction between sound and image; therefore considering the relationship will give a more comprehensive understanding than an analysis of the individual elements. It is also worth re-noting that this book promotes a form of examination that supports forensic analysis and in so doing recognises that previous forms of film theory, that privilege one element of film language over another, are ultimately deficient as they do not address the transformative relationship.

My approach for best dealing with how audio-visual space is created, represented and perceived in musical numbers is fivefold. Firstly, the issue of the movement into and out of musical numbers will be addressed. The delineation of musical numbers or song sequences is a multifaceted theoretical concern. Delineation is only possible when one recognises what the musical number is being demarcated from, be it narrative, non-musical moments, the change in relationship with the audience, or some other aspect.

Secondly, I will consider how the operetta can both complicate and aid in theorising on the musical genre more widely, both in general terms and, more specifically, with regards to understanding the interaction of audio-visual elements in the comprehension and theorising of spatial relations. Study of the operetta, and indeed opera theory more widely, is often excluded from wider studies of the musical. Ruminating on the reasons for this general omission is not without difficulty; theoretical discussions on the musical are marked more by an absence of opera theory rather than the issues having been addressed and disregarded as a line of relevant theorising. One could posit that it is due to either a belief in their essential differences and therefore theorising will have little in common, or a lack of desire to share territory with a 'separate' discipline. The issue is not one of the foci of this book, however, and thus whilst there is an acknowledgement of the lack of theoretical boundary crossing, I will not adhere to such a demarcation. Theories on opera and the operetta can prove useful tools in an analysis of musicals and film more widely; there is a long tradition of theorising on the relationship between music, dialogue, images and mise-en-scène, nowhere more evidently than in Richard Wagner's own work on the *Gesamtkunstwerk*, and these will be utilised in this chapter.[1] Furthermore, they offer a useful addition to the theories concerning the movement into and out of musical numbers.

Thirdly, I will directly address the issue of gestalt theory, specifically how it aids and affects the understanding of audio-visual space within song sequences. The chapter will develop the theories and issues discussed in preceding chapters and place it within the context of the wider relationship between sound and image.

Fourthly, I will discuss the wider issues of perception that are both connected to and built upon those understood in gestalt theory. Issues surrounding neurology and perceptual comprehension of sound and image in conjunction with one another will be examined with a focus on the creation and representation of space: how the interaction between the two elements are perceived and help in the formation of an understanding of the musical numbers.

Finally, I will look at a series of musical numbers to demonstrate examples of the utilisation of the theories previously discussed. It will also continue to demonstrate and promote another of the primary foci of this book; namely, forensic analysis and virtual reconstruction. The examples for this chapter include a number from *Umbrellas of Cherbourg* (1964) and *Billy the Kid and the Green Baize Vampire* (1987).[2] There are several reasons for these filmic examples. Firstly, they are exemplars of a range of different musicals, thus continuing and extending my aim to look at the broad spectrum of the genre rather than restrict analysis to a smaller group. The purpose of such an intention is to establish a mode of reading the musical genre, and musical numbers specifically, as a whole. By not limiting the range of films, one can begin to understand to what extent the creation and representation of space in musical numbers varies across the spectrum.[3]

The first example, *Umbrellas of Cherbourg*, is an operetta, completely through-sung with an almost constant musical score composed by Michel Legrand. Issues of delineating musical numbers from that which surrounds them will be important to a discussion of its space, so too will be the relationship between music and image particularly in terms of understanding the construction of space as a unified entity. *Umbrellas of Cherbourg* demonstrates how theories surrounding opera can be of use to an understanding of the musical genre.[4] *Billy the Kid*, conversely, continues the trend of a musical made by a director, in this case the social realist Alan Clarke, who neither focused on, nor made another film within, the genre; *Dancer in the Dark* is another such example. Such films often demonstrate a playing with the musical's conventions that, whilst not absent from the genre as a whole, frequently display a different relationship with its history and traditions.

Secondly, the filmic examples chosen in this chapter not only are demonstrative of the range of the musical genre in terms of form, but also of the genre's international variations. The breadth of the examples, both within this book more widely and within this specific chapter, will prevent the readings from being restricted solely to Hollywood productions; thus enabling the promotion of a methodology for the genre rather than specific national variations. Additionally, as the focus is on abstract aesthetic representation of space, it is important to illustrate that language is not an insurmountable barrier to spatiotemporal perception. Undoubtedly there will be many viewers of the films, such as *Umbrellas of Cherbourg*, who are familiar and fluent in the relevant (in this case French) languages but this will not be the case across the board. Although it is essential to acknowledge that no demographic, or audience, is homogenous, it is also essential to re-note that I am using an abstract audience. This abstract audience recognises potential cultural/social/political/economic variations that may have an impact on perceptions of space, but takes as its primary exemplar the author of this book: me. My primary aim is to promote a mode of analysis that focuses on forensic analysis of musical numbers with a view to understanding abstract aesthetics; an abstract audience enables a paradigm to be created that aids this objective.

As this chapter's primary focus is on understanding *audio-visual* space, it is important to provide examples of musical numbers that could also be included in previous chapter's analysis. This is true of the films chosen throughout this book. Though each chapter may emphasise a variety of different aspects of space, each looking through a different 'lens' or 'mic' and thus drawing a range of findings, they would all experience different conclusions if analysed through the more comprehensive and the ultimate gestaltist reading of audio-visual analysis. Thus, both *Umbrellas of Cherbourg* and *Billy the Kid* are exemplars of their different positions on the spectrum lending breadth to the analysis. Whilst *Umbrellas of Cherbourg* may lend itself to an analysis of, for instance, Wagner's *Gesamtkunstwerk* due to its being closer in nature to Wagner's ideas on the medium, so too does *Billy the Kid*. What can be applied to one example of the musical genre can be applied to all; the issue is in discerning to what degree.

Previous chapters have dealt with the issues associated with delineating musical numbers at a rudimentary level. To achieve an understanding of audio-visual space it is important to take the issues to a more in-depth level and analyse its implications for, and construction by, the negotiated audio-visual space. It is to this end that the chapter now turns: to the movement into (and indeed out of) musical numbers.

Movement into Musical Numbers

Defining what is and is not a musical number is rife with difficulty. Indeed, analysing the temporal structure of the musical genre more widely is not without issue. Rick Altman has argued that the musical genre has a structure that is based upon a dual-focus narrative.[5] He states that such a structure 'requires the viewer to be sensitive not so much to chronology and progression [...] but to simultaneity and comparison'.[6] Such a structure that Altman is describing is one that is narrative centric in its construction. Though he states that 'the traditional approach to narrative assumes that structure grows out of *plot*, the dual-focus structure of the American film musical derives from *character*', Altman is still privileging narrative's place in structural construction due to character development.[7] As has been previously detailed, this book eschews narrative in favour of abstract aesthetics. This notwithstanding, Altman's arguments are of use when placed within the wider context of the musical genre: that of subverting traditional temporal structures. The example of *New Moon* (1940) Altman utilises, demonstrates that the film is not 'a continuous chain of well-motivated events but a series of nearly independent fragments [...]'.[8] These 'independent fragments' are the musical numbers, the sites where filmic structure and meaning are established.[9] The musical numbers are thus the focus of the genre, rather than the narrative. This variance in temporal structure from other Hollywood films, for Altman's focus is the American film musical rather than the genre more widely, though highlighting the peculiarities of the genre, does little to aid in the delineation of musical number from that which surrounds it.

How does one begin defining the parameters of the musical number? Perhaps a good starting point, if only to show how problematic the idea is, is to use Altman's notion of the 'audio-dissolve'. In his book *The American Film Musical*, Altman cites the moment in *Top Hat* when Fred

Astaire's movements cease being driven by the character's motivations and become driven by the music. Here Altman focuses on a useful but highly problematic moment. Before Astaire begins to move and 'sing' in time to the music, he has arguably already begun the musical number; he has set it up, the signs have already been produced for the spectator that a musical number will occur. These signs are not limited to a single filmic text, but rather are formed from prior knowledge of musicals and stars.

Momentarily leaving this to one side and returning to that singular moment of the audio-dissolve can provide an insight into the believed focal point of a musical number and how it differs from that which surrounds the number. Of particular importance is the attention that Altman gives to the music of the scene. Is one, therefore, to interpret a shift in primary signification from the visual to the aural or sonic as a defining characteristic of the musical number, as its moment of beginning? How would this work in an operetta where music has held a more prominent role throughout? Furthermore, the ocularcentrism implied for the shift in 'primary signification' to take place sits ill with gestalt theory's understanding of the importance of the unifying audio-visual relationship over the individual elements of sound and image. Put succinctly, for a shift to sonic primacy to take place, there is an assumption that until this point image has been the primary mode of signification.

Additionally, Altman's audio-dissolve makes no apparent distinction regarding the nature of the newly privileged music. Does it matter if the audio is diegetic or non-diegetic? Indeed, how does one distinguish the two without the use of a visual signifier as to the music's source, an issue important to both Chion's notion of the acousmêtre and Kerin's 'superfield'? Does this even matter? Ben Winters in his piece 'The Non-Diegetic Fallacy' has argued that labelling music as 'non-diegetic' threatens to separate it from the narrative and thus denies it an active role in shaping the course of on-screen events.[10] This focus on narrative as primary mode of signification is an issue. Though Winters is not discussing the musical genre specifically, it remains conspicuous by its almost complete absence. He briefly states that with musicals, audiences have little difficulty believing that music occupies the same narrative space as the characters, but it is a shame that Winters does not fully explore how or why.[11] The status of narrative in musical numbers should be questioned. Film theory's general lack of questioning of these seemingly 'impossible' spaces—song sequences—may be due to their being physically perceived by audiences, enabling us a level of autonomy over the space. I will now turn to theories surrounding opera and argue that not only can they offer fruitful readings of different realms of space, but they can also add more nuance to subsequent spatial studies of embodied spectatorship.

Opera

I have made it clear that the musical genre should be considered along a spectrum rather than as a clearly delimited genre. As such, many films can be considered under the rubric of the musical. These range from 'films by any other name'—for instance Quentin Tarantino or Pedro Almodóvar films that emphasise musical sequences at particular points in the narrative—to the backstage musical, from the integrated, to opera and operetta. The issue of delineation of the space of the musical number becomes further complicated when one considers the implications that viewing the musical genre as a spectrum can have, for not only is the position of the sequences in the 'narrative' various, but so too the emphasis of sensual primacy.

One such implication occurs when one looks at the opera or operetta: the division between musical number and 'narrative' moments have been obscured; what the audience are left with in this 'sub-genre' is perhaps rather a distinction between recitative and aria—an issue I will return to subsequently. The questions that arise from this, however, are: if music is constantly present then is the notion of the audio-dissolve complicated further? Is a shift to audio primacy possible, or is it rather that the sound's position does not change, but rather the image's place in sensory perception does? To answer these questions it is worth looking at the relationship between the different elements of opera and how they are synthesised.

The opera theorist Egon Wellesz has argued that 'opera has no uniform development. The relation of its component parts to each other is perpetually shifting. A period in which the dramatic element is exaggerated is followed by one in which text and music have equal rights'.[12] For Wellesz, there is no uniform relationship between the elements of opera language. Put simply, the history of the art has seen many changes in emphasis. He continues and states, 'an era in which the stage is neglected is followed by one in which special attention is paid to it'.[13] The reason for this shifting relationship between the different components of opera no doubt has much to do with changing sensibilities towards art more generally throughout the many years of its history. This notwithstanding, Wellesz claims that

> Opera does not obey the same laws as the other musical forms. The fact that it is a combination of text, décor, production, and music, elements which must be welded together so as to make a single, unified impression on the audience, means that opera has laws and aesthetic principles of its own.[14]

I contend that many of these attributes are more widely found in the musical genre, particularly so if one considers it as more a topology than a taxonomy. Though, as Chapter 3 argues, there is no such thing as an 'original' version of a musical—and indeed film more widely—one might reason that during a musical number each element of film language, be it sound, mise-en-scène, cinematography and such like are working towards a particular desired effect; albeit unique to each film. What is undoubtedly a truism is that, like opera, musicals are 'a combination of text, décor, production, and music, elements which must be welded together [...]'.[15] Thus, a musical number is the epitome of film's audio-visual nature.

In *Opera in Theory and Practice, Image and Myth*, Lorenzo Bianconi and Giorgio Pestelli have stated that

> The basic accusation is that opera has subverted the fundamental principle of classical drama itself and of its so-called closed form, which would have the author completely divorced from the action and the characters completely independent onstage, as if operating in a self-sufficient world and 'closed off' from any external influence. The intrusion of music shatters this complete coherence, destroys realism, and expels what Saint-Évremond calls 'l'esprit de la representation'. In making the characters sing, the composer lends them his own voice, and it is toward this, not to the thoughts of the hero, that the attention of the listener is directed, the listener seeing in the characters the figure of the author, as the only person truly onstage.[16]

A number of interesting points of note arise from this extended quote. Firstly, if it follows that the musical spectrum in general shares many of the same attributes as opera more specifically, then the musical is an 'open form'. Secondly, the music destroys realism (it is important here to note the lack of ambiguity with which Bianconi and Pestelli credit the term 'realism'), thirdly, that the introduction of music makes sound become the audience's primary focus; and finally, that it is the author, not the character that is 'heard' on stage in these moments.

All of these 'condemnations' of opera can be applied to the musical more widely, and more particularly its representation and perception of space; however, far from being condemnations they are arguably misunderstood virtues of the genre. For instance, the notion of open form is in many respects caught up with the second criticism of opera, that its deployment of music destroys the perceived realism of the narrative. Film scholarship has a long tradition of theorising issues of realism, however it is not my aim to add to this debate.[17] My exploration into and promotion of a methodological approach for studying spatial representation and perception, endorses the interpretation of space as being physically felt, and indeed traversed with a level of autonomy, by audiences. As such, my understanding of space rather negates the issue of realism being 'destroyed' by the introduction of music. If one considers that the space between audience and diegesis is traversed and merged through both a haptic and embodied spectatorship reading, then a consequence of this is that the experience by the audience is no less 'real' than their existence in the theatrical space as an external audience.

The final two issues raised by Bianconi and Pestelli, that music becomes the audience's primary focus and so too the author rather that performer, are surely linked. Again, a spatial reading of the musical spectrum renders their complaints less problematic. Some form of song sequences in the musical are not only expected but a requirement of the genre, and thus arguably less disruptive to audience absorption than Bianconi and Pestelli give it credit. As such, although it is certainly possible for music to be the audience's primary focus, it does not necessarily follow that its effect should be working contrapuntally to the image. Furthermore, the premise that the introduction of music promotes the author's voice over that of the performer's, is not only illogical but also flawed and again hinges on the notion of a prevention of audience absorption.

Robert Donington, conversely, has argued that the different elements of opera—mise-en-scène, dialogue, music, et al.—act as symbols that should be viewed in a complementary relationship to one another. These symbols, he states, are both conscious and unconscious and make their way into opera in two ways: 'One way is unplanned and results from the innately image-forming disposition of the human psyche'.[18] He argues that it is in human nature to ascribe meaning to images and that '[…] however autonomous the material, it is still only the material, and will need to be worked over with conscious craftsmanship. The artist may not know *why* he does it the way he does, but he must certainly know *how*'.[19] The second way for symbols to enter opera, Donington claims, is much rarer: 'Here there is planning for the purpose, and the symbols themselves may be largely, though never wholly, conscious and deliberate'.[20] In this case the artist not only knows how but also why: 'The unconscious still crucially contributes to the formation of the symbols, but the conscious contributes crucially as well'.[21]

Donington's focus on the symbol, conscious and unconscious, though not without issue, particularly in his understanding of symbols as universally understood, raises an interesting point as to how the symbolism of the various elements work together.

> Words can obviously be symbolical; music in my opinion also; staging has possibilities which today are better relished than understood. But in opera it is the partnership of these different components which counts and they do need to blend together as a matter of intrinsic style. In this partnership, words are the most articulate component, music the most expressive, and staging the most localising.[22]

Whilst arguing that the different elements work in unity together, Donington is also suggesting that words, or one might say lyrics, are the primary conveyors of information. This raises two key points: firstly, that in an art form that also conveys visual information, opera's meaning is conveyed through sound; and secondly, that within sound itself there is a hierarchy of meaning or primacy. With ease one could transpose these arguments onto the musical genre more widely. It is important to note, however, that Donington believes that, although these various elements of sound exist in a hierarchy, they are also working together.[23]

As befits the central tenet of this book, and more specifically discussed in Chapter 3, sound should be seen as a gestalt: though the individual parts may have different emphases the summation of all the elements works to a unified whole. Donington's focus on the interplay between the different types of sound does not discount the image's role in symbolism. He argues that 'the total symbolism which is opera will not add up unless the staging is basically compatible in style with the words and the music'.[24] Donington thus sees the musical elements of opera as the central and primary focus of audience engagement. Additionally, he takes this idea further and argues that in filmed opera, and one could extend this to film musicals more generally, the use of close ups

> put at great hazard all that theatrical distancing which gives to the singer the magic of his otherness. The nearer we get [...] the more [they] look like an actor and the less like an archetype. What we gain in intimacy we may lose in numinosity.[25]

For Donington it is important to keep the mythic symbolism at the forefront of audience interpretation, to thus keep a distance between the 'reality' of the audience and the 'reality' of the performance. This can be seen in contrast to Adrienne McLean's work as discussed in Chapter 4, whereby the performer is able to exert a level of control over the filmic space by presenting themselves as consummate performers.

What then becomes of embodied spectatorship and the space between audience and the musical number? Sam Abel's book *Opera in the Flesh: Sexuality in Operatic Performance* provides an interesting counterpoint and one more in keeping with the porous boundaries of spatial realms.[26] Abel's book seeks to explore what happens to the audience's body physically and erotically when watching opera; a brave line of theorising that privileges his own experiences in an attempt to seek understanding. Though not explicitly stated by Abel, such a book is tacitly exploring the relationship between different spaces. The guiding premise behind Abel's subsequent theorising is that there should be a distinction between drama and theatre. Although also looking at theatre in the literal sense of focusing on live performance, Abel also defines the term as 'a performed physical exchange between singer and audience'.[27] Drama, conversely, may have more focus on form.[28] These highly ambiguous definitions notwithstanding, Abel is emphasising the focus on excess and spectacle, a charge to be levelled at the musical number more widely: 'The fact that opera unites music, verbal narrative, and theatrical presentation—its necessary elements—when any one of these media constitutes an art form, creates a sense of excess consumption'.[29]

Opera, like musicals more widely, push the boundaries of audiences' willing suspension of disbelief. For Abel, this does not cause a problem for the art form; rather it is defined to a large degree by its highly contrived conventions. Musicals, like opera, have performers sporadically bursting into song (or dance) and thus Abel argues that

> The psychological theories of audience identification and sympathy, which inform so much contemporary performance and film criticism and which depend so heavily on the assumption that the audience accepts the spectacle as reality, do not work neatly for opera.[30]

One way in which these theories do not work, Abel argues, is as follows:

> [The] psychological process of audience identification becomes distorted in opera. First of all, since many audience members cannot follow the words of the libretto (either because they do not speak the language of because technical requirements of singing or the volume of the orchestra blur the words), the familiar channels that present the discursive information necessary for identification function erratically.[31]

Here perhaps lies a difference between opera and the musical genre more widely, though perhaps more subtle than at first it might appear. Whilst it is arguably the general assumption when watching an opera that the audience might not know the language, unless they are proficient in several—largely European—languages, the same is not the case for musicals as a whole. Not only does this highlight the great variety existing in the genre, but also the complexity. Furthermore, musicals, be it those made in Hollywood or elsewhere in the world, do often cross their native geographical boundaries and will thus be seen by audiences who do not share in the language. Whether it is as a result of a diasporic community or festival distributions amongst other means, musical audiences are wider than those proficient speakers of the language. Subtitling, like in many operas staged today, is one way in which understanding may still be permitted.[32]

I am suggesting that one way that space can be understood is through embodied spectatorship, a key question must therefore be: what happens to embodied spectatorship if identification is, as Abel claims, distorted? The issue of identification is an interesting one, not least because it is often used within the context of narrative readings of films. It is important, however, to recognise that identification should not be restricted in this way. Chapters 3 and 4 have demonstrated how sound and images respectively enable forms of embodied spectatorship. Abel states that 'opera seduces me into its reality and then refuses to give me a solid grounding for my identity'.[33] This 'reality' can be seen in a variety of ways, but most succinctly in the opposition between Bertolt Brecht's *Verfremdungseffekt* and Richard Wagner's concept of the *Gesamtkunstwerk*.[34] On the subject of the *Verfremdungseffekt* Abel has argued that:

> This confusion of identification is not the same thing as the disruption of audience identification that Bertolt Brecht outlines in his theory of alienation, the *Verfremdungseffekt*. Brecht sets out to upset the traditional identification process of realism, to encourage the audience to stay outside the narrative frame, so they may make a detached political judgement

about the story and its social implications. But opera does not set up such boundaries. Opera does not ask me to stay outside its narrative frame. Opera fully expects me to enter its world, to identify with its central characters, all of them; there is no Brechtian disengagement here, but rather excess engagement.[35]

Though Abel might be maintaining that excess is the key—this would certainly help a reading of embodied spectatorship—his claim that opera does 'not ask me to stay outside its narrative frame' needs elucidating.[36] The excess alluded to, though not requiring a removal from narrative involvement, enables a movement of the audience 'beyond' the narrative; however slight a distinction. The importance of narrative for identification should be questioned, particularly in a musical context: do audiences only identify with characters within a particular context and audience specific moral milieu? Abel thinks not. His belief is that the singing character, regardless of character traits (protagonist or antagonist), takes precedence. 'Music', he states, 'obscures the narrative and my ability to judge its emotional effects, because my desire for the music overwhelms any feelings I might have about the narrative'.[37]

Richard Wagner's concept of the *Gesamtkunstwerk* is an interesting theoretical concern that explicates on the core issues that Abel is discussing. Here, rather than creating a distinction between operatic elements, broadly placed into visual and aural categories, Wagner is placing their relationship in the foreground and their ability to work towards a unified goal: *Musikdrama*.[38] Whilst *Gesamtkunstwerk* can be translated several ways, the emphasis here will be on the 'total work of art'.[39] Although Wagner's interests lie in opera, he has frequently been discussed in terms of film music. Scott D. Paulin has stated that, 'The claim on unity and totality represents more of an ideological neo-Wagnerism than any influence on the level of technique or aural surface. To the extent that film music is or has been Wagnerian, it has largely been as a sort of wish fulfilment'.[40] Through looking at a predominantly American body of literature, Paulin's argument is that there has been a 'tendency to overvalue Wagner' and use his work as a form of theoretical fetish object, a disavowal of the lack of unity in film due to the heterogeneity of the cinematic apparatus.[41] Thus film is different from theatre; just as Walter Benjamin argued for an understanding of film as a form of mechanical reproduction, Wagner was writing under the rubric of live theatre.[42] The same is true of opera and filmed opera, be it a filmed live performance or a production designed for cinema, of which *Umbrellas of Cherbourg* would be an example. Wagner's concept of the *Gesamtkunstwerk* is not without issue, even within his own writings. As Paulin states:

> If the need to redefine the relationship of the arts within some totality is a recurrent topos in Wagner's writings, however, the solution to the problem cannot be located at a stable point. [...] The change is clear: from an apparently equal "collaboration" between music and poetry in [1851], to the valorisation in 1879 of music's active role in bringing about the transfiguration of opera into music drama.[43]

Wagner's initial conception of the *Gesamtkunstwerk* was that of a synthesis of music and drama on an equal level whereby music should not attempt to 'prescribe the aim of Drama'.[44] This status quo between music and drama is altered in 1854, when the balance shifts in favour of music, particularly instrumental music.[45] Paulin describes how Wagner's view adjusts to the understanding that 'music is to maintain an on-going commentary on the drama but is not strictly tied to the language [...]'.[46] Even this tie to language ultimately changes in *The Ring* cycle (1848–1874), with motifs appearing in the orchestra that do not appear in the voice.[47] It is clear to see that Wagner's concept of the *Gesamtkunstwerk* was more of a goal than a complete theoretical concern: 'In no way' as Paulin attests, 'did it represent a coherent strategy, nor could Wagner have satisfied its requirements as an abstract concept of total unity. Simply put, it was a goal, the route to which Wager frequently redefined'.[48]

With such vagueness in Wagner's own conception of the term, it is therefore not surprising that theoretical use of Wagner's *Gesamtkunstwerk* represents an ideological neo-Wagnerism wish fulfilment than a concrete and accurate use of his paradigm.[49] As such, Wagner cannot have sole authorship of the subsequent meanings his ideas have come to have.[50] A consequence of which are various adaptations of his ideas, as can be seen in the transferral of theatre to cinema. Both the similarities and differences between theatrical opera and cinema are numerous, though can be simplified to issues of heterogeneity. Scott D. Paulin is worth quoting at length:

> Like opera, film is a heterogeneous form that combines a number of artistic practices. Unlike an opera, however, a film is also a heterogeneous body of material comprising separate shots of photographic footage edited together (after the invention of the splice), to which has usually been added either

live musical performance, or (after the transition to sound at the end of the 1920s) a soundtrack including some combination of dialogue, sound effects, and music. The imperative for synthesis is therefore of heightened urgency in the case of film, almost always an art with 'multiple authors' and the resultant risk of rupture.[51]

The emphasis on synthesis in cinema thereby permits the blurring of the boundaries of the heterogeneous material resulting in a unified whole, harking back to Wagner's earlier formulation of the *Gesamtkunstwerk*. Despite this, as David Schroeder has maintained: 'With a musical essence predetermining the visual images and giving them an inherent musical quality, a filmmaker would also then want to present the audience with actual musical sounds that would come as close as possible to unlocking the musical essence underlying the cinematography'.[52] As Schroeder explains, this would often be achieved through the creation of a working temp-track shared between the composer and director at the beginning of filming.[53] The music in such cases is often used to establish mood, tone, space and place, and enable the emotions of the scene to be drawn out through the complementary workings of cinematography and music.

At this juncture it is important to return to the previously mentioned distinction between recitative and aria, for they both highlight one aspect of the balance that such a synthesis should address and demonstrate the heterogeneous nature of both artistic media. Like Altman's 'audio-dissolve', this distinction is not without issue, particularly when one considers there is no one definitive form of either aria or recitative. This notwithstanding, in *Opera and Drama* Wagner argues that 'The musical basis of Opera was—as we know—nothing other than the *Aria*'.[54] With regards to the aria, Bianconi and Pestelli have stated that:

> [...] the aria was the most thorny problem area, a tangle of glaring contradictions. Its generous dimensions, its location at the end of a scene (with the obligatory exit of the character singing it), and its effect of being suspended pointed the way toward the charge that it was the main obstacle to the development of the plot; whatever its inherently musical merits, it remained virtually unconnected to the dramatic context.[55]

Bianconi and Pestelli's conception of the aria is that it is in many respects not only separate to the plot, but a hindrance to it. Furthermore, it is a space for the performer to exhibit their singing skills and thus takes it into the realm of Adrienne McLean's work on performance space. Winton Dean, however, provides more nuance to the aria's relationship to narrative. In regards to late baroque opera he states that '[...] plot development was virtually confined to the recitative (the outer action) and emotional expression to the arias (the inner action) [...]'.[56] This distinction perhaps better reflects the balance between plot and plot motivation, between simultaneity and chronology, as Altman would contend. This separation is arguably why, as Jeremy Tambling suggests, Hollywood films (and musicals more generally) have been able to pull from opera, particular arias. He states that

> Hollywood's refusal to film operas but its willingness to plagiarise music and arias for stories of its own devising indicates its need to erase from even the sentimental Italian operas of the nineteenth century the oppositional elements that make up the conflictual drama of opera [...].[57]

The conflicts referred to are the constantly negotiated relationships between libretto and orchestral music, and elements of music and mise-en-scène. Hollywood's willingness to 'borrow' from operas also illustrates its ability to separate elements in a clearly demarcated manner. As Chapter 3 demonstrates, problems abound when one considers the concept of the 'original'. The same is true of film more generally. As Tambling describes, '[...] there is no primary, authoritative text, and [...] texts remake themselves and are remade [...]'.[58] This is certainly the case in the Hollywood's appropriating of operatic texts. A consequence of this is that meaning is ascribed through context. Thus, an operatic piece used in a film musical not only takes on connotations from the opera, but also its location in the film. An example of overt filmic 'borrowing' would be *Carmen Jones* (1954), though this is a reimagining of the original narrative. This is not always the case, however, in filmic operas or operettas; as Jacques Demy's *Umbrellas of Cherbourg*, original operetta, demonstrates.

UMBRELLAS OF CHERBOURG

Umbrellas of Cherbourg is an entirely sung operetta, the result of which is the distinction between musical number and 'narrative' moments has been obscured. If music is constantly present, then the notion of the audio-dissolve is complicated further. Michel Legrand's music permeates the film from the opening scene to the finale. There are very few instances of diegetic music being visually signified, a trip to an opera and a café, yet music is still present, and seemingly heard by a collective group; after all, the characters are able to converse in song using the same musical melodies and rhythms.

The source of the music is often a point of issue with musicals; frequently a source of music is not given, and what should be non-diegetic music is heard by all—both the spectator and characters, whether a part of the singing or an internal audience member. In *Umbrellas of Cherbourg*, perhaps the source of the music is the character themselves, in which case would this negate the music driving the musical number if the characters themselves are driving the music? Altman's audio-dissolve gives a privileged position to the place of the music within the fictitious world of the film itself, rather than in relation to the external spectator. Music will be heard elsewhere throughout the course of the film, but it is apparently this internal music—this 'meta-diegesis'—that distinguishes a musical number from its surroundings; an issue further complicated by *Umbrellas of Cherbourg*. The external audience takes its cue from the characters—they sing and or dance—but from where do the characters take theirs? This is not merely meta-diegetic sound heard by a single character, but frequently a communal act heard by several simultaneously. They must make a distinction between the non-diegetic music heard only by the audience and the non-diegetic music they too experience. What is this distinction and does it still exist in an operetta?

If there is constant singing, is the audience experiencing a constant state of negotiated meta-diegesis? Negotiated in terms of who the primary singer is at any given moment, and thus driving that music. In which case, are these films without any non-diegetic music at all? Does *Umbrellas of Cherbourg* contain any music that only the external audience can hear? This of course presupposes that the characters can indeed hear the music they are singing to, but how could they not—if only internally—if their actions and singing are being driven by that music? Perhaps it is the distinction, between the internal and external, that contains the key.

The operetta is arguably one long song sequence or musical number, yet still people point out individual musical moments. In *Umbrellas*, for instance, 'I Will Wait for You' was not only a stand out moment in the film, emotionally and musically, but has been sung by such performers as Liza Minnelli, Johnny Mathis and Matt Monroe. Amongst the constant music and singing, 'I Will Wait for You' has been singled out, a beginning and end found and a distinction made between the song and that which surrounds it. Is this the distinction between recitative and aria, and if so, how was it made?

Reinhard G. Pauly has described the distinction between aria and recitative: 'Often, in Baroque and Classic opera, the division into recitative and aria was both textual and musical—prose carried the action forward in recitatives, while poetry served for the more reflective, lyrical, and emotional aria texts'.[59] For the sake of simplicity, I include under the rubric of aria duets and ensemble sequences, and as recitative any instance where the words are driving the music; where the pattern of speech is of primary concern (even though recitative does itself exist along a spectrum). In other words, recitative is the sung speech of the characters, and aria the expression of their emotions. This distinction is highly problematic and again returns to the notion of interiority and exteriority, of diegetic and non-diegetic. This issue is further complicated if one looks at the opening sequence of the film. It is important now to turn to another of the virtual reconstructions, VR 2; an example of a virtually recreated version of the opening sequence. I have chosen this musical moment, 'Mechanics' scene, as it is an example of recitative and arguably less common across the whole musical genre spectrum. The music continues through from the opening credits where strings and double bass have been dominant. The camera is positioned, as demonstrated in VR 2 at 6 seconds, in a medium shot looking through a busy street to a man, facing the camera, outside the garage. As the double bass scales down, diegetic bell sounds can be heard, before a jazz band is introduced. The camera cuts to a close-up of the gentleman before following him into the garage. It is at this point the singing of tunefully banal conversation starts. The music before this point has been the dominant sound heard, the introduction of the singing, however, causes a reduction in the volume of the orchestra in order to aurally favour the singing. This, whilst demonstrating an inconsistency in the spatiality of the sounds of the orchestra, enables a closer proxemic relationship with the characters singing. This proxemic relationship is further enhanced by slight variation in the volume of the different singers; for instance, as demonstrated by VR 2, as Pierre is further away from the original gentleman when he starts singing, his volume is marginally lower. This changes throughout the number. The camera's medium shot provides the audience with much visual information about the space of the garage. The mise-en-scène shows it to be a spacious building with bare walls and much metallic equipment; in short, a room that might echo. The slight echo on the voices of the singers and indeed the orchestral music, which does not use a close-miked sound, enhances this visual information. This changes when the camera and characters enter the washroom, as demonstrated by VR 2 from 1 minute 20 seconds onwards. Thus, both the images and sounds within the opening 'Mechanics' sequence, are working together to provide a rational space for the scene. This sequence would be an example of recitative due to the 'exterior' nature of the tone and content of the lyrics. Using Pauly's term, this is 'prose' carrying the narrative forward. The issue, however, is that this is still a musical number in the strictest sense: music is at the fore, there is an element of spectacle about it, and characters are singing. The sequence not only permits an understanding of the actual space of the scene, but also aptly demonstrates a different type of space: space within the musical score. By varying the volume of the different aspects of the soundtrack, a choice has been made as to what to manipulate the audience to focus upon, be it score or libretto at any given moment. This raises an interesting question of not only how these elements are perceived, but also how their particular choice aids in representation. In order to answer these issues it is worth considering Laura Marks' work in this area.

Perception

There is a multiplicity of ways that modes of perception can affect one's understanding of the audio-visual media's space presented. I have so far demonstrated an array of views on perception encompassing, and sensitive to, both sound and image and their interaction. As has been stated, the central tenet of gestalt theory is that the whole is more than the sum of its parts, and thus though gestalt is the overarching theoretical framework of this book, it does not necessarily follow that other forms of perception are counterintuitive to this theory. Indeed one particular notion that it is worth drawing attention to is that of 'enfolding-unfolding aesthetics' as developed by Laura Marks. I have so far drawn on Marks' work within the context of embodied spectatorship and sensual analysis, and I will continue to utilise this fecund theoretical bent; here, however, Marks' understanding of the senses and mediation is discussed. Put simply, Marks describes enfolding-unfolding aesthetics as images in a position to 'unfold' information and thus connect it back to the world.[60] Marks discusses this largely in narrative terms; for instance, as images that are often required to be 'read' rather than perceived.[61] Although I am not concerned with narrative readings of films, it is important to note in Marks' argument that the sensually perceived is mediated. 'These days,' Marks states,

> [M]any of the images that appear to our senses are not more than the effects of the information that generated them. The graphical user interface (GUI) of computers—a set of images that index actions of information manipulation—is directed to our eyes and ears, but this perceptual experience is simply the medium through which we receive information.[62]

In terms of narrative, this mediation is largely seen in the form of signs that are encoded rather than as isolated sensual phenomena, thus images are chosen to tell a narrative from a plethora of other image choices. Images 'unfold' both from the world and information. Marks argues that

> For cinema studies, enfolding-unfolding aesthetics proposes a theory of representation and narrative as unfolding. The image unfolds from the world. An additional level, information, sometimes intervenes; so that while information unfolds from the world, the image unfolds from information. Cinematic conventions, insofar as they obviate the necessity of really seeing and hearing a film, operate as information.[63]

Her concept of enfolding-unfolding aesthetics, Marks argues, attempts to readdress the issue of where the images that viewers perceive come from. There is a distinction that Marks makes between the 'universe of images' and 'images'.

> [A]morphous, unarticulated and imperceptible as such. The events that occur here are momentary, passing in a flash and leaving no trace—unless they are—captured as information or image [the latter]. The universe of images contains all possible images in a virtual state, and certain images arise from it, becoming actual.[64]

'Actual images' are those that are realised on screen, i.e. mediated and having undergone semiotic processes. Narrative is a form of mediation as it causes images to be chosen that best convey the information that helps its cause. Thus, the images of cinema are always mediated and 'unfolding' as they have been chosen to best convey a particular viewpoint. The question that thus arises is twofold: firstly, is the same true of sensory perception of sound? Secondly, how does this affect our understanding of space in musical numbers? It is important to return briefly to the distinction between images and the universe of images. Marks makes use of Charles Sanders Peirce's epistemology that argues that

> The universe of images is a First, a unity unknowable in itself. Information, a Second, implies a struggle by which certain results are actualised, and not others. The image that arises from information is a Third, relaying the universe of images (First) through information (Second). The image points out relationships, teaching us something about how information is selected from the universe of images. Being triadic, enfolding-unfolding aesthetics avoids some of the pitfalls of dualistic theories of representation.[65]

To such a triad the representation of space can be applied; space is perceived through the relationship between the images chosen to best create the desired spatial realms, these are then perceived sensually. Thus, as Marks claims, 'what we experience with our senses', and in this case it is space, 'is simply the end result of processes of information that are ultimately more significant than perceptible images'.[66]

Marks' idea of an enfolding-unfolding aesthetics provides a further nuance to this book as it highlights the issue of mediated sensory experience, integral to an analysis of cinematic space. Like many theories it has fallen short at discussing sound and has continued the ocularcentrism prevalent in film. Many theories that privilege sensory experience utilise a discourse that highlights the 'purity' of this form of perception, of which I am guilty also. What is important to note, however, is the level of mediation. Sensory perception and readings of films offer an alternative to the Cartesian cognitive position, which will be returned to later, as it is 'unmediated' by the brains' 'higher' cognitive processes; a more 'natural' reaction without encoding, i.e. it is an unconscious reaction. What Marks' has illustrated, however, is that no image is unmediated. Rather, that there are realms of mediation that exist at different stages of perception. This book, therefore, following Marks' ideas, largely focuses on stimuli that are felt with the senses (we could call this 'Level 1 Mediation') before being cognitively encoded ('Level 2 Mediation'); thereby acknowledging the mediated nature of all images.

It is important to return to the issue of ocularcentrism. The rhetoric used in discussing Marks' ideas, both by Marks herself and my examination of it, has hitherto maintained a focus on the image. This should not be the case. Previous chapters have dealt with the variations in sensory perceptions, for instance how gestalt theorises the perception of different stimuli, and it is thus important to continue this trend with Marks' work. Such an enfolding-unfolding aesthetics should deal with sound also. Like images it has realms of mediation, and furthermore, exploring either images or sound in a film context does a disservice to both. By analysing the audio-visual relationship, not only is mediation compounded, but it is also arguably on occasion challenged through its inherent nature as a synthesis. Like images, sound can be split into Marks' triadic form of representation: the filmic soundtrack signifies the third that has arisen from the information that has been chosen (second). Like the image, the chosen sound(s) indicate relationships from a potential multitude, what we might call the 'universe of sounds'. These sounds are also mediated. The challenge to the triad arises when sounds and images are synthesised and film is acknowledged as audio-visual. Though there is no work on the effect of exploring Marks' work on enfolding-unfolding aesthetics in an audio-visual light, it does illustrate the difficulties inherent to recognising and following gestalt theory's central approach.[67] Despite its inability to yield 'easy' answers, it is an avenue that should be encouraged; for it reveals that there is much still to learn about filmic representation.

How Marks' work on enfolding-unfolding aesthetics applies to the study of the space of film musical numbers is an essential point. As the 'Introduction' demonstrates, the representation of space is a multifaceted area of study with several components, one of which is the perception of space: how space is perceived by audiences and how this affects their relationship to that space. As I contend, there are many realms of space, not just that between performer and the mise-en-scène of the musical number. The perception of space by the audience is important for understanding how that space (between performer and mise-en-scène) is considered, but also how the seeming gap between the onscreen space and the space of the cinema is bridged. By understanding the audio-visual relationship, and space as mediated, it enables us to illustrate that at every stage of film production, the 'gap' between audience and screen has already been bridged; it is not self-contained, but, rather, made with the audience in mind.

Being cognizant of this, it is wise to return to the issue of ways in which the spatial realm between screen and audience is bridged and traversed. I have looked at how independently image and sound can be read in a haptic manner and this chapter will now turn to how such theories can be utilised and taken further to read the audio-visual space. Furthermore, the theory of haptics will be placed into the wider context of embodied spectatorship using the work of the theorist Anne Rutherford.[68]

Embodied Spectatorship and Haptic Space

In her essay 'Cinema and Embodied Affect', Anne Rutherford described scientific film theory as a 'debilitating heritage' that, alongside the phenomenological concepts of embodiment, 'have persistently thwarted the articulation of an aesthetics of embodiment which recognises the full resonance of embodied affect in the experience of cinema spectatorship'.[69] Rutherford creates a distinction between scientific film theory and embodied spectatorship and its theoretical grounding; a distinction that many theorists would perhaps not agree with, indeed this book argues that they are not mutually exclusive. Rutherford takes exception to scientific theory of the body that bases its findings on what is essentially cadaverous; the body is discussed in terms of the 'anatomy', which she argues is best categorised as on the dissection table.[70] Like many notions that this study takes issue with, such an understanding of the body omits the way it interacts with lived experiences. This is perhaps a symbolic way of summarising the methodology that this book is seeking to promote. Whilst theories of the body that Rutherford deems problematic may be considered as scientifically accurate, they do not take into account the interactions at play. It is an exemplar of how an audio-visual understanding will be different from approaches that look either solely at sound or image. This notion of the body stems from the German term '*Körper*' that refers to 'the structural aspects of the body, the objectified body and also the dead body or corpse'.[71] This theory has been corrupted in the translation into English as it fails to take into account the alternative German concept '*Leib*', which refers to the living body with feelings.[72] Rutherford argues that 'the erasure of the distinction between these two concepts [*Körper and Leib*] has masked the implications of the concept of *Leib*, the experiential potential of *Leib* as embodied affect, for a cinematic aesthetics of embodiment'.[73] Thus, an understanding of embodiment should make allowances for this latter concept.

Rutherford discusses how a shift occurred from the model above to one that 'derives its principles and claim to authority from physiology'.[74] Jonathon Crary argues that sense receptor based theories have been replaced by the subjective understanding of vision.[75] The former,

Rutherford claims, assumes that the eye simply registers information from the external world. Crary calls this 'new integration of the subjective ground of vision a "corporeal" concept of vision'.[76]

A central issue of theories of embodiment is the site of vision, Rutherford states that it is an epistemological question as to whether the sensations that audiences 'perceive as visual derive from external, so-called objective realities, or whether they derive internally, from the subject'.[77] There is an inherent difference, however, between the terms 'subjective' and 'embodiment'. Although not mutually exclusive, they do represent different experiences. 'Subjectivity,' Rutherford claims, 'is not coterminous with embodied experience—it is only one component, one narrowly-defined layer of experience, which does not approximate the heterogeneous and conflicting multidimensionality of the lived body'.[78] An understanding of embodiment is therefore multifaceted, and haptics is one way that audiences may experience it. Theories of embodiment are important for understanding how the space between screen and audience is blurred, shared; indeed, separate spatial realms being paradoxically coterminous with one another.

As I have stated throughout, I am concerned purely with the space of musical numbers as distinct from narrative. A consequence of this removing of a dominant theoretical framework is the promotion of an alternative mode of reading films, namely through abstract aesthetics. How embodiment can be read in an aesthetic manner is thus a significant question to deal with. In fact, embodied spectatorship offers a variety of ways in which aesthetics can be understood. Peter Brooks uses the term 'aesthetics of embodiment' to analyse how the body can be a site of signification; how bodily gestures can be used to carry meaning.[79] Whilst Brooks is discussing the body on screen as a point of signification, what he does not clarify is whether he believes the same may be true of the spectator's body. It is a combination of both that this book utilises: the filmic body and the audience's. Previous chapters have demonstrated both how the performer's body can be read spatially as a point of signification (for instance through proxemics), and how the audience's body can be used to carry meaning (e.g. haptics). Unlike Brooks, Rutherford argues for aesthetics of embodiment that is more concerned with this (spatial) relationship between the embodied spectator and the screen.[80]

A significant point to raise here is that Brooks' aesthetics of embodiment requires an onscreen body, and he is not the only theorist who promotes such an approach. Rutherford uses Linda Williams' work on 'body genres', such as porn or horror, to demonstrate how their approach differs. In essence, Willams' work analyses the effect that a body on screen can have on the spectator.[81] Rutherford argues that 'while [Williams] does propose a dimension to this experience that goes beyond a simple mimicry of those viewed bodies, her analysis and discussion of embodiment relies on the presence of the human body on the screen'.[82] Rutherford's aesthetics of the body focuses on movement, vision, tactility and their connection to affective experience. 'The understanding of this relationship', she argues, 'stems from how the body or embodiment is conceptualised as the existential ground of perception. Two terms—kinetic vision and visual kinaesthesis—form the pivotal points of two vastly different paradigms of visual perception which underpin understandings of cinema based on divergent concepts of embodiment'.[83] It is key to again highlight the ocularcentric rhetoric that Rutherford is utilising and that dominates theories of embodiment more widely.

Kinetic vision and visual kinaesthesis are important notions both based on vision, more precisely ambulatory vision; namely, 'being able to see objects and move around a room without stumbling or bumping into obstacles'.[84] Though they might share the focus on ambulatory vision, Rutherford summarises how they approach embodiment very differently. It is worth quoting the distinction she sees between them at length. On kinetic vision she states that:

> The theory of kinetic vision, or vision-in-motion, developed by nineteenth century sculptor, Adolf Hildebrand, stems directly from the laboratory of the physiologists and their affiliation with the motion studies of Marey, Muybridge and others. Hildebrand's model derives from an analysis of the biological mechanics of stereoscopic vision in the perception of an observer moving towards an object. In its application to cinema, the eyes of a beholder or observer moving through space provide the prototype of a perception of motion which is supposedly duplicated by the mobile camera's ability to simulate or represent perceptual cues of depth and movement. This analogy is extended with the assumption that, just as the camera is equated with the eye of the beholder moving through a physical space, so the spectator in cinema identifies his or her subject position totally with the point of view of the camera [...]. As Mary Ann Doane claims [...], '[t]here is a certain metonymic slippage between vision, the image, the eye and the 'I' of subjectivity', and this slippage has formed the shaky foundation of one of the dominant paradigms of film theory.[85]

Kinaesthetic vision, however, she describes as a combination of factors that create the wider vision:

> The eye, says [James] Gibson, is just an anatomical structure, only one component of the process of vision, and [Gibson] replaces the model of perception derived from physiological optics with what he terms an ecological approach to perception, one which emphasises the process of visual kinaesthesia. As Gibson puts it, 'vision is kinaesthetic in that it registers movements of the body just as much as does the muscle-joint-skin system and the inner-ear system'.[86] Vision, he claims, picks up movements of the body or part of the body relative to the ground. (He includes stasis of the body as one form of movement). This information he calls proprioception. 'The [inherited] doctrine that vision is exteroceptive, in other words that it obtains "external" information only, is simply false', he argues: '[v]ision obtains information about *both* the environment and the self'.[87] Theories of motion perspective, he claims, are only 'an abstract way of describing the information at a moving point of observation'.[88]

Much as was discussed in Chapter 4, Gibson sees vision as an environmental process; an important means of locating oneself in the environment. Unlike Marks' enfolding-unfolding aesthetics, Gibson believes that what people perceive is the actual environment rather than data: 'the significance of surfaces in relation to our body'.[89] It is at this juncture that haptics becomes important with regards to the understanding of embodiment and space.

Sue Cataldi in *Emotion, Depth, and Flesh* uses the phenomenologist Maurice Merleau-Ponty's work to point out that the latter did not theorise the link between 'his view of emotionally 'blind' apprehension [and] tactile perception or emotional feeling' and thus does so herself, thereby linking Gibson's notion of haptics (in this case the body's movements contributing to the formation of vision) with Merleau-Ponty's understanding of emotion.[90] Rutherford believes that this link that Cataldi creates provides the most fecund paradigm for an understanding of 'affective experience and its relationship to the embodied vision of cinema spectatorship'.[91]

For many theorists it is the notion of movement, as discussed in previous chapters, which is so instrumental to comprehending a variety of theories ranging from physical affect to emotion. For Cataldi, it is Gibson's understanding of inhabiting a spectacle, or what one might call 'space', that is useful to her consideration of emotion. Emotion is an integral component of embodiment and thus the synthesising of space between cinema auditorium and cinematic filmic space. Cataldi's definition of an emotion is defined as a crossing and remaking of boundaries between oneself and me here, foremost of which is that emotions can be felt by cinema audiences as a result of the movement from screen through cinema auditorium; thus a shared space defined by movement. Cataldi claims that 'the deeper the emotional experience the more blurred and de-bordered the world-body border becomes, the more we experience ourselves as belonging to or caught up in the flesh of the world'.[92] In essence, the more heightened the emotions, the more the space is synthesised. As outlined previously, musical numbers are sites of excess, both in terms of film language and their effect on the audience and thus, following Cataldi's paradigm, provide particularly instructive examples of haptic cinema. The reading of space through an understanding of haptics becomes an increasingly viable and convincing methodology when one considers the multiple ways it may be utilised.

The very core of the word 'emotion' implies a movement; a movement through space. Glen Mazis states that:

> E-motion is taken up within the body, the body as the affective space…and the term feeling points [to this], the etymology in its root in the Icelandic falma means to grope. Through feeling in its emotional sense the body moves forward gropingly into the world, not as self-sufficient…but rather as touching things in order to be touched back. The hand in groping is an openness, a gaping waiting for a reciprocal touch from the world […].[93]

Rutherford argues that such points can move theorists towards an understanding of film theory that has previously been lacking: film theory needs to make the move 'from the concern with sensation or with emotion understood as sentiment organised along the axis of narrative identification, or with desire, to an understanding of embodied affect, in the theorisation of spectatorship'.[94] Embodied vision should be reconceptualised, she claims, as inherently tactile and thus an affective process.[95]

It is clear from such arguments that there is a growing body of supporters who advocate touch as an essential element of film theory. Rutherford is promoting the notion of embodiment as a central paradigm of spectatorship in which haptics plays a role. Whilst I concur that such a focus on the body and multi-sensory analysis should be at the forefront of film theory, particularly that of space, the inverse is true: that haptics should be seen as encompassing a broader spectrum of ideas of which embodiment is one. Haptics should be seen more broadly, not just as a means of touching cinema, but of interacting with its spaces, and as a form of spectatorship and reading films. These spaces are frequently seen through movements, and, as Rutherford justly claims:

> This movement is not conceived as a physical movement across a physical space: no empirical measurement can discern it, nor can an optical model define it. This is a movement interior to both the gritty materiality of the body's location in space, and simultaneously to the carnality of an idea or experience. It is a movement of the entire embodied being towards a corporeal appropriation of or immersion in a space, an experience, a moment. It is a movement away from the self, yes, but away from the self-conceived as the subject, in so far as this concept is a cognitive or disembodied one—a movement out of the constraints of the definable, knowable—a groping towards a connection, a link-up with the carnality of the idea, the affect of the body, the sensible resonances of experience. It is a movement towards—a movement of the world towards our grasp, or of our beings towards potency. It is an erotics of the image, a dilation of the senses, a nervous excitation—an eye-opening sure—but more than that an opening of the pores, a quickening of the pulse.[96]

There is much discussion, both in this book and the rhetoric of the theories it is applying, to the movement between spaces and the crossing of boundaries, be it in the way a performer moves from one space to another, e.g. diegetic to meta-diegetic, or the manner in which the audience interacts with the filmic space. To enable the crossing of such boundaries, delineation must occur. It does not necessarily follow, however, that these delineations are not in a state of flux or porous. Although they might be seen to delineate space, they should not be seen as barriers but more as markers. One such marker, particularly important when discussing haptics and how it enables embodied spectatorship, is the skin. The skin of the audience should be a concept rather than a definitive article. The term 'epidermis' is perhaps more suited to the latter, the former is used as a metaphor. Rutherford asks the key question of how we should understand the skin:

> Is it a container, keeping in the subject and keeping the object out, on the other side? Is the spectator thick-skinned, impervious to the vibrations set up on the screen on all but the most blatant level, or is the skin permeable, a membrane that mediates a contact with the world, a tactile being in the

world, that can respond to the flux of textures, of temperatures, can glow, can bristle and tremble, can even relinquish its boundaries in an osmosis of feeling and sensation?[97]

An important question that should be raised at this juncture is where these feelings are located; by which it is meant, are they diegetic, non-diegetic, meta-diegetic or indeed none of these traditional filmic terms?

BILLY THE KID AND THE GREEN BAIZE VAMPIRE

Now that I have suitably defined what the haptic is and how it can provisionally be used to understand space within an audio-visual context, it is worth turning to another filmic example: *Billy the Kid and the Green Baize Vampire*. The film's story concerns Billy the Kid, played by Phil Daniels, who is an up-and-coming snooker player managed by T.O, played by Bruce Payne. As T.O is in debt, he organises a game of snooker between Billy and the world champion Maxwell Randall, played by Alun Armstrong, (who also just happens to be a vampire). Not only is there a lot of money riding on the game, but whoever loses must never play snooker again.

It would be false to call this film a financial success. The film had a large budget of £2.7 million from various financers, but though it was exhibited in cinemas it was really on television that it debuted.[98] Though the reasons for Alan Clarke taking on this project, or its relative failure, are not the issues here, one might hazard that the latter was due to a combination of factors, such as the playing with the musical genre's conventions (and indeed synthesising various other genres, for instance the gangster genre), lack of a clear audience, needing and failing to appeal to an overseas market, artificial sets and lack of catchy musical numbers. One important point to be taken from this is the reaffirmation of the musical genre as a spectrum rather than a homogenous category of film. By which it is meant, though *Billy the Kid* perhaps lacks several of the elements that many audiences may deem the appeal of a musical film, it is still very much within the genre.

The reason for raising the issue of *Billy the Kid*'s financial failure is to highlight the film's seeming inability to connect with audiences, whether on TV or at the cinema. I am promoting and arguing that films' audio-visual space can be read in a multi-sensory manner, in this case with a focus on haptic experience, which invites an interaction between the audience and the film. I would further claim that a film like *Billy the Kid*, which intentionally distances the audience (as musicals often do through a lack of perceived 'naturalism'), still allows for this spatial experience that permits audience absorption, negotiation and interaction with its musical numbers.[99] In short, a haptic and embodied form of spectatorship.

Taking a number from the film as an example, namely, 'Super-Sonic Sam's Cosmic Café', [VR 3], one can see a number of devices that would traditionally be dichotomous with audience absorption, such as sparse sets, clear lack of location filming, all but direct address to the camera and extreme lighting; in short, visual elements of film language. How is a haptic relationship and mode of viewing thus created?

The number takes place largely within two locations: a corridor and a room containing people playing video games. The two locations are crossedited. The camera movement is minimal and very simplistic, either largely following behind the journalist and henchman walking along the corridor, or providing static, medium close-ups of the people playing games. More complicated camera movement is introduced once the two parties represented by the cross-cutting come together in the same location, at which point the audience are provided with a full pan around the characters. The singing in the number is largely chant-like, particularly from the secondary characters, and the music is non-naturalistic, with electronic reverb and mainly percussive; in keeping with the hypnotic state of the characters playing the video games. Once the journalist enters the room with Billy, the location does not change again until the end of the number. The music, scenery, and indeed musical number as a whole, is repetitive. One might reasonably ask: how can a haptic reading of this musical number be achieved? It is two-pronged and dependent upon understanding the musical number as a synthesis, a gestalt in which the whole is more than the sum of the parts; the musical number is an audio-visual experience. It allows a haptic reading both because it invites a sense of touch and allows the audience to enter and negotiate the space, thus covering the two sides to haptic readings: haptic images and haptic spectatorship permitted as a result of the number's audio-visual relationship. There are many ways that this is achieved; both audio and visual. When these elements are combined, however, a cohesive multi-sensory space is created. In order to demonstrate this, two aspects, one from image and sound respectively, will be explored.

It is first imperative to break down this number to a suitably forensic level, another means of analysis worthy of promotion. Using Yuri Tsivian's Cinemetrics software, which allows the user to monitor shot length and type, one can see that there were 27 shots in total.[100] A haptic reading can begin to take place with help from the data gathered, for instance, the average shot length is 8.8 seconds but there are three longer shots that stand out. What this demonstrates is that there is, on average, a relatively slow rate of editing, which in turn allows the audience to absorb the visual elements of the film and begin to visually explore. It is not as simple as this, however. It is not possible to state that because of a longer shot that arrives a quarter of the way through the number, the audience is able to 'enter the scene' in a haptic manner. It is, however, helped by the camera, particularly in the first of the longer shots that arrives at 59 seconds into the number and lasts 39.3 seconds.

This shot sees the camera continue to follow the journalist and man that is established in a previous shot; they enter the room and the camera pans around them shifting what has traditionally been an over-the-shoulder shot of the journalist to a front-on. The journalist has until this point in the number been the audience's pseudo-guide. They have followed her from the previous musical number, to shots in the car, through repeated shots of walking through corridors and into the room. She has taken the audience through the veritable maze of the location and edits, with lack of establishing shots, to Billy.

As the number progresses, the camera increasingly comes to align the audience with the journalist. Thus, as she walks through the dark hallways, the audience do also. Previous shots, such as a medium close-up of Billy, which is repeated throughout the number, seem to bend time and align themselves spatially with the future point-of-view position on the journalist.

The audience is thus occupying a series of different spaces, the space of the cinema (or home), the camera P.O.V and also the journalist's. On top of this, I would add a fourth space that reflects a further viewing position: that of the game playing extras. These characters are absorbed in their arcade games much as the audience is (to varying degrees) with the film. The audience, much like game players, are not passive, despite their initial appearance. They are perceptually processing and interacting with their game, much like the audience is with this musical number. One way this interaction can be seen is through the use of sound and it permitting a haptic reading, which I now turn to.

The spectrograph (Fig. 5.1) demonstrates the changes in sound volume throughout the number. What this simply demonstrates is a rather unvaried sonic geography, at least in terms of volume. There is a quieter

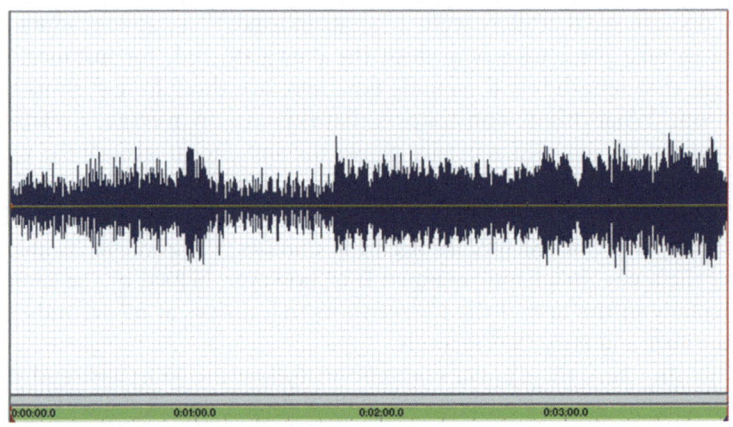

Fig. 5.1 Spectrograph demonstrating sound levels in 'Supersonic Sam's Cosmic Café' number

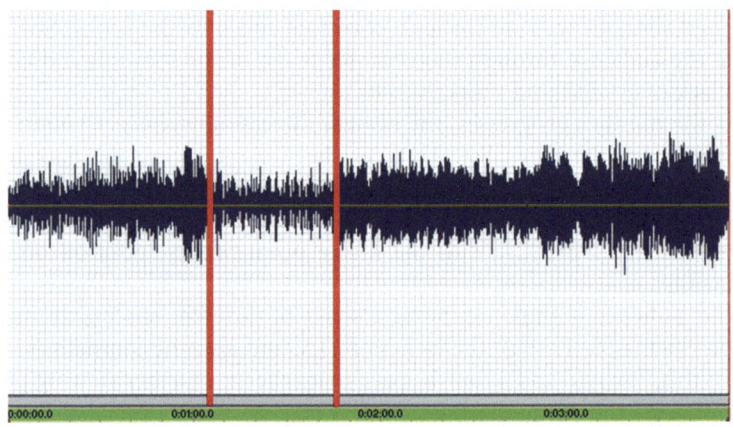

Fig. 5.2 Spectrograph demonstrating quieter section of 'Supersonic Sam's Cosmic Café' number

section about two quarters of the way through, which correlates with the aforementioned shot—the journalist entering the same room as Billy—in which dialogue rather than singing comes to the fore.

Other than this section (Fig. 5.2), the music continues with a 4/4 time signature being driven by percussion, which for much of the time is the dominant musical sound. This is being accompanied by the changing of the game players and the sounds of the video games that they are playing. The almost paradoxical close-miked sound alongside electronic reverb not only links the sound and visuals together more closely (for they emphasise the use of technology by the secondary characters), but also plays with the space of the scene. The lyrics that Billy sings often mirror, to some degree, the actions and situation of the journalist: for instance 'The light, the sound, all rattle round, spooky but sublime', abstractly linking the sonic and visual realms. When this musical number is watched, it has a physical effect on me: I tap my feet to its rhythm, I occasionally join in with the words, and my hands have been known to play a virtual arcade game, much as many people may air guitar to a Jimi Hendrix song. In such situations, the audience, like the arcade game players, are interacting with the scene, processing it neurologically. A consequence of this is a breaking down of the boundaries between the audience and the screen, the space is bridged and the boundaries blurred. Robynn Stilwell calls this crossing the 'fantastical gap' in her aptly named essay 'The Fantastical Gap between Diegetic and Nondiegetic'.[101] She states that

> The phrase 'fantastical gap' seemed particularly apt for this liminal space because it captured both its magic and its danger, the sense of unreality that always obtains as we leap from one solid edge toward another at some unknown distance and some uncertain stability—and sometimes we're in the air before we know we've left the ground.[102]

I want to take Stilwell further and argue that firstly, not only is it a diegetic/non-diegetic dichotomy, but a trifecta in which the diegetic status of the audience is called into question; and secondly, that one way in which this 'magic' can be explained is through a haptic reading; an understanding that the space between audiences and film is negotiated, traversed and indeed confused, both through inviting a sense of touch and promoting a mode of spectatorship. Sounds are physical, demonstrated in one way through the development of THX technology to standardise cinema sound's effects on audiences. By feeling the repetitive sounds of 'Super-Sonic Sam's Cosmic-Café' number, the audience are interpreting them physically as well as mentally processing them. The boundary between the audience and the diegetic space of the number has been breached; there are no longer distinct spaces, but spaces that can be negotiated, shared with the characters on the screen and felt physically.

Exploring embodied spectatorship and haptics enables theorists to begin to comprehend the nuanced spatiality of musical numbers and of film more generally. Space is not merely something represented to the audience, but is perceived, interacted with and explored. It exists as part of an active relationship that is far more complex than at first it appears. Furthermore, spatial analysis provides an opposition to the dominant Cartesian cognitive position, which maintains that perception takes place in the mind. As an understanding of haptics and embodied spectatorship illustrates, this is not always the case. Perception takes place across the whole body, often before it goes through a process of mental cognition. Thus, spatial readings should take into consideration a multifaceted approach to analysis.

Notes

1. Wagner was not the first to use the term, which has been attributed to K. F. E. Trahndorf's essay of 1827. This chapter's use of the term will be derived from Wagner's use that was discussed in the following texts: Richard Wagner, *Art and Revolution*, trans. William Ashton Ellis (Gloucester: Dodo Press, 2008). The original essay was published in 1849; Richard Wagner, *Richard Wagner's Prose Works VI: The Artwork of the Future (1895)*, trans. William Ashton Ellis (Whitefish: Kessinger Publishing, 2008). The original was published in 1849.
2. Subsequent references to *Billy the Kid and the Green Baize Vampire* will also be as *Billy the Kid*.
3. The degree of this variation within the musical spectrum will be the subject of later work. The current book is aimed at first assessing the spatial field of the musical genre in terms of abstract aesthetics before further work can be done.
4. Subsequent references to *Umbrellas of Cherbourg* will also be as *Umbrellas*.
5. Altman, *The American Film Musical*, p. 19.
6. Altman, *The American Film Musical*, p. 19.
7. Altman, *The American Film Musical*, p. 21.
8. Altman, *The American Film Musical*, p. 21.
9. Altman, *The American Film Musical*, p. 27.
10. Winters, "The Non-diegetic Fallacy: Film, Music, and Narrative Space," p. 224.

11. Winters, "The Non-diegetic Fallacy: Film, Music, and Narrative Space," p. 229. When narrative is the primary focus of analysis, Winters' piece is particularly useful for its consideration of the interaction between sound and image. Winters' recent exploration of the different realms of diegetic space, particularly in terms of how it is shared between audience and performer, offers a development of his argument: one that is not inherently restricted to narrative readings. See Ben Winters, *Music, Performance, and the Realities of Film: Shared Concert Experiences in Screen Fiction* (London: Routledge, 2014).
12. Egon Wellesz, *Essays on Opera*, trans. Patricia Kean (London: Dennis Dobson LTD, 1950), p. 123.
13. Wellesz, p. 123.
14. Wellesz, p. 106.
15. Wellesz, p. 106. There is a small body of work that has looked at the relationship between film and opera, for examples, see: Jeremy Tambling, *Opera, Ideology and Film* (Manchester: Manchester University Press, 1987); David Schroeder, *Cinema's Illusions, Opera's Allure: The Operatic Impulse in Film* (London: Continuum, 2002); Marcia J. Citron, *Opera on Screen* (New Haven: Yale University Press, 2000); Jeongwon Joe, *Opera as Soundtrack* (Burlington: Ashgate, 2013).
16. Lorenzo Bianconi, and Giorgio Pestelli, (eds), *Opera in Theory and Practice, Image and Myth*, trans. by Kenneth Chalmers and Mary Whittall. Vol. 6, *The History of Italian Opera* (Chicago: The University of Chicago Press, 2003), p. 16.
17. Many theorists throughout the history of Film Studies have attempted to deal with the issues inherent to realism. A good starting point for a broad introduction to the debates can be found in Leo Braudy and Marshall Cohen, (eds), *Film Theory and Criticism*, 6th edn (Oxford: Oxford University Press, 2004). Here a number of seminal essays by theorists such as André Bazin, Siegfried Kracauer, and Noel Carroll et al. can be found.
18. Robert Donington, *Opera and Its Symbols: The Unity of Words, Music, and Staging* (London: Yale University Press, 1990), p. 5.
19. Donington, p. 5.
20. Donington, pp. 5–6.
21. Donington, pp. 5–6.
22. Donington, p. 9.

23. Donington, p. 10.
24. Donington, p. 13.
25. Donington, p. 189.
26. Sam Abel, *Opera in the Flesh: Sexuality in Operatic Performance* (Oxford: Westview Press, 1996).
27. Abel, p. 5.
28. Abel, p. 5.
29. Abel, p. 17.
30. Abel, pp. 20–21.
31. Abel, p. 32.
32. One has only to look at a local art house cinema to see that live opera performances are streamed into cinemas with subtitles on screen, or at regional theatres that host opera companies such as the Welsh National Opera, to see that subtitling is provided.
33. Abel, p. 32.
34. Richard Wagner, *Art and Revolution*. Originally published in 1849.
35. Abel, p. 33.
36. Abel, p. 33.
37. Abel, p. 35.
38. Richard Wagner, *Opera and Drama* 1852 <http://users.belgacom.net/wagnerlibrary/prose/wlpr0063.htm#d0e1920> [date accessed 18/11/2013].
39. Stephen Moss, "A-Z of Wagner: G is for *Gesamtkunstwerk*", *The Guardian*, 18th April 2013, [accessed 18/11/2013].; See also Adrian Daub, *Tristan's Shadow: Sexuality and the Total Work of Art after Wagner* (Chicago: University of Chicago Press, 2013) for more information of Wagner's ideas of the 'total work of art' and how they can be seen in the aesthetics of opera.
40. Scott D. Paulin, "Richard Wagner and the Fantasy of the Cinematic Unity: The Idea of the *Gesamkunstwerk* in the History and Theory of Film Music", in James Buhler, Caryl Flinn, and David Neumeyer, (eds), *Music and Cinema* (Hanover: University Press of New England, 2000), 58–84, (p. 59).
41. Paulin, p. 59. It is not the subject of this book to attempt to analyse film music's form and function on a universal level, to attempt to delineate film music from film sound, or indeed to analyse its changing forms across generic borders—however porous they may be. This notwithstanding, a distinction must be made

between film music on a broad level and that used in the musical genre. As such, I make no claim that the use of Wagner's *Gesamtkunstwerk* in the musical would be true of all film music. See Jeongwon Joe and Sander L. Gilman, (eds), *Wagner and Cinema* (Bloomington: Indiana University Press, 2010) for more information regarding academic literature on Wagner's influence on the cinema.
42. Benjamin, pp. 791–811.
43. Paulin, p. 60.
44. Paulin, p. 60; Wagner, *Opera and Drama*, in *Richard Wagner's Prose Works*, p. 8.
45. Paulin, p. 60.
46. Paulin, p. 61.
47. Paulin, p. 61.
48. Paulin, p. 61.
49. James Buhler, Caryl Flinn, David Neumeyer, (eds), *Music and Cinema* (Middletown: Wesleyan University Press, 2000), p. 59.
50. Paulin, p. 62.
51. Paulin, p. 62.
52. Schroeder, pp. 6–7.
53. Schroeder, pp. 6–7.
54. Wagner, *Opera and Drama 1852*.
55. Bianconi, p. 29.
56. Winton Dean, *Essays on Opera* (Oxford: Clarendon Press, 1990), p. 78.
57. Tambling, p. 47.
58. Tambling, p. 23.
59. Reinhard G. Pauly, *Music and the Theatre: An Introduction to Opera* (New Jersey: Prentice-Hall, Inc., 1970), p. 14.
60. Laura U. Marks, "Information, Secrets, and Enigmas: An Enfolding-Unfolding Aesthetics for Cinema", *Screen*, 50 (2009), 86–98. (87).
61. Marks, p. 86.
62. Marks, p. 86.
63. Marks, p. 87.
64. Marks, p. 88.
65. Marks, p. 89; Charles Sanders Peirce, "The Principles of Phenomenology" in Justus Buchler, (ed.), *Philosophical Writings of Peirce* (New York, NY: Dover, 1955), pp. 74–97.

66. Marks, p. 87.
67. There is also a lack of theorising of Marks' ideas of enfolding-unfolding aesthetics with regards to sound.
68. This book does not explore the work of Gilles Deleuze. Whilst he is an important theorist for Film Studies and for image and movement more specifically, his ocularcentric approach does not parallel mine. He does, however, provide ideas to be explored at a later date. See: Gilles Deleuze, *Cinema 1: The Movement Image* (London: Athlone, 1986); Gilles Deleuze, *Cinema 2: The Time Image* (New York: Continuum, 2005); Gilles Deleuze and Felix Guttari, *A Thousand Plateaus: Capitalism and Schizophrenia*, trans by Brian Massumi, (Minneapolis: University of Minnesota Press, 1987).
69. Anne Rutherford, "Cinema and Embodied Affect", in *Senses of Cinema* (2003). <http://sensesofcinema.com/2003/feature-articles/embodied_affect/>[date accessed 09/07/2013].
70. Rutherford.
71. Thomas Ots, "The Silenced Body—The Expressive *Leib*: On the Dialectic of Mind and Life in Chinese Cathartic Healing", in Thomas Csordas, (ed.), *Embodiment and Experience: The Existential Ground of Culture and Self* (Cambridge: Cambridge University Press, 1994), p. 117.
72. Rutherford.
73. Rutherford.
74. Rutherford.
75. Jonathan Crary, *Techniques of the Observer: On Vision and Modernity in the 19th Century*, (Cambridge, Mass. & London: MIT Press, 1990), p. 45.
76. Rutherford; Crary, p. 45.
77. Rutherford.
78. Rutherford.
79. Peter Brooks, "Melodrama, Body, Revolution", in J. Bratton et al. (eds.), *Melodrama: Stage—Picture—Screen*, (London: BFI, 1994); Rutherford.
80. Rutherford.
81. Linda Williams, "Body Genres", *Film Quarterly* 44: 4, Summer, 1991.
82. Rutherford.
83. Rutherford.

84. "FAQ-ROP", Vision Research: ROPARD Foundation <http://www.ropard.org/ropard-home/information-for-parents/faq-rop> [date accessed 12/03/2014].
85. Rutherford; Mary-Ann Doane, "When the direction of the force acting on the body is changed: The moving image", *Wide Angle*, 7: 1 & 2, 1985, p. 61.
86. James J. Gibson, *The Ecological Approach to Visual Perception*, (Boston et al.: Houghton Mifflin & Co., 1979), p. 183.
87. Gibson, p. 183.
88. Gibson, p. 183; Rutherford.
89. Gibson, p. 183.
90. Sue Cataldi, *Emotion, Depth, and Flesh: A Study of Sensitive Space: Reflections on Merleau-Ponty's Philosophy of Embodiment*, (Albany: State University of New York Press, 1993), p. 109.; Rutherford.
91. Rutherford.
92. Cataldi, p. 115.
93. Glen A. Mazis, *Emotion and Embodiment: A Fragile Ontology*. (New York: Peter Lang Publishing Inc., 1993), pp. 29–30.
94. Rutherford.
95. Rutherford.
96. Rutherford.
97. Rutherford.
98. Dave Rolinson, "The World Within a Frame", Commemorative Booklet, *Billy the Kid and the Green Baize Vampire*, 2006 release, UK, Network.
99. See Feuer, *The Hollywood Musical*.
100. See http://www.cinemetrics.lv/cinemetrics.php for more information regarding Cinemetrics [Accessed 13/08/2013].
101. Stilwell, "The Fantastical Gap between Diegetic and Nondiegetic", p. 186.
102. Stilwell, "The Fantastical Gap between Diegetic and Nondiegetic", p. 187.

CHAPTER 6

What Next?

At the start of this book I made it clear that there was one overarching emphasis; namely, understanding and analysing the representation of space and promoting it as a valid methodological approach in Film Studies. I have always felt that the best way of achieving this was by focusing on a single generic case study, namely the musical, despite my belief that such an approach could and should be applied more widely to film, paying attention to any potential generic, national, auteurist, etc. idiosyncrasies.

The processes I have used to attempt to accomplish the promotion of this spatial methodology are multifaceted and so too are the inherent difficulties, particularly if one considers the particulars of the chosen case study. One example of this is the need to understand and assess the representation of space during song sequences.[1] This is a result of the wider theorising on the musical genre being concerned more with narrative-centric readings focusing predominantly on visual representation. Such hegemonic theorising has recently taken a turn towards re-evaluating canonical musicals in light of alternative readings.[2] Whilst this provides fecund scholarship, which adds much to the study of the musical genre, particularly in terms of providing social and cultural relevance, it omits a deeper understanding of the aesthetics of film language. Put simply, when such discourses are used, any analysis of film language is almost solely restricted to understanding how it aids and supports a particular narrative reading (be it a feminist, Marxist or a queer theory reading, amongst others). Such a mode of film theory not only presupposes that the narrative is the dominant aspect of musicals (and indeed films more widely) for theorists, but, furthermore, for audiences too.[3] As made clear in Chapter 1, I am not disavowing such narrative readings, but rather seeking to provide an alternative methodology that, when followed, challenges the dominance of narrative in Film Studies whilst providing original and interesting results. By removing the focus on narrative a dominant framework for understanding film language has been lifted, thus permitting a variety of readings that would otherwise be impossible.

Furthermore, my particular focus on spatial analysis enables an exploration into the interactions between the space of the musical number and audiences; a relationship that has multiple implications for understanding musicals and films more widely. Indeed, by highlighting an analysis of both sound and image and their symbiotic relationship, one can not only begin to understand the space of musical numbers more accurately, but also illustrate the importance of understanding the audio-visual nature of musicals; an aspect all too often overlooked. A particular focus on musical numbers, rather than whole musicals, further encourages a renunciation of narrative; for not only does it assist in a re-evaluation of the formal structure of musicals—namely the emphasis on spectacle—but it also enables a closer analysis of the key aspect of the genre, specifically the interaction between sounds and images.

Though in this book I have taken the musical genre as a case study, I am concerned with the promotion of this spatial methodology more widely. In films existing outside the musical's generic spectrum, musical numbers could be replaced most obviously with scenes that have a focus on spectacle, whether this is an explosion in an action film, or a tense attack in a horror film. Although this does not have to be the case, indeed any film can be read using this spatial approach. This book has been my attempt to move the discussion in a new direction; as such it is incomplete, at times speculative and not always fully implemented. What I have suggested, however, are the theoretical tools you might use, the considerations you would have to be attuned to, and how they might be brought together. It is my strong hope that others will continue the discussion, challenge the ideas and suggest alternatives.

In this concluding chapter I want to address a number of areas: firstly, an examination of the approaches that I have adopted alongside other potential avenues that I could have taken. Secondly, how the work in this book could be fruitfully placed alongside other scholarship. Thirdly, I want some discussion of where I hope others will take this work and how it might be engaged with.

In order to provide a methodological approach to the examination of the representation of space, I used forensic analysis. With the removal of an overarching narrative framework my focus thus became the abstract aesthetics of film style when explored through the lens of space. The intention of providing an alternative reading to narrative resulted in another principal framework being imposed: space. The term 'abstract aesthetics' is in many respects misleading and open to misinterpretation. A true exploration into abstract aesthetics would require the elimination of any central framework, be it space or narrative, and I can only hazard a guess at what the findings might be, or, indeed, how they would be interpreted. The lens of space therefore becomes an alternative interpretive model to narrative. The justification for the use of the term 'abstract aesthetics', despite the possibility of its misleading the reader, is due to my abandonment of hegemonic readings when analysing elements of film language. In short, though not abstract in the strictest sense, I have used it ironically to refer to the apparent understanding that there are no readings outside that of narrative.

The use of forensic analysis promotes a return to close textual analysis of films and an understanding of their formal construction. It encourages film style to be the focus of an analysis, rather than in the service of an already formed understanding. One might query how many theorists begin their analysis of a particular film with an interpretation already in mind, only subsequently examining film style to support their reading rather than using it as the starting point to understanding. As so little has been written about spatial understanding of films, its theoretical framework—or 'shorthand'—has not been developed: you do not start with a spatial understanding of a film, but rather discover it through forensic analysis.

The forensic analysis used is multifaceted so that its usefulness for a variety of readings can be clearly demonstrated. Any new framework, in this case spatial understanding, necessitates different ways of looking at data in order to aid in interpretation. More established forms of close analysis notwithstanding, including shot-by-shot analysis and tabulations, it was essential that close analysis be developed in new ways: one such example includes the use of virtual reconstructions.[4] The motivation for creating these virtual reconstructions and using them in the study of musical numbers was threefold. Firstly, it was an attempt to introduce new uses of software to the study of musicals (and film more widely). One of the paradoxes of Film Studies is that theorists, this book being a case in point, must discuss moving images and heard sounds using only words and few images, particularly in terms of publications: static descriptions of a very un-static artistic medium. The introduction of animated modes of the presentation of data enables different forms of interpretation, not least due to the ability of the animation to reveal what static images cannot: the movement of the camera and performers within the set design or filmed location, and the relationship between them as seen, in the case of those in this study, from a static 'bird's-eye view'.

This undoubtedly links to the second reason; namely, analysis should be making more use of the developments in computing technology to aid the examination of film language. Although one could place this within the larger move towards digital media and, more particularly, the digitisation of the film industry, the desire of this book was more particularly to make a positive impact towards not only bringing film theory up to date, but moving it into new and innovative areas. As a cultural industry and an art form, film's place seems assured, though changing in form and function. It therefore follows that Film Studies should create new forms of analysis that not only utilises the possibilities now open to it in terms of software, but challenges other disciplines to do the same. Animated virtual reconstructions are my attempt at challenging traditional Film Studies analysis and moving it forward into new territory.[5] The virtual reconstructions are in the early stages of development, however, and further discussions as to their usefulness and uses needs to be had by myself and others.

Thirdly, notwithstanding the need to 'update' Film Studies, there is much to be said about the presentation of data enabling new readings. The virtual reconstructions were compiled through the positing together of the different aspects of film language, be they camera angles, editing or sound. As such, new examples of film language were not revealed; however, by presenting known data in original ways, new relationships between the different elements can begin to be discovered. These virtual reconstructions are not meant to offer all-encompassing data for an analysis of the musical sequences (indeed, as I mentioned previously, they are very much in their aesthetic infancy), but rather to be an aid to understanding the constantly changing formation of space. I want to briefly turn to the specific examples used in order to discuss their usefulness in the study of space, the problems that arose in their creation and indeed how they can be developed further in future.

I have used three virtual reconstructions, each focusing on a specific musical number: 'Fancy Free' from *Top Hat*, 'Supersonic Sam's Cosmic

Café' from *Billy the Kid and the Green Baize Vampire*, and 'The Mechanics Sequence' from *Umbrellas of Cherbourg*. The particular choice of these numbers for the virtual reconstruction is, however, another matter. It was important to demonstrate a different aspect of filmic space with each virtual reconstruction, hence not only their appearance in two different chapters, but also their slightly different emphasis. Due to *Top Hat*'s context—relevant to which is not only the historical period in which it was made, but also the subsequent technical limitations and developments that arose from this—and the performance style of Fred Astaire, it became clear that the key aspect of space to be examined more closely with the help of the virtual reconstructions was the performers' interaction with the wider mise-en-scène and the camera. Consequently, though there is much to be said about the interaction between sound and image within this number and reconstruction, the focus was on visual elements almost exclusively. One reason for this is due to the slower rate of editing. Chapter 3 demonstrates that a film such as *Dancer in the Dark* proved impossible for a virtual reconstruction with the time and resources available due to the high speed of editing and lack of spatial coherence (as discovered through the initial attempt to virtually reconstruct the 'Cvalda' number).[6]

Whilst recognising that Astaire and Roger's nine film collaborations at RKO during the 1930s are not just exemplars of the musical genre in the classical period, but rather still remarkable canonical films, they do highlight a number of spatial tropes existing within the genre. One such example is the medium-long shot of the dancing performer(s). In 'Fancy Free', once Astaire has started his tap dance, the camera moves from the previous position it has taken (a series of medium shots of Astaire's face and upper torso) to the more regular use of a medium-long shot. As Jane Feuer argues in *The Hollywood Musical*, this front on positioning of the camera, allowing the non-diegetic audience the best view of the performer, is akin to that of the theatrical audience.[7] Feuer's work on the seemingly spontaneous creation of proscenium arches in order to create an interchange between consummate professional and amateur is important to the spatial relationship with the audience.

Such a negotiation between professional/amateur and the spectator often results in a front-on view for the audience, permitting the creation of a shared space. This shared space, although replicating that of the theatre in which the filmic audience takes the place of the diegetic theatrical audience, does not have to be so detached. The space between audience and performer, though shared in such front on instances, has the possible result of an 'othering'. The audience is not the performer (however amateur or professional the presentation may be) and though there is a shared space, it comes with the caveat of distinct roles. This is, however, a reductive view that fails to take into account the transformative power of sound. The sonic geography of the scenes, particularly with the move away from stereo sound towards multi-channel sound technologies, although maintaining the role distinction between audience and performer, enables an 'immersion' that was previously only hinted at in primarily a visual way. Put simply, cinema sound that permits a more varied sonic geography with various acoustic sources (i.e. speakers in the cinema), subverts the front on nature of the proscenium arch. If the sound the audience experiences in the cinema no longer chimes with the visuals presenting an orchestra, singer or performer in front of them, then the shared space is further complicated.

The front-on view of the performer is further challenged when the audience is permitted a changing view, one more in line with the immersive sonic realm they have the ability to experience. This changeability is aptly demonstrated by Lars von Trier's *Dancer in the Dark* in which the camera is frequently handheld, the editing rate though variable, is high, and the camera angle is often impossible to replicate in the theatre. Thus the audience is offered a more 'immersive', but paradoxically, less possible visual space; they are able to move within the action of the number often never establishing one singular point of view. A consequence of this paradoxical space, which is not only impossible in the theatre but also in 'real life', is that sound provides grounding through its near constant presence.

In the second virtual reconstruction, from *Umbrellas of Cherbourg*, it was important to focus upon sound and its relationship to the image; to understand the scene in an audio-visual manner. A different type of musical than *Top Hat* and *Billy the Kid and the Green Baize Vampire*, *Umbrellas of Cherbourg* has a near constant musical score. In the opening scene the audience is immediately confronted with characters that are singing alongside each other. There has been no establishing of narrative before this point and no traditional moment of 'audio-dissolve'. It was important for this virtual reconstruction to demonstrate who was singing at any given moment and their relationship to the camera, particularly as sonically there is much information for the audience to synthesise. As Chapter 5 demonstrates, there is a change in the volume of the instrumental music each time a character sings. A consequence of this is that the instrumental music alone is not a reliable gauge of proxemics. Subsequently, analysing both the scene and the virtual reconstruction with a view to its audio-visual relationship was crucial.

The final virtual reconstruction was from *Billy the Kid and the Green Baize Vampire*. Like *Umbrellas of Cherbourg*, this virtual reconstruction was again used to highlight audio-visual spatial relationships. The emphasis of this reconstruction, however, was to highlight the role of the journalist in negotiating the audio-visual space. Both the music and the camerawork in the number are repetitive, thus by demonstrating this with the virtual reconstruction, one can begin to analyse how embodied spectatorship and negotiated spatial realms can be achieved in a musical number that offers very little variation.

In this book I have attempted many approaches to both understanding and analysing space, ranging from the aforementioned animated virtual reconstructions, to proxemic analysis, close shot-by-shot analysis, cinemetrics and spectrographs. Though these demonstrate that there are a range of methods for exploring spatial representation, they have been utilised with a view to understanding space on a theoretical level and are, as such, not the only approach that could have been taken. Though I discuss technological issues, it is not the subject of this book. It would be a fruitful avenue to explore further, however. The objective of this study was first to provide an overarching assessment and an initial methodological approach for understanding the representation of space in musical numbers before examining how technological developments affected said spatial relationships. It was for this reason that a particular sub-genre or period of the musical genre was not looked at more specifically. Once tropes and spatial representations were found, future research could scrutinise the more particular arrangements of each period or formal structure upon the wider musical spectrum.

Though there is much still to discover with regards to the representation of space in musical numbers, paying particular attention to the interaction between sound and image, this research has achieved a number of aspects that should have an impact on Film Studies generally, and more specifically the study of the musical genre. I have illustrated that a non-narrative based approach is not only possible, but can be achieved in numerous ways. Furthermore, the study has demonstrated that by using space as an overarching framework, new understandings of aesthetics and musical numbers more widely can be found. Moreover, it has shown that by using a spatial analysis, the researcher has a number of tools in their arsenal that will take Film Studies' analysis into the computer era.

I have built upon the theoretical approaches regarding space used by the Affrons and C. S. Tashiro and taken them further. Although the former were more particularly interested in mise-en-scène, with the latter also bringing in aspects of framing to his analysis, they all have stopped short at examining the implications for the relationship between the audience and cinematic space. By framing such a negotiation of shared space within the wider work of embodiment, by theorists such as Vivian Sobchack and Anne Rutherford, I have attempted to provide an analysis of space that is less reductive. Not only does it move away from a sole focus on mise-en-scène and framing, it has purposefully advanced theories of embodied spectatorship into the realm of sound and music. The musical, as is film more widely, is an audio-visual medium and should be understood and examined as such.

As a result of the findings of this book there are a number of implications for the study of the musical genre and filmic space. The first stems from this study's understanding of the genre as existing along a spectrum; a topology rather than a taxonomy. Genre theory has long been a dominant theoretical framework within Film Studies and the musical, despite being an archetypal genre, has often been overlooked in genre analysis due to the genre's inability to provide easy adherence. Despite the venerable work by theorists such as Rick Altman, who has made active attempts at understanding the musical's formal structure within the larger framework of genre theory, most critical work on the genre seeks not to explore its position as a genre but rather begins with the assumption that it is an agreed-upon category. Whilst in this book I am not arguing that the musical is not a genre, I would claim that it does not fit unproblematically into categorisations, be it industrial, production or theoretical. By understanding the musical genre as a topological spectrum, easy generic categorisation and understanding is arguable further problematised; particularly when one sees that films that were once not considered under the musical paradigm now can be. It is, however, not my desire to provide easy answers. Indeed, in many respects I take issue with theoretical approaches that attempt to do so.

By removing the dominant theoretical framework of narrative, the ability of analysis to provide easy answers has been further reduced. Whilst no analysis is straightforward, the understanding of 'easy answers' here refers to those already known before the analytical breakdown takes place. Again the issue of how many theorists already know their findings before acquiring support for their arguments is returned to. I wanted to move away from these approaches and favour one where findings and understanding may only come after analysis has taken place. It is not by chance that narrative has become one of the dominant theoretical models for film analysis, for it enables a guaranteed interpretation based upon the theorist's individual approach, be it Marxist, Feminist or any other. A spatial reading, conversely, offers uncertainty; what purpose can space play if not to aid the narrative? Once one stops attempting to understand narrative, and more specifically in this case spatial representation and its effect on narrative, one can begin to understand its other effects on the audience. This study has taken a gestalt approach to understanding musicals, which undoubtedly favours audience perception and comprehension.

Though gestalt theory has been all but lost to Film Studies, due to the supremacy of cognitivism, it can still offer much, particularly in relation to spatial understanding free from narrative influence.[8] Like spatial analysis, gestalt theory cannot offer easy answers; undoubtedly a factor in its lack of theoretical prevalence. Gestalt's primary mantra is that 'the whole is more than the sum of the parts'; alternatively, cognitivism is founded upon an understanding of the organising principles of sensory perception; the stimulus does not issue a response rather the organisation of the stimuli does.[9] The stimulus is, therefore, mediated in order to illicit understanding.

By analysing the representation of space and its effect on audiences, theories of spatial interaction thus become valuable, particularly those relating to the haptics and embodied spectatorship. Through their use it is clear that they pose a threat to the hegemony of the Cartesian cognitive position; by focusing on the body's reaction to spatial perception, the supplementary position of the body in film theory is challenged. Furthermore, as Vivian Sobchack has identified, a claim often levelled at phenomenological film theory is that it is too subjective. [10]

This has been my attempt to make an active contribution towards rectifying this critical position. By illustrating how theories of embodied spectatorship can not only be objective, but also deliver profound readings that provide understanding into audience perception of space, I have demonstrated that the dichotomous relationship between the body and the mind should be reconsidered. No longer should it be the case that cognitivism and narration should be the unquestioned de facto hegemonic tools at the film theorist's disposal. Though, like with narrative, I am not asserting that cognitivism should be avoided, I do maintain that there are other theoretical avenues that should be explored and both cognitivism and narration should not be used as if they were without issue. This becomes particularly significant when you consider that cognitivism's essential belief in the status of the mind is challenged by the body's ability to react instinctively, without 'mental mediation'.

A further desired consequence of this study is to establish a sensory approach to film theory into the mainstream. Despite a growing body of work by theorists, such as Laura Marks, Jennifer M. Barker, Anne Rutherford, et al, a sensory approach to Film Studies is still relatively marginal. This book demonstrates that the theoretical approaches of sensory-based film theory can be used to provide new and innovative readings of film that challenges the dominant theoretical order. Indeed, as this book's title suggests, I have promoted the idea that a spatial reading of film is best understood through the senses; that audiences feel space, even negotiate and participate in its construction and representation.

The desire to challenge the current hegemony is further exemplified by my use of a cross-disciplinary approach as typified by utilising theories found within Opera Studies and Anthropology for instance, the latter relating to theories of proxemics. A result of the introduction of the new theoretical framework to filmic analysis of abstract aesthetics, within this study it is space and the senses, is the requirement of openness to theoretical avenues not traditionally related to Film Studies. If new opportunities for scholarly discourse are not introduced into the discipline, as is true of any discipline, then calcification occurs. It is therefore essential to bring to the study of film new modes of analysis. Whilst within every discipline there is a degree of self-protectionism—a delineation of space that is unique to that subject alone—there is much that other subject areas can offer, be it methodological or theoretical approaches. Theories of opera have long been concerned with the relationship between the various constituent parts: libretto, musical composition and set design, amongst others. The analysis of the relationship between these various different elements has often been put into the service of narrative. Thus, though there is little crossover between those studying film musicals and those studying opera, the same preoccupations can be found in both disciplines. By introducing theories found in the study of opera to a spatial analysis of the film musical, a better emphasis can be placed upon sound.

Despite opera's preoccupation with narrative, or 'drama' since the seminal work of Richard Wagner, a rudimentary element of opera is understood to be sound. Though there is much debate as to the role that sound should play, particularly with regards to the breakdown between libretto and musical score, there is a fundamental understanding that music and sound are at the heart of the art form; arguably the most important element, essential to opera. Theoretical discourse on the film musical, however, often omits sound. There is a growing body of scholarly work on sound in cinema. Though these offer a range of findings, and often provide fundamental challenges to the understanding of canonical films that had previously developed through visual analysis, they often state explicitly that they offer sound and music analysis of films. There is an understanding that these are deliberate attempts to study sound and music by specialists, it is not yet part of the general vernacular of every film scholar as it should be. It is hoped that one day every film scholar will analyse film's audio-visual nature, rather than having a delineated theoretical sect that dedicates their time to it.

Anthropology's theory of proxemics, not only provided a methodological approach for analysing space, but enabled a continuation of close filmic analysis as promoted by this study. Edward T. Hall's numerous tables and graphs to aid in the recording of space, demonstrated that by recording spatial data in a new way and applying it to a new medium could reveal much about space and audiences' perception of it. An important point to note at this junction is that this recording of space is two-pronged. Whilst his tabulations provide a means of recording the different uses of space, for instance the spatial interaction between Astaire and Rogers in 'Waltz in Swing Time', they also enable the recording of perceptual space. The same can be said of the animated virtual reconstructions. As with Hall's tabulations, the virtual reconstructions enable an understanding of perceived space that, whilst distinct from the 'actual' space of the set design/location, is arguably more significant.

As previously stated, I might have taken alternative approaches for the exploration into the representation of space in musical numbers. The justification for the chosen approach, one based upon abstract aesthetics and not restricted to a particular country's/director's/sub-genre's/period's output, is that it permits an assessment of the spatial tropes found within the wider genre. This notwithstanding, there are a number of implications for future research that arise from this and I hope others will pursue. As this book has established methodological approaches for the analysis of filmic space, future research might build upon its findings and turn its attention to how, for instance, technological developments within different historical periods change the perception and representation of space. One can imagine that the development of the Steadicam, digital technologies and the resurgence of 3D amongst other technological developments, alters in various ways the representation of space within musical numbers and film more widely. Culturally diverse paradigms should also be explored. Although I have not restricted myself to the Hollywood musical, I have also not had the opportunity and space to investigate whether the musicals of different national cinemas vary spatially and whether there are recurring tropes. Further research may well turn to a re-exploration and re-appraisal of more traditional forms of analysis, for instance: what might be discovered if a particular auteur's films were explored using a spatial methodology? Or, indeed, how we might incorporate a spatial reading with an analysis of narrative.

The possibilities for subsequent research, which builds upon the methodological approaches developed here, are wide-ranging. Perhaps the most obvious of them all, however, is the expansion away from the musical, or any genre specific study, and into Film Studies more generally. I have explored musical numbers in order to demonstrate how spatial readings can be achieved; future research need not be so restricted. A spatial methodology is robust enough to be up to the challenge of being applied to any filmic examples, whether they focus on a particular director's oeuvre, a filmic period, a country's output or indeed a combination thereof. A spatial reading is both thorough enough to be applied to single films and robust enough to be adapted to fit the specific needs of the individual scholar.

My aim here has been to demonstrate what we are left with when we remove narrative readings. This is of course based upon the understanding that we react to and read films on multiple levels: though we follow the narrative, we also simultaneously appreciate the film on an aesthetic audio-visual level. A spatial reading, understood through the senses, is the best way of understanding, exploring and analysing this parallel aesthetic realm.

Notes

1. Other genres undoubtedly have their own peculiarities, whether this is an example of violence in the horror genre or fight scenes in martial arts films. Scenes need not be spectacular, however. Indeed, however mundane the scene (or film) it can be analysed using a

spatial methodology. Scenes with a focus on spectacle, however, offer more obvious examples and help with my need for clarity.
2. See Cohan, *The Sound of Musicals*. Chapters include: Rick Altman, "From Homosocial to Homosexual: The Musical's Two Projects", pp. 19–29, in which he reassess his work on the musical in terms of the establishing of heterosexual relationships, and Sean Griffin, "Bloody Mary is the Girl I love: U.S. White Liberalism vs. Pacific Islander Subjectivity in *South Pacific*", pp. 104–113, in which various political readings are evaluated.
3. It is important to restate that musicals question narrative-centred assumptions through their focus on spectacle, sound and music.
4. All virtual reconstructions used in this book were created by the University of Southampton archaeologist Matthew Harrison, details of which can be found here: "Matthew Harrison", Digital Humanities<http://digitalhumanities.soton.ac.uk/people/matthew-harrison#profile> [date accessed 21/11/2013]. These reconstructions were achieved through the help of a University of Southampton Digital Humanities grant.
5. The video essay is another form of analysis that, whilst still in relative infancy, appears to be bearing fruitful results.
6. It is the intention of future research to develop the use of animated virtual reconstructions further, at such a time a reconstruction of *Dancer in the Dark* will be attempted again.
7. Feuer, p. 26.
8. Since Rudolph Arnheim's work there have been very few theorists who have favoured gestalt theory. See Donnelly, *Occult Aesthetics*.
9. Wolfgang Kohler, *Gestalt Psychology: An Introduction to New Concepts in Modern Psychology* (New York: Liveright Publishing Company, 1947), p. 200.
10. Sobchack, *Carnal Thoughts: Embodiment and Moving Image Culture*, pp. 59–60.

Bibliography

Abel, Sam. 1996. *Opera in the Flesh: Sexuality in Operatic Performance*. Oxford: Westview Press.
Affron, Charles. 1995. *Sets in Motion*. New Brunswick: Rutgers University Press.
Altman, Rick. 1981. *Genre: The Musical*. London: Routledge.
———. 1989. *The American Film Musical*. Bloomington: Indiana University Press.
———. 1992. Sound Space. In *Sound Theory, Sound Practice*. New York: Routledge.
———. 1999. *Film/Genre*. London: BFI.
———. 2002. The American Film Musical as Dual-Focus Narrative. In *Hollywood Musicals: The Film Reader*, ed. Steven Cohan, 41–52. London: Routledge.
———. 2010. From Homosocial to Homosexual: The Musical's Two Projects. In *The Sound of Musicals*, ed. Steven Cohan, 19–29. Basingstoke: Palgrave Macmillan.
Andrew, J. D. 1984. *Concepts in Film Theory*. Oxford: Oxford University Press.
Arnheim, Rudolf. 1986. *New Essays on the Psychology of Art*. London: University of California Press.
———. 1992. *Towards a Psychology of Art: Collected Essays*. Berkeley: University of California Press.
Babington, Bruce, and Peter William Evans. 1985. *Blue Skies and Silver Linings: Aspects of the Hollywood Musical*. Manchester: Manchester University Press.
Bacci, Francesca, and David Melcher (ed). 2011. *Art and the Senses*. Oxford: Oxford University Press.
Balász, Bela. 2004. The Close up. In *Film Theory and Criticism*, 6th edn, ed. Leo Braudy, and Marshall Cohen, 314–315. Oxford: Oxford University Press.

Baldassare, Mark. 1978. Human Spatial Behavior. *Annual Review of Sociology* 4: 29–56.
Barker, Jennifer M. 2011. Touch and the Cinematic Experience. In *Art and the Senses*, ed. Francesca Bacci, and David Melcher. Oxford: Oxford University Press.
Barsacq, Léon. 1978. *Caligari's Cabinet and Other Grand Illusions: A History of Film Design*. New York: New American Library.
Beck, Jay, and Tony Grajeda (ed). 2008. *Lowering the Boom*. Urbana: University of Illinois Press.
Benjamin, Walter. 1969. The Work of Art in the Age of Mechanical Reproduction. In *Illuminations*. New York: Schoken Books.
Bergfelder, Tim, Sue Harris, and Sarah Street (ed). 2007. *Film Architecture and The Transnational Imagination*. Amsterdam: Amsterdam University Press.
Bianconi, Lorenzo, and Giorgio Pestelli, eds. 2003. *Opera in Theory and Practice, Image and Myth*. Trans. Kenneth Chalmers, and Mary Whittall. The History of Italian Opera, Vol. 6. Chicago: The University of Chicago Press.
Bordwell, David. 1985. *Narration in the Fiction Film*. Madison: University of Wisconsin Press.
———. 1988. *The Classical Hollywood Cinema*. London: Routledge.
———. 2005. *Figures Traced in Light: On Cinematic Staging*. Berkeley: University of California Press.
Bordwell, David, and Kristin Thompson. 2004. *Film Art: An Introduction*, 7th edn. London: McGraw-Hill.
Braudy, Leo. 2004. Acting: Stage vs. Screen. In *Film Theory and Criticism*, 6th edn, ed. Leo Braudy, and Marshall Cohen, 429–435. Oxford: Oxford University Press.
Braudy, Leo, and Marshall Cohen (ed). 2004. *Film Theory and Criticism*, 6th edn. Oxford: Oxford University Press.
Brooks, Peter. 1994. Melodrama, Body, Revolution. In *Melodrama: Stage—Picture—Screen*, ed. J. Bratton et al. London: BFI.
Bruno, Giuliana. 2002. *Atlas of Emotions*. New York: Verso.
Buhler, James, Caryl Flinn, and David Neumeyer (ed). 2000. *Music and Cinema*. Hanover: University Press of New England.
Carman, Taylor. 2013. Foreword. In *Phenomenology of Perception*, ed. Maurice Merleau-Ponty, vii–xvi. London: Routledge.
Cataldi, Sue. 1993. *Emotion, Depth, and Flesh: A Study of Sensitive Space: Reflections on Merleau-Ponty's Philosophy of Embodiment*. Albany: State University of New York Press.
Cavell, Stanley. 2004. Audience, Actor, and Star. In *Film Theory and Criticism*, 6th edn, ed. Leo Braudy, and Marshall Cohen, 345–347. Oxford: Oxford University Press.

Cecchi, Alessandro. 2010. Diegetic Versus Nondiegetic: A Reconsideration of the Conceptual Opposition as a Contribution to the Theory of Audiovision. *Worlds of Audiovision*. www-5.unipv.it/wav/pdf/WAV_Cecchi_2010_eng.pdf. Accessed 4 June 2011.

Charles, Carlos López. *Transduction between Image and Sound in Compositional Processes*. Mexico: Mexican Centre for Music and Sonic Arts. http://www.ems-network.org/ems09/papers/charles.pdf. Accessed 8 May 2012.

Chion, Michel. 1994. *Audio-Vision: Sound on Screen*. Trans. Claudia Gorbman. New York: Columbia University Press.

Christie, Ian. 2012. "Suitable Music": Accompaniment Practices in Early London Screen Exhibition from R. W. Paul to the Picture Palaces. In *The Sounds of the Silents in Britain*, ed. Julie Brown, and Annette Davidson, 95–110. Oxford: Oxford University Press.

Cinemetrics. http://www.cinemetrics.lv/cinemetrics.php. Accessed 18 Dec 2012.

Citron, Marcia J. 2000. *Opera on Screen*. New Haven: Yale University Press.

Cohan, Steven (ed). 2002. *Hollywood Musicals: The Film Reader*. London: Routledge.

——— (ed). 2010. *The Sound of Musicals*. Palgrave Macmillan: Basingstoke.

Condon, William S. 1979. Neonatal Entrainment and Enculturation. In *Before Speech: The Beginning of Interpersonal Communication*, ed. M. Bullowa, 131–148. New York: Cambridge University Press.

Crary, Jonathan. 1990. *Techniques of the Observer: On Vision and Modernity in the 19th Century*. Cambridge, MA: MIT Press.

Daub, Adrian. 2013. *Tristan's Shadow: Sexuality and the Total Work of Art after Wagner*. Chicago: University of Chicago Press.

Dean, Winton. 1990. *Essays on Opera*. Oxford: Clarendon Press.

Deleuze, Gilles. 1986. *Cinema 1: The Movement Image*. London: Athlone.

———. 2005. *Cinema 2: The Time Image*. New York: Continuum.

Deleuze, Gilles, and Felix Guttari. 1987. *A Thousand Plateaus: Capitalism and Schizophrenia*. Trans. Brian Massumi. Minneapolis: University of Minnesota Press.

Dilla, Geraldine P. 1924. Music-Drama: An Art Form in Four Dimensions. *Music Quarterly* X: 492–499.

Doane, Mary-Ann. 1985. When the Direction of the Force Acting on the Body is Changed: The Moving Image. *Wide Angle* 7(1–2): 42–58.

Donington, Robert. 1990. *Opera and Its Symbols: The Unity of Words, Music, and Staging*. London: Yale University Press.

Donnelly, K. J. 2007. *British Film Music and Film Musicals*. Basingstoke: Palgrave.

———.. 2014. *Occult Aesthetics: Synchronisation in Sound Film*. Oxford: Oxford University Press.

Doyle, Peter. 2005. *Echo & Reverb: Fabricating Space in Popular Music Recording 1900–1960*. Middletown: Wesleyan University Press.

Durant, Alan. 1988. Review: Unheard Melodies. *Popular Music* 7: 339–342.
Dyer, Richard. 1985. Entertainment and Utopia. In *Movies and Methods Volume 2: An Anthology*, ed. Bill Nichols, 220–232. Berkeley: University of California Press.
Ellis, W. D. 1950. *A Source Book of Gestalt Psychology*. London: Routledge.
FAQ-ROP. Vision Research: ROPARD Foundation. http://www.ropard.org/ropard-home/information-for-parents/faq-rop. Accessed 12 Mar 2014.
Feuer, Jane. 1993. *The Hollywood Musical*, 2nd edn. London: Macmillan Press.
Fischer, Lucy. 2003. *Designing Women: Cinema, Art Deco and The Female Form*. New York: Columbia University Press.
Forensic. *Oxford Dictionaries*. http://oxforddictionaries.com/definition/english/forensic. Accessed 7 Oct 2013.
Gallafent, Edward. 2002. *Astaire and Rogers*. New York: Columbia University Press.
Gibson, James J. 1979. *The Ecological Approach to Visual Perception*. Boston: Houghton Mifflin.
Goldmark, Daniel, Lawrence Kramer, and Richard Leppert (ed). 2007. *Beyond the Soundtrack: Representing Music in Cinema*. London: University of California Press.
Goldstein, E. Bruce. 2005. Pictorial Perception and Art. In *Blackwell Handbook of Sensation and Perception*, ed. E. Bruce Goldstein. Oxford: Blackwell Publishing.
Gorbman, Claudia. 1998. *Unheard Melodies*. London: BFI.
Griffin, Sean. 2010. Bloody Mary is the Girl I love: U.S. White Liberalism vs. Pacific Islander Subjectivity in South Pacific. In *The Sound of Musicals*, ed. Steven Cohan, 104–113. Basingstoke: Palgrave Macmillan.
Grimani, A. Bass Management and the LFE Channel. *Sound and Vision*. http://www.soundandvision.com/content/bass-management-and-lfe-channel. Accessed 24 Feb 2014.
Gunning, Tom. 2003. *The Silent Cinema Reader*. London: Routledge.
Hall, Edward T. 1963. A System for the Notation of Proxemic Behaviour. *American Anthropologist* 65(5): 1003–1026. New Series, Selected Papers in Method and Technique.
———.. 1965. *The Silent Language*. New York: Premier Books.
———.. 1989. *The Dance of Life*. New York: Doubleday.
Hall, Stuart, and Paddy Whannel. 1964. *The Popular Arts*. London: Hutchinson Educational.
Hammond, Michael, and Linda Ruth Williams (ed). 2006. *Contemporary American Cinema*. Maidenhead: Open University Press.
Harrison, Matthew. *Digital Humanities*. http://digitalhumanities.soton.ac.uk/people/matthew-harrison#profile. Accessed 21 Nov 2013.
Hatwell, Yvette, Arlette Streri, and Édouard Gentaz. 2003. *Touching for Knowing: Cognitive Psychology of Haptic Manual Perception*. Philadelphia: John Benjamin's Publishing.

Hediger, Heini. 1955. *Studies of the Psychology and Behaviour of Captive Animals in Zoos and Circuses*. London: Butterworth.
Holman, Tomlinson. 2007. *Surround Sound: Up and Running*. London: Taylor and Francis.
Hubbard, Phil, Rob Kitchin, and Gill Valentine (ed). 2004. *Key Thinkers on Space and Place*. London: Sage Publications.
Hyam, Hannah. 2007. *Fred and Ginger: The Astaire—Rogers Partnership 1934–1938*. Great Britain: Pen Press Publishers.
Jameson, Fredric. 1991. *Postmodernism, or, the Cultural Logic of Late Capitalism*. London: Verso.
Joe, Jeongwon. 2013. *Opera as Soundtrack*. Burlingtong: Ashgate.
Joe, Jeongwon, and Sander L. Gilman (ed). 2010. *Wagner and Cinema*. Bloomington: Indiana University Press.
Jordan, Randolph. 2005. Big Fun in My Living Room. *Squalid Infidelities 3*, May 16. http://www.synoptique.ca/core/en/articles/jordan_squalid3. Accessed 24 Feb 2014.
———. 2009. The Visible Acousmêtre: Voice, Body and Space Across the Two Versions of *Donnie Darko*. *Music, Sound and the Moving Image* 3(1): 47–70, Spring.
Katz, David. 1950. *Gestalt Psychology: Its Nature and Significance*. New York: The Ronald Press.
Kerins, Mark. 2011. *Beyond Dolby (Stereo): Cinema in the Digital Sound Age*. Bloomington: Indiana University Press.
Kohler, Wolfgang. 1947. *Gestalt Psychology: An Introduction to New Concepts in Modern Psychology*. New York: Liveright Publishing Company.
Lant, Antonia. 1995. Haptical Cinema. *October* 74: 45–73, Fall.
Lastra, James. 1992. Reading, Writing, and Representing Sound. In *Sound Theory: Sound Practice*, ed. Rick Altman, 65–86. New York: Routledge.
Lefebvre, Henri. 1993. *The Production of Space*. Trans. Donald Nicholson-Smith. Oxford: Blackwell.
Mather, George. 2011. *Essentials of Sensation and Perception*. London: Routledge.
Marks, Laura U. 2009. Information, Secrets, and Enigmas: An Enfolding-Unfolding Aesthetics for Cinema. *Screen* 50(1): 86–98.
Marshall, Bill, and Robynn Stilwell (ed). 2000. *Musicals: Hollywood and Beyond*. Exeter: Intellect Books.
Mazis, Glen A. 1993. *Emotion and Embodiment: A Fragile Ontology*. New York: Peter Lang Publishing.
McClinton, Katharine Morrison. 1986. *Art Deco: A Guide for Collectors*. New York: Clarkson N. Potter.
McLean, Adrienne. 2004. *Being Rita Hayworth: Labor, Identity, and Hollywood Stardom*. London: Rutgers University Press.
Merleau-Ponty, Maurice. 2012. *Phenemonology of Perception*. London: Routledge.

Mordden, Ethan. 1981. *The Hollywood Musical*. New York: St Martin's Press.
Morin, Edgar. 2005. *The Stars*. Minneapolis: University of Minnesota.
Moss, Stephen. 2013. A–Z of Wagner: G is for Gesamtkunstwerk. *The Guardian*, April 18. Accessed 18 Nov 2013.
Movie Measurement and Study Tools Database. http://www.cinemetrics.lv/index.php. Accessed 19 Feb 2014.
Mulvey, Laura. 1975. Visual Pleasure and Narrative Cinema. *Screen* 16(3): 6–18, Autumn.
———. 1996. *Fetishism and Curiosity*. London: BFI.
Ots, Thomas. 1994. The Silenced Body—The Expressive *Leib:* On the Dialectic of Mind and Life in Chinese Cathartic Healing. In *Embodiment and Experience: The Existential Ground of Culture and Self*, ed. Thomas Csordas, 116–136. Cambridge: Cambridge University Press.
Pallasmaa, Juhani. 1991. *The Architecture of the Image: Existential Space in Cinema*. Helsinki: Building Information Rakennustieto Oy Helsinki.
Panofsky, Erwin. 2004. Style and Medium in the Motion Pictures. In *Film Theory and Criticism*, 6th edn, ed. Leo Braudy, and Marshall Cohen, 289–303. Oxford: Oxford University Press.
Paulin, Scott D. 2000. Richard Wagner and the Fantasy of the Cinematic Unity: The Idea of the Gesamkunstwerk in the History and Theory of Film Music. In *Music and Cinema*, ed. James Buhler, Caryl Flinn, and David Neumeyer, 58–84. Hanover: University Press of New England.
Pauly, Reinhard G. 1970. *Music and the Theatre: An Introduction to Opera*. Englewood Cliffs, NJ: Prentice-Hall.
Peirce, Charles Sanders. 1955. The Principles of Phenomenology. In *Philosophical Writings of Peirce*, ed. Justus Buchler, 74–97. New York: Dover.
Reay, Pauline. 2004. *Music in Film*. London: Wallflower.
Recommended Guidelines for Presentation Quality and Theatre Performance for Indoor Theatres. 2000. http://www.film-tech.com/warehouse/manuals/TAPGUIDELINES.pdf. Accessed 10 Sept 12.
Rolinson, Dave. The World Within a Frame. Commemorative Booklet. *Billy the Kid and the Green Baize Vampire*. 2006 release, UK, Network.
Rubin, Martin. 1993. *Busby Berkeley and the Tradition of Spectacle*. New York: Columbia University Press.
Rutherford, Anne. 2003. Cinema and Embodied Affect. In *Senses of Cinema*. http://sensesofcinema.com/2003/feature-articles/embodied_affect/. Accessed 9 July 2013.
Sacks, Oliver. 2006. The Power of Music. *Brain: A Journal of Neurology* 129: 2528–2532.
Schroeder, David. 2002. *Cinema's Illusions, Opera's Allure: The Operatic Impulse in Film*. London: Continuum.

Sedgewick, H.A. 2005. Visual Space Perception. In *Blackwell Handbook of Sensation and Perception*, ed. E. Bruce Goldstein, 128–167. Oxford: Blackwell Publishing.
Sergi, Gianluca. 2004. *The Dolby Era*. New York: Manchester University Press.
Shiffrar, Maggie. 2005. Movement and Event Perception. In *Blackwell Handbook of Sensation and Perception*, ed. E. Bruce Goldstein, 272–310. Oxford: Blackwell Publishing.
Shore, Brad. 1998. *Culture in Mind: Cognition, Culture and the Problem of Meaning*. Oxford: Oxford University Press.
Smith, Jeff. 2009. Bridging the Gap: Reconsidering the Border Between Diegetic and Nondiegetic Music. *Music and the Moving Image* 2(1): 1–25, Spring.
Sobchack, Vivian. 1991. *The Address of the Eye: A Phenomenology of Film Experience*. Princeton: Princeton University Press.
———. 2004. *Carnal Thoughts: Embodiment and Moving Image Culture*. London: University of California Press.
Staiger, Janet. 1989. Reception Studies: The Death of the Reader. In *The Cinematic Text: Methods and Approaches*, ed. R. Barton Palmer, 353–367. New York: AMS Press.
Stilwell, Robynn J. 2001. Sound and Empathy: Subjectivity, Gender and the Cinematic Soundscape. In *Film Music: Critical Approaches*, ed. K. J. Donnelly, 167–187. New York: Continuum.
———. 2007. The Fantastical Gap between Diegetic and Non-Diegetic. In *Beyond the Soundtrack: Representing Music in Cinema*, ed. Daniel Goldmark, Lawrence Kramer, and Richard Leppert, 184–202. London: University of California Press.
Tambling, Jeremy. 1987. *Opera, Ideology and Film*. Manchester: Manchester University Press.
Tashiro, C.S. 1998. *Pretty Pictures: Production Design and The History Film*. Austin: University of Texas Press.
Théberge, Paul. 2008. Almost Silent: The Interplay of Sound and Silence in Contemporary Cinema and Television. In *Lowering the Boom*, ed. Jay Beck, and Tony Grajeda, 51–67. Urbana: University of Illinois Press.
The Image. *Oxford English Dictionary*. http://www.oed.com/view/Entry/91618?rskey=4fYlie&result=1&isAdvanced=false#eid. Accessed 7 Feb 2013.
The History of Film: 1940s. *Film Site*. http://www.filmsite.org/40sintro5.html. Accessed 19 Dec 2013.
Tsivian, Yuri. Intolerance Study. http://www.cinemetrics.lv/tsivian.php. Accessed 19 Feb 2014.
van Leeuwen, Theo. 1999. *Speech, Music, Sound*. London: Macmillan Press.
Vernallis, Carol. 2004. *Experiencing Music Video: Aesthetics and Cultural Context*. New York: Colombia University Press.

Wagner, Richard. 1852. *Opera and Drama*. http://users.belgacom.net/wagnerlibrary/prose/wlpr0063.htm#d0e1920. Accessed 18 Nov 2013.
———. 1995. *Opera and Drama*. Lincoln: University of Nebraska Press.
———. 2008a. *Art and Revolution*. Trans. William Ashton Ellis. Gloucester: Dodo Press.
———. 2008b. *Richard Wagner's Prose Works V1: The Artwork of the Future (1895)*. Trans. William Ashton Ellis. Whitefish: Kessinger Publishing.
Watson, Michael O. 1970. *Proxemic Behaviour: A Cross-Cultural Study*. Paris: The Hague.
———.. 1972. *Symbolic and Expressive Uses of Space: An Introduction to Proxemic Behaviour*. Module in Anthropology, Vol. 20, 1–18. Reading, MA: Addison-Wesley.
Wellesz, Egon. 1950. *Essays on Opera*. Trans. Patricia Kean. London: Dennis Dobson.
Whittington, William. 2007. *Sound Design and Science Fiction*. Texas: University of Texas Press.
Williams, Alan. 1980. Is Sound Recording Like a Language? *Yale French Studies: Cinema/Sound* 60: 51–66.
Williams, Linda. 1991. Body Genres. *Film Quarterly* 44: 4, Summer.
Winokur, Mark. 1996. *American Laughter: Immigrants, Ethnicity, and the 1930s Hollywood Film Comedy*. New York: St Martin's.
Winters, Ben. 2010. The Non-diegetic Fallacy: Film, Music, and Narrative Space. *Music & Letters* 91(2): 224–244.
———. 2014. *Music, Performance, and the Realities of Film: Shared Concert Experiences in Screen Fiction*. London: Routledge.
Wollen, Peter. 2002. *Paris Hollywood: Writings on Film*. New York: Verso.
Wood, Michael. 1989. *America In The Movies*. New York: Columbia University Press.
Žižek, Slavoj. 1989. Looking Awry. *October* 50:30–55, Autumn.

Filmography

An Affair to Remember. Leo McCarey. Twentieth Century Fox. 1957.
Because of Him. Richard Wallace. Universal Pictures. 1946.
Billy the Kid and the Green Baize Vampire. Alan Clarke. ITC. 1987.
Carefree. Mark Sandrich. RKO. 1938.
Carmen Jones. Otto Preminger. Carlyle Productions. 1954.
Dancer in the Dark. Lars von Trier. Pain Unlimited GmbH Filmproduktion. 2000.
Down to Earth. Alexander Hall. Columbia Pictures. 1947.
Evergreen. Victor Saville. Gaumont British Pictures Corporation. 1934.
Follow the Fleet. Mark Sandrich. RKO. 1936.
Footlight Parade. Lloyd Bacon. Warner Bros. 1933.

Gilda. Charles Vidor. Columbia Pictures. 1946.
Intolerance. D. W. Griffith. Triangle Film Corpotation. 1916.
Jaws. Steven Spielberg. Zanuck/Brown Productions. 1975.
Kill Bill: Vol. 1. Quintin Tarantino. Miramax Films. 2003.
Les Misérables. Tom Hooper. Universal Pictures. 2012.
Mamma Mia!. Phyllida Lloyd. Universal Pictures. 2008.
New Moon. Robert Z. Leonard. MGM. 1940.
Oklahoma!. Fred Zinnemann. Samuel Goldwyn Company. 1955.
Roberta. William A. Seiter. RKO. 1935.
Seven Brides for Seven Brothers. Stanley Donen. MGM. 1954.
Swing Time. George Stevens. RKO. 1936.
The Big Sleep. Howard Hawks. Warner Bros. 1946.
The Red Shoes. Michael Powell, Emeric Pressburger. The Archers. 1948.
Top Hat. Mark Sandrich. RKO. 1935.
Umbrellas of Cherbourg. Jacques Demy. Parc Film. 1964.
Vertigo. Alfred Hitchcock. Paramount Pictures. 1958.
Volver. Pedro Almodóvar. Canal+ Espana. 2006.
Wild at Heart. David Lynch. PolyGram Filmed Entertainment. 1990.

INDEX

A
Abel, Sam, 151–3, 176n26
acousmêtre, 16, 17, 43–5, 67, 146
aesthetics
    abstract aesthetics, 1, 4–9, 11, 13, 20, 29, 34, 90, 100, 144, 145, 164, 174n3, 183, 190, 191
    enfolding-unfolding aesthetics, 159–62, 166, 178n67
An Affair to Remember (1957), 19
Affron, Charles, 105, 135n58, 188
Almodóvar, Pedro, 147
Altman, Rick, 145, 146, 155–7, 188, 193n2
aria, 17–19, 147, 155, 158
Arnheim, Rudolf, 32, 33, 45n5, 45n9, 107, 193n8
Art Deco, 105, 106, 109, 121–4, 132, 135n60, 138n131
Art Nouveau, 105, 121, 122, 124
Astaire, Fred, 4, 10, 19, 23, 42, 75, 90, 91, 100–10, 112, 114–17, 120, 121, 123, 124, 126–33, 135n41, 135n51, 146, 185, 191
audience, 1, 5–7, 11, 14–18, 20, 22, 34, 36, 37, 40–2, 50, 51, 53, 54, 56, 58, 59, 61, 63–9, 71, 72, 74–81, 83n14, 86n77, 90–4, 96–9, 102–21, 127, 130–3, 134n10, 141, 142, 144, 146–53, 155, 157, 158, 162, 164, 167–71, 173, 174, 175n11, 182, 185, 186, 188–91
audio dissolve, 10, 16, 19, 35, 36, 69, 73, 145–7, 155–7, 186

B
Balász, Béla, 114, 137n96
Baldassare, Mark, 12, 25n39, 38
Barker, Jennifer M., 14, 26n50, 59, 60, 96, 97, 134n32, 190
Barsacq, Léon, 12, 25n42
Because of Him (1946), 34
Benjamin, Walter, 26n49, 41, 48n55, 153
Bergfelder, Tim, 26n55, 41, 42, 48n54, 101, 102, 105–8

Note: Page numbers followed by "n" refer to footnotes.

Berkeley, Busby, 5, 24n11, 36, 113
Bianconi, Lorenzo, 148, 149, 155, 175n16
The Big Sleep (1946), 19
Billy the Kid and the Green Baize Vampire (1985), 23, 143, 169–74, 174n2, 179n98, 185–7
Björk, 67, 69, 72, 73, 76–81
body
  Korper, 163
  Leib, 163, 178n71
  skin, 14, 59, 60, 115, 166, 168
Bordwell, David, 13, 24n22, 25n44, 30, 51, 70, 82n6, 87n88
Braudy, Leo, 107, 115, 117, 136n87, 137n102, 137n103, 175n17
Brecht, Bertolt
  Verfremdungseffekt, 152
Brooks, Peter, 164, 178n79
Bruno, Giuliana, 14, 26n48, 41, 42, 96, 103

C

Carefree (1938), 110, 113, 117, 120
Carman, Taylor, 59, 84n31
Carmen Jones (1954), 156
Cataldi, Sue, 166, 167, 179n90
Cavell, Stanley, 112, 136n87
Cecchi, Alessandro, 35, 46n18
Charles, Carlos López, 70, 86n87
Chion, Michel, 16, 24n14, 43, 60, 61, 66, 67
cinemetrics, 20, 21, 72, 90, 170, 187
Clark, Carroll, 101
cognition, 1, 174
cognitivism, 1, 189, 190
Cohan, Steven, 4, 5, 7, 9, 11, 23n6, 24n12, 101, 111, 123, 131, 193n2
communication, 12, 38, 120, 125, 126, 129
Condon, William, 129, 139n154
Crary, Jonathon, 163

D

dance, 10, 17, 19, 73, 106, 107, 109–11, 116–9, 123, 124, 126–33, 151, 157, 185
Dancer in the Dark (2000), 22, 49, 52, 67–82, 144, 185, 186, 193n6
Day, Doris, 4
Dean, Winton, 156, 177n56
Deneuve, Catherine, 68
dialogue, 15, 17, 33, 36, 53, 62, 64, 108, 111, 130, 143, 149, 155, 172
diegesis
  diegetic, 2, 15, 16, 34–6, 50, 56, 57, 60, 62, 66–9, 71, 73, 76, 77, 96, 106–9, 146, 157, 158, 168, 169, 173, 175n11, 185
  meta-diegetic, 10, 15, 16, 35, 36, 50, 67, 69, 87n99, 157, 168, 169
  non-diegetic, 10, 15, 34–6, 56, 57, 67, 69, 76, 96, 109, 146, 157, 158, 169, 173, 185
Dilla, Geraldine P., 17, 26n64
direct address, 36, 37, 111, 112, 170
Doane, Mary-Ann, 179n85
Dolby Surround Sound (DSS)
  Low-Frequency Effects (LFE), 57–60
  5.1 system, 18
Donington, Robert, 149, 175n18
Donnelly, K. J., 10, 15, 16, 24n10, 25n29, 26n56
Down to Earth (1947), 113
Doyle, Peter, 70, 76, 80, 86n86
drama, 17, 18, 130, 131, 148, 151, 154–6, 190
Durbin, Deanna, 34
Dyer, Richard, 19, 27, 86n77
dynamic space, 39, 42

E

Ellis, W. D., 30, 45n1, 174n1
engagement

emphatic engagement, 118, 119, 121
   kinaesthetic involvement, 118
Evergreen (1934), 106
experience, 1, 14, 18, 19, 31, 32, 40,
   42, 43, 46, 55, 56, 58–60, 64,
   65, 68–70, 78, 79, 81, 91, 94,
   95, 98, 99, 102, 107, 109, 118,
   119, 122, 125, 128, 144, 149,
   151, 157, 160, 161, 163–70, 186

F
Feuer, Jane, 7, 10, 11, 111, 113–7,
   119, 120, 130, 185
Fischer, Lucy, 105, 121–3, 130,
   135n60
Follow the Fleet (1936), 131
Footlight Parade (1933), 113
forensic analysis, 4, 6, 20, 53, 57, 68,
   71, 89, 90, 142–4, 183

G
Gallafent, Edward, 103, 131, 135n51
Garland, Judy, 4
genre, 2–11, 13, 16, 19, 20, 23, 23n7,
   23n9, 24n10, 29, 35, 45, 51, 63,
   64, 68, 70, 72, 86n77, 90, 91,
   97, 109–11, 113, 117, 131,
   142–50, 152, 158, 165, 169,
   174n3, 177n41, 181, 182, 185,
   187, 188, 191, 192, 192n1
Gentaz, Édouard, 14, 26n49, 40, 41, 97
Gesamtkunstwerk, 18, 143, 144,
   152–5, 177n41
gestalt, 1, 21, 22, 30–3, 42, 44, 45n2,
   45n5, 49, 57, 64, 65, 68, 70–2,
   75, 76, 80, 89, 97, 141–4, 146,
   150, 159, 162, 170, 189
Gibson, James, 134n15, 166, 179n86
Gilda (1946), 19
Goldstein, E. Bruce, 93, 133n4,
   134n14, 134n15

Gorbman, Claudia, 5, 10, 15, 16, 35,
   36, 69, 108
Grimani, A., 58, 59, 84n28
Gunning, Tom, 9, 25n27

H
Hall, Edward T., 12, 20, 25n38,
   37–40, 90, 112, 116, 124–9,
   133n1, 138n134, 191
Hall, Stuart, 40, 47n51
Harris, Sue, 26n55, 41, 42, 48n54,
   101, 102, 105–8
Hatwell, Yvette, 14, 26n49, 40, 41,
   96, 97, 134n32
Hayworth, Rita, 10, 132
Hediger, Heini, 46–7n32, 127,
   138n134
Hyam, Hannah, 100, 135n41

I
immersive, 18, 69, 186
Intolerance (1916), 20, 21

J
Jordan, Randolph, 18, 27n69, 83n15

K
Katz, David, 31, 32, 45n6, 64, 65
Kerins, Mark, 18, 24n14, 27n66, 44,
   55–7, 60–3, 65, 67, 68, 71,
   83n19

L
Lant, Antonia, 14, 26n54, 41, 42
Lastra, James, 18, 27n69
Lefebvre, Henri, 11, 12, 25n36, 33, 34
Les Misérables (2012), 4
libretto, 152, 156, 159, 190

listening, 44, 59, 66, 79, 100, 106
  acousmatic listening, 17, 50, 81

M

Mamma Mia! (2008), 5
Marks, Laura, 14, 96, 97, 159–62, 166, 177n60, 178n67, 190
Marshall, Bill, 4, 5, 9, 23n7
Mather, George, 93–6, 134n16
Mazis, Glen, 167, 179n93
McClinton, Katherine, 121–4, 138n131
McLean, Adrienne, 10, 25n34, 132, 151, 156
Merleau-Ponty, Maurice, 59, 60, 84n31, 84n32, 166, 179n90
Metaxa, Georges, 127
mise-en-scène, 13, 33, 71, 89, 92, 101, 110, 120, 123, 143, 148, 149, 158, 162, 185, 188
Mordden, Ethan, 130, 139n164
Morin, Edgar, 115, 137n101
movement, 13, 14, 23, 32, 37, 40–2, 57, 59, 71, 74, 79, 81, 91–4, 96, 102–4, 106–8, 110, 114, 120–2, 126, 142, 143, 145, 146, 153, 165–8, 170, 178n68, 184
Mulvey, Laura, 113, 114, 133n6
music, 3, 5, 8–10, 15–17, 19, 26n56, 31, 33, 35, 36, 43, 44, 46n28, 49, 51, 53, 56, 60, 62–4, 68–71, 73–7, 79, 81, 87n99, 101, 104, 106, 108–11, 129, 130, 143, 146–51, 153–9, 170, 172, 177n41, 186–8, 191
musical, musical number, 4, 8, 10, 16, 19, 20, 22, 33, 34, 37, 44, 51, 72–5, 78, 82, 101, 110, 113, 119, 121, 142, 145–8, 151, 156, 157, 159, 162, 170, 171, 173, 182, 184, 187

N

narrative, 1, 5, 6, 8–13, 16, 19, 21, 29, 34, 35, 42, 46n28, 49, 51, 61, 64, 68, 70, 74, 82, 85n58, 87n88, 97, 100–6, 108–11, 114, 120, 121, 132, 133, 141, 142, 145–7, 149, 151–3, 156, 159, 160, 164, 167, 175n11, 181–3, 186–90, 192, 193n3
New Moon (1940), 145

O

Oklahoma! (1955), 16
opera, 17–19, 23, 142, 143, 147–58, 175n15, 175n16, 176n32, 190, 191
operetta, 19, 111, 142, 143, 146, 147, 156, 157
orchestra, 16, 17, 50, 53, 75, 111, 114, 117–19, 152, 154, 158, 186

P

Pallasmaa, Juhani, 41, 48n57
Panofsky, Erwin, 115, 137n102
Paulin, Scott D., 153, 154, 176n40, 176n41
Pauly, Reinhard G., 158, 177n59
perception, spatiotemporal, 144
performer, 10, 11, 16, 22, 36, 76, 81, 83, 108, 110–14, 116–21, 131–3, 149, 151, 155, 157, 162, 164, 168, 175n11, 184–6
Pestelli, Giorgio, 148, 149, 155, 175n16
Pierce, Charles Sanders, 161, 177n65
Polglase, Van Nest, 101
proscenium arch, 10, 114, 116–18, 120, 131, 185, 186
proxemics, 12, 33, 37–40, 47n32, 76, 78, 80, 118, 124, 126, 138n134, 164, 186, 190, 191

R

recitative, 17, 18, 147, 155, 156, 158, 159
The Red Shoes (1948), 19
The Ring cycle (1848–1874), 154
RKO, 23, 90, 100, 101, 105, 115, 132, 185
Roberta (1935), 131
Rogers, Ginger, 19, 23, 42, 75, 90, 91, 100–3, 105–11, 114–24, 126–33, 191
Rubin, Martin, 5, 24n11, 107
Rutherford, Anne, 163–8, 178n69, 179n85, 188, 190

S

Sacks, Oliver, 81, 87n102
Schroeder, David, 155, 175n15
Sedgewick, H. A, 91–4, 133n4, 134n10
senses, 2, 13, 14, 26n47, 26n63, 40, 43, 58, 69, 82, 89, 94, 95, 98–100, 110, 159–61, 168, 190, 192
Sergi, Gianluca, 18, 19, 27n66, 27n67
set design, 12, 13, 17, 37, 74, 87n91, 90–2, 101, 103–5, 110, 121, 184, 190, 191
Seven Brides for Seven Brothers (1954), 34
Shiffrar, Maggie, 93, 134n14
Shore, Brad, 118, 137n109
Sobchack, Vivian, 14, 26n53, 58, 61, 84n25, 96–100, 188, 189
sound
  stereo sound, 5, 186
  surround sound, 5, 18, 55–8, 60, 61, 65, 66, 69, 71, 83n19
space
  audio-visual space, 16, 17, 21, 23, 141–79, 187

dynamic space, 39, 42
sound space, 15, 18, 21, 22, 49–87, 100, 141
visual space, 21, 22, 43, 44, 60, 71, 73–5, 89–139
spatial, 2–4, 7, 8, 12, 16–18, 20, 21, 23, 29, 30, 33, 34, 37–40, 44, 45, 46n32, 49–54, 56, 57, 62, 63, 66, 68–72, 74–7, 79, 81, 90–3, 101, 102, 127, 133, 138n134, 141, 142, 147, 149, 151, 158, 161, 162, 164, 170, 171, 174n3, 181–3, 185, 187, 189–3
spectacle, 9, 151, 159, 166, 182, 193n1, 193n3
spectator, 10, 12, 14, 15, 53, 55, 57, 59, 60, 65, 82, 92, 107, 111, 112, 118–20, 146, 157, 164, 165, 168, 185
spectatorship
  embodied spectatorship, 37, 50, 58, 63, 67, 69, 71, 82, 83n18, 92, 94, 96, 110, 134n10, 147, 149, 151–3, 159, 163, 164, 168, 174, 187–9
  immersive, 18, 69, 186
Stilwell, Robynn, 4, 5, 9, 23n7, 36, 46n28, 58, 64, 84n26
Street, Sarah, 41, 42, 101–8
Streri, Arlette, 14, 40, 41, 96, 97
superfield, 44, 60–3, 146
Swing Time (1936), 23, 121–4, 126, 127, 129, 130, 132, 133, 191
synaesthesia, 95, 96, 99, 104

T

Tambling, Jeremy, 156
Tarantino, Quentin, 147
Tashiro, C. S., 12, 13, 25n41, 34, 42, 102, 104, 107, 108, 188

technology, 5, 18, 42, 53, 54, 56, 57, 66, 71, 75, 83n19, 83n20, 85n70, 93, 102, 105, 173, 184
Théberge, Paul, 68, 69, 86n78
Thompson, Kristin, 30, 51, 70, 87n88
touch, 14, 40, 41, 58, 61, 81, 94, 100, 105, 110, 126–8, 167, 168, 170, 173
Tsivian, Yuri, 20, 21, 27n75, 72, 170

U
ultrafield, 44, 60–3
Umbrellas of Cherbourg (1964), 23, 143, 144, 154, 156–9, 185–7

V
van Leeuwen, Theo, 50, 51, 75, 76, 82n1
Vernallis, Carol, 69, 70, 74, 86n82
Vertigo (1958), 93

virtual reconstructions, 2, 20, 21, 90, 103, 143, 158, 183–7, 191, 193n4, 193n6
von Trier, Lars, 52, 67, 68, 75, 87n91, 186

W
Wagner, Richard, 17, 18, 26n65, 143, 144, 152–5, 174n1, 176n39, 177n41, 190
Watson, Michael O., 38, 39, 47n37
Wellesz, Egon, 147, 175n15
Whittington, William, 66
Williams, Alan, 24n14, 52–4
Williams, Linda, 165
Winokur, Mark, 124, 138n132
Winters, Ben, 35, 46n23, 146, 175n11
Wood, Michael, 110

Z
Žižek, Slavoj, 66, 86

The manufacturer's authorised representative in the EU is Springer Nature Customer Service Centre GmbH, Europaplatz 3, 69115 Heidelberg, Germany. If you have any concerns regarding our products, please contact ProductSafety@springernature.com

Printed and bound by CPI Group (UK) Ltd, Croydon, CR0 4YY
23/03/2026
02076750-0002